"This book is a brilliant achievement. Frema Engel, a thought leader, continues to heighten our awareness of the impact of workplace violence while illuminating strategies to offset its' devastating impact."

– **Ingrid Taylor, MSW, RSW, CTS**
Director of Trauma Management
Ceridian Integrated EAP and Work-Life Services

"Through riveting examples and thoughtful commentary, Frema Engel's *Taming the Beast* provides a critical reminder of the high cost of threatening and violent behavior, as well as the pivotal role that managers can play in promoting a respectful—and safe—workplace."

– **Rebecca A. Speer, Esq., Principal**
Speer Associates/Workplace Counsel

"*Taming the Beast* is an essential and practical read for those who want to break and prevent the cycle of violence in the workplace. Frema Engel provides a valuable resource for all levels of the organization—from workers to managers—to help them understand that workplace violence is a preventable organizational problem."

– **Anthony Pizzino, National Health and Safety Director**
Canadian Union of Public Employees

"*Taming the Beast* clearly explains how we've become so tolerant of violence and offers tools to combat it. It should be a reference manual in every business. I know that I'll be referring to mine for years to come. Besides illuminating the depths of violence in the workplace, it offers us the tools to combat it. My hat goes off to Frema Engel who has obviously done her homework."

– **M. Lynne Jacob**
MLJ Coaching & Consulting

"**F**rema Engel led the workplace violence field long before others realized how deeply organizations need this information—and these solutions."

– **Ingrid Norrish**
Creative Meeting & Marketing Services

"**I**f you are new to the issue of workplace violence and need comprehensive, clearly written information, *Taming the Beast* is a must-read. Frema Engel's incisive, down-to-earth approach makes it easy for anyone to understand, manage, and grapple with workplace violence."

– **Henri Derome, Director**
Human Resources and Administrative Services
Batshaw Youth and Family Centres

"*T*aming the Beast* is one of the most comprehensive and well written books on workplace violence to come out of North America. It is especially helpful with its analysis on how organisations and unions need to play a key role in the prevention and management of such violence."

– **Vaughan Bowie, Author**
Coping with Violence: A Guide for the Human Services

"**B**y unmasking workplace violence, Frema Engel has spurred us to break our silence and act. Her book is an indispensable guide for the people and organizations who respond to this violence and, through them, its victims. Thanks Frema, for sharing your rich experience and insight with us."

– **Arlène Gaudreault, Lecturer in Victimology**
University of Montreal, School of Criminology

Second Edition
Revised and Updated

TAMING
THE
BEAST

Getting Violence Out of the Workplace

Frema Engel

National Library of Canada Cataloguing in Publication

Engel, Frema
Taming the beast: getting violence out of the workplace/Frema Engel – 2nd ed.

Includes bibliographical references

ISBN 0-9682998-3-0

1. Violence in the Workplace – Prevention. I. Title

HF5549.5.E43E54 2004   658.4'73   C2004-901209-6

Ashwell Publishing
6980 Cote St. Luc, Suite 907
Montreal, Quebec
Canada H4V 3A4

ATTENTION: Quantity discounts are available for bulk purposes.

Tel: 514-989-9298
Toll free: 1-800-363-6435
Fax: 514-989-9150
E-mail: sales@fremaengel.com

Printed and bound in Canada

FIRST EDITION – 1998
SECOND EDITION – 2004

Cover design: A2Zeegraphix
Desktop Publishing: Josée Valcourt
Communications: Textex

The material in this publication is provided for general information purposes only. If legal or other expert assistance is required, the services of a competent professional should be sought. The analysis contained herein represents the experience and opinion of the author, but neither the author nor the publisher is responsible for the results of any action taken on the basis of information found in this work nor for any errors or omissions. Although case examples are based on actual events, identifying information has been altered to protect the parties involved, with the exception of parties or events that have been publicized by the media.

Acknowledgements

Taming the Beast could never have been conceived without the thousands of people who have shared their stories, pain and triumphs with me. Although this book is about them, it is really for them. I was able to write it because of what they let me learn from them.

Several colleagues and friends have shown what true friendship is really about. Over the two years, Rolande Marquès and Beverley Robinson helped me sharpen my thinking and test out new ideas and approaches. My new friend Ruth Selwyn stimulated my thinking, challenged me to reach deeper inside myself and helped me express my ideas in a clearer way. Linda August is my sounding board, helping me articulate my ideas and giving me steadfast support. Robert Frank listens attentively and turns rambling thoughts into succinct copy. With attention to detail and great patience, Josée Valcourt miraculously pulled everything together. Cathy Doucet, Rita Tenenbaum, Suzanne Belson, Lynda Goldman, Lynne Jacob and Miriam Pearl: their efforts and contributions helped raise this project to a new level. Because of the dedication, hard work and inspiration of all these good people, *Taming the Beast* is a much more balanced, improved and radically different book from its first edition.

I would like to especially thank the people who supported this project with their endorsements. Their enthusiastic accolades have convinced me that this book is worthwhile and makes a difference.

Special thanks to the Engel clan: Sydney, David, Josie, Avra, Allen, Jodi, Randy and Samantha. Through thick and thin we show what families are all about. My last comment is for David, who long ago taught me how to grow an idea. He reminded me that trees grow from acorns, but to make them strong, you have to pay attention and keep watering them. And so it is with this book—it took love to conceive it, lots of nurturing to grow it and conviction about its worth to let it fly free.

For Samantha Bethany

*May her generation experience only
respect and collaboration in the workplace.*

Table of Contents

Introduction

In April 1995, the Oklahoma City bombing forever changed the face of American work life. With the collapse of the Federal building, the deaths of so many adults and the destruction of the daycare center where employees had just dropped off their babies and preschool children, came the stark realization that terrorism can strike at the workplace.

While some people had said at the time that what happened in Oklahoma City was an anomaly and that employees and businesses should not have cause for concern, in fact this terrorist action was just one more twist in a growing problem confronting our workplaces worldwide—the problem of violence. Moreover, little did we know at the time that this incident would pall in comparison to what would follow. The destruction of the World Trade Center on September 11, 2001 with close to three thousand deaths and countless injuries of innocent people at work, brought the reality of terrorism to unimaginable heights.

When I first began researching the topic of workplace violence in the early 1990's for the First Edition of this book, it was difficult to find broad-based studies and national statistics. Things changed rapidly. A flurry of studies and surveys in the mid 1990's, mostly coming from the United States and Britain, examined the extent of the problem and provided an initial understanding of what workplace violence was all about. Now workplace violence has gained recognition as a major global occupational health and security problem. Along with this has been research, clarification of definitions, post-incident programs and services, training, and management initiatives to control or prevent incidents.

Workplace violence is not only about terrorism and murder, although this is what captures media attention. It is really about the more subtle forms of abuse which occur daily in many workplace relationships. Despite anti-harassment or zero tolerance policies adopted by many workplaces, for the most part, more subtle forms of violence are ignored, tolerated and even permitted to develop. Violence takes its toll—in fear, stress and health problems. Violence also negatively affects performance, teamwork and customer service. When violent behavior is not stopped, it usually gets worse.

Taming the Beast: Getting Violence out of the Workplace is based on incidents and experiences of real people whom I have helped for close to two decades. These people come from every type of organization and from every level of the organization. Among them are CEO's, executives and senior managers, people on the front-line, professionals, salespeople and support staff. They work in banking, retail, health care, education and social services and are employed in some of our largest corporations and institutions. Working with them has enabled me to see patterns and trends in violent behavior and how workplace culture can contribute to abusive conduct.

This book examines the nature of work-related violence and explains what happens to people who go off to work believing they are protected and safe, only to be confronted with an overwhelming violent experience. It describes what goes on at work where violence is a problem and what can make a work site a dangerous place. It explores how organizational culture can help set the stage for violence. It explains how certain attitudes of employees and senior managers can contribute to violence. This book also analyzes the impact of abuse, harassment, physical attacks and other forms of violence on employee health, job performance, customer service, organizational effectiveness and the bottom line. Lastly, it offers practical suggestions and recommendations on how to stop the violence.

In writing the original version in 1998 and this second edition, I have drawn on my many years of experience counseling employees, developing training programs, and consulting with executives and senior managers to help them control and prevent workplace violence. These experiences have helped me to recognize certain signs in organizations that lead to abusive behavior, and to understand how to control violence and transform hostile workplace cultures into vibrant, respectful, collaborative environments.

Taming the Beast: Getting Violence out of the Workplace highlights the dilemmas, reactions and problems employees face, and what they and their families go through as a result of exposure to traumatic workplace incidents. For CEO's and managers who are increasingly forced to deal with disruptive, dysfunctional and violent behavior at work, I explain why this happens and offer a concrete, practical guide to manage the problem. For people who are confronted with on-the-job violence, I offer a confirmation that certain disturbing experiences are actually forms of violence. For employees and families victimized by work-related violence, I describe how violence affects people's professional and personal lives and provide concrete coping strategies. I also discuss the other side of the equation: when staff abuse vulnerable people in their care. Finally I address the challenges. What will it take to create a violence-free workplace? What must CEO's and their executives do to make this happen? How can we reverse this trend?

A comment on the writing style and the victims' stories. In order to facilitate the reading, I have used the masculine as a generic term of reference. In order to maintain the confidentiality of the people and organizations cited in the examples, I have omitted or camouflaged identifying information, without changing the facts. What is important are not the names of the victims and the work sites, but the facts and the actual violence. These are described as they happened.

This book was written for all levels of employees in workplaces everywhere. Let me be clear about one thing. I do not believe that all workplaces have problems with violence. Many workplaces do not tolerate violence of any kind. Others respond to unanticipated incidents effectively. Nor do I believe that all employees or employers are either victims or offenders, or that all clients are abusive. However, as the reader will come to realize, workplace violence is now, and has been for a long time, a disturbing problem for many employees and managers. We must therefore continue our efforts to find better solutions to this social problem that has become identified as a major occupational health and security issue and has a major impact on the global economy.

Workplace violence is not a chance happening. No matter what type of job we hold or where we work, we must become aware of the risks associated with work-related violence, what it can do to us and how we can deal with it. For we never know when we can become an unsuspecting target, or when our nice quiet job can suddenly turn into a nightmare.

Frema Engel
February 2004

PART ONE

THE STAGE

- 1 -
Backdrop of Fear: Violence in Society

After a day or a weekend off, it's the start of another week of work. People who enjoy their jobs often feel a charge of excitement knowing that work is about to begin again. Others view work as another chore to be done. Their salary pays the rent, buys food and clothes and sometimes provides a little extra for fun times.

For many people though, the start of a new shift or workweek means the dread returns. They spend the night tossing, turning or lying awake, waiting for morning to come. The night triggers a sick feeling in the pit of the stomach, a pressure-building headache or overall uneasiness. Just the thought of work creates anxiety, for this may mean facing an abuser, from whom escape is impossible, or once again confronting a living nightmare that they cannot put out of their minds. These people, like Jane and Robert whose stories follow, have been victims of workplace violence.

Jane, a 34-year-old single mother with two children to support, works in a high-risk occupation. A bank teller, she has been the victim of five holdups over a three-year period. The last one occurred two months ago. None of them were "violent," that is to say, the robbers fired no shots and did not physically injure anyone. Yet every time, they displayed a weapon. In the last holdup, the robber passed her a note. Jane could not put out of her mind what it said: "Holdup. Hand over your money. No noise or I'll kill you. Obey or you're dead."

The robber had been agitated and Jane had become nervous. Suddenly she saw herself laying dead and her children left motherless. She froze for a couple of seconds and he swore at her. She had trouble unlocking and opening her cash drawer. He swore at her again. After what seemed like an eternity, but was really only a couple of seconds, she got the drawer open and gave him the money.

When it was over, the reaction set in. Jane began to shake and feel cold. She was sick to her stomach. She cried uncontrollably and kept reliving the holdup in her mind. She felt lucky to be alive.

Weeks later, Jane began to brood about being killed the next time. "After all," she explained, "he seemed so jumpy, he could have shot me, just by mistake." She could not put the image of that gun pointed at her out of her mind and she kept hearing the robber swear at her. Each Sunday night she became a mass of nerves. She knew she could not face going to work at the bank, but jobs were hard to come by and she had nowhere else to go.

Jane is not alone in her predicament. She is one of the millions of people who work in banks, transportation, communication and utility services, supermarkets, convenience stores, pharmacies, service stations and other retail establishments. Working with money makes employees prime targets for holdups. Robbers believe they are stealing from a business. Rarely do they think about the cashier's emotional suffering. They seem to think that if they do not fire a shot or "hurt" anyone, the robbery will be a fleeting inconvenience for the employees. Yet Jane, like thousands of other cashiers, developed *holdup trauma* and became psychologically scarred from the incident. Her life became totally disrupted and she could no longer function properly. Although she did not understand it yet, she was suffering from post-traumatic stress disorder (PTSD). What she did know was that she could not handle another robbery. She lived with the dread of it happening again.

Jane is a victim of workplace violence. So is Robert, a 46-year-old senior marketing manager of an electronics corporation.

Bill, Robert's director for the past eight months, had a reputation for brilliance. He also was known to be abusive and a bully. Lately he began criticizing Robert and screaming at him in front of his co-workers. He never gave him any direction, yet often tore Robert's work apart. In a recent meeting Bill got angry because he did not like Robert's presentation and he lashed out at him. "You idiot," he screamed. "Can't you for once get it through your thick skull that what we're supposed to do is sell a product? People would have to be fools to buy anything from you. For a college graduate you sure are stupid. For once why can't you get things right?"

Robert felt shocked, angry, embarrassed and fearful. Not usually at a loss for words, he became tongue-tied. He dared not respond. He worried that if he did, his employer would tell him that if he did not like it there, he could leave. Robert could not do that. He knew he should find another job, but he had worked for the company for twelve years and he felt he had too much of his career invested there. Besides, his confidence was so low, he was sure no one would hire him.

At a time when Robert should have been excited about his career, he was depressed. He could not see a way out. He hated Bill, but dared not complain to anyone at work about the treatment he was receiving from his boss. He would be seen as a wimp, or someone who could not take the "heat." So he kept his mouth shut and hoped one day Bill would leave or pick on someone else.

Sunday nights became unbearable. He felt sick, had diarrhea and could not sleep. Beer became his solace. Robert started yelling at his wife and children. Once a pleasant guy who had been easy to live with, he became surly and exhausting to be around.

The stories of Jane and Robert are common. For many employees, violence at work is a horrible reality. Many employees experience violence, either because the nature of their jobs places them at risk, or because they are targets of another person's abusive behavior.

That employees may be victims of violence and that violence in the workplace is a problem of major proportion, may seem greatly exaggerated. Surely the cases of Jane and Robert are isolated incidents? Sadly, they are not. Certain occupational groups, particularly those in the military, law enforcement and correctional institutions have to control violence—and they are prime targets. Yet every working person, in every type of job and in every conceivable setting, is also a potential target. This means that we are all at risk of some form of violence during our working years. Even more important, many of us will also experience multiple episodes of work-related violence.

That workplace violence should be such a huge problem is understandable when we think about the kind of societies we live in and the violence that surrounds us. Violence is rampant throughout the world: in our homes, on our streets, in our schools, in our communities and between countries. Daily news reports in every large city provide evidence of the troubled times in which we live. The reports are brutal and graphic. A day does not go by without a story about a rape, assault, shooting, stabbing, hostage-taking incident, murder, suicide bombing, terrorist activity, or act of war. Not only are these actions committed by adults, but by children as well.

The stories we read about are only the tip of the iceberg. They are the cases where journalists follow the story, people report the violence, or the assailants get caught.

Yet most incidents are unreported and therefore go unnoticed. Each day thousands of women are beaten by their male partners, and female adolescents and young adult women are date-raped. Children of both sexes are physically, sexually and psychologically abused by parents, relatives, family, friends, teachers, baby-sitters and other people entrusted to take care of them. Despite public awareness of the problem, many incidents take place behind closed doors and are unreported.

Family violence has long been recognized as a pervasive global problem. In the United States alone, an estimated 960,000 incidents of violence were committed against women by a former spouse, boyfriend or girlfriend. Four million women are physically abused by their husbands or live-in partners each year.[1] In 2001, an estimated 3 million referrals concerning the welfare of 5 million children were made to child protective services. Of these 903,000 children were found to be victims of child abuse or neglect.[2] Elder abuse is also an alarming problem, with estimates ranging from 1-2 million cases per year.[3]

Recently workplace violence has gained recognition as a pervasive global problem. Many strides have been made since the early 1990's when workplace violence came into the public spotlight.

Although efforts have been made to understand, manage and prevent incidents, this is still a problem that most employees handle on their own. The problem is huge and widespread. If this were an illness, it would be considered to be of epidemic proportions. While at work, employees in every conceivable setting suffer harassment, intimidation, physical assault and acts of crime. The assailants are superiors, subordinates, colleagues, clients and total strangers.

SOCIETY'S CANCER

How could the workplace be spared from violence?

Violence is all around us and many people live in fear. It curtails our activities and restricts our freedom. We try to live in "safe" neighborhoods. We avoid walking the streets alone at night. Some of us fear taking the subway or bus. Others avoid crowds. Many people do not even feel safe in their own homes.

How many of us double and triple lock our doors or install an alarm system to prevent a break and entry? How many people are afraid to leave a window open at night for fear of an intruder getting in? What about the violence many of us experience right in our homes—psychological, sexual and physical abuse, not from strangers but from loved ones?

One of life's mysteries relates to violence and the reasons so many people are aggressive and brutal. One has to wonder whether violence is a condition of the human species, or whether eons of genetic programming as protectors, hunters and warriors have produced a violent society. This does not explain though, why some people are violent and others, who have been abused or witnessed violence as children, are not. What is it about our society that pushes desperate people over the edge? Why do we tolerate so much violence?

Some people believe that men, who commit most of the violence, have been socialized to become that way. The phrase "boys will be boys" is a common statement used to excuse violent male behavior. This social acceptance of male violence is an important factor. However, many other social factors increase frustration, intolerance, desperation and hopelessness, all of which may lead to violence.

One such factor is poverty. How can we expect people to show restraint when so many of them are unemployed, homeless, hungry and sick, or when the gap between the poor and the rich is so wide? We cannot expect people to be civil when to live means fighting for survival. We cannot presume that people can be tolerant and respectful of others when they have no hope that things will change for themselves in the future.

Another factor is exposure to violence at home. Children, who have witnessed violence or have been victims themselves, learn that abusive behavior is normal.

Economic and social conditions and life experiences may be leading causes of violence. Yet it is our acceptance of violence as part of our lives that allows it to flourish. Despite all the industrial, scientific and technological advances human beings have made, the area where we have advanced the least is our ability to settle our differences nonviolently and live in peaceful coexistence.

We seem to have a love-hate relationship with violence. Our fascination and our addiction to it are evident. Finding a movie without violent scenes is hard. Not only is the violence graphic, our imagination shows no limits in creating and enjoying horrific events. Strangely, the aggressors become our heroes. They abuse, assault, rape, commit armed robbery, torture and murder people—and we glorify them.

The entertainment business seems obsessed with violent movies. Why does Hollywood produce them? Simply because the public's appetite for violent entertainment translates into box office successes. Two examples of this insatiable appetite for violence, which incidentally, grossed Hollywood more than $100 million in 1996, the year of their release, are a success by Hollywood's standards. To date, Eraser has grossed $234 million and Ransom, $308 million. Two films highly rated for strong violence released in 2003 were Bad Boys II and Kill Bill: Vol.1.[4] Both films are on their way to strong box office successes.

The entertainment industry gives us what we want. Since the public cannot seem to get enough stories about man's aggression and depravity, Hollywood obliges with even more blood, gore and bodies to appease our ever-increasing appetites.

Yet when people actually commit the type of horrific and brutal acts depicted in our films and enacted by our movie or television heroes, we become enraged.

Our feelings toward violence and violent people seem confused. While on the one hand we profess to abhor the display of aggressive behaviors and violence, in reality our actions show a blasé acceptance and tolerance for such conduct.

We permit access to firearms and other weapons that kill. We use a band-aid approach to fix social problems that induce people to become violent. These problems include unemployment, poverty, homelessness, alcoholism, and drug abuse. We have not succeeded in creating the kind of societies where all people, but especially the youth, the marginalized, and the disadvantaged, have a hope for a better future. We have not done enough to take care of the mentally ill who, left without support, wander alone and aimlessly on the streets. We have been unsuccessful in eradicating blind hatred and intolerance for people different from ourselves. We continue to wage war rather than pursue peace. We permit inequities and injustices that breed resentment or a resigned acceptance of a bleak existence. We allow inequities to exist in our justice systems, reflecting instead racial, sexual and economic biases in verdicts and in sentencing practices. Most important, we fail to handle offenders consistently.

In our efforts to be a civilized society, we look for reasons to excuse or justify offenders' behavior. They are too sick to know what they were doing, had horrible childhoods, did not intend to do what they did, live in tremendous distress, or were too drunk or mentally incapacitated at the time. We accept a litany of excuses.

However no excuse, no matter how good, justifies the intent of the offender's behavior—which is to harm, cause injury or threaten the lives of others. Excusing behavior away does only one thing: it relieves people of their responsibility for their actions. By reducing offenders' sentences, we give them and potential offenders mixed messages about violent behavior and actions, and our tolerance for it.

Our passive acceptance of the problems related to violence and our denial and inattention to the conditions that push people toward aggressive behavior exacerbate the situation. Add to this our permissive and inconsistent approach in dealing with offenders, and an inability to engage in successful conflict resolution—the stage is set for even more hostility, brutality and wanton abuse.

THE SPILL OVER

With so much violence permeating our cities, communities and family life, it is only natural for it to spill over into our workplaces. As microcosms of a larger society, workplaces are not immune. In many workplaces, harassment, disruptive behavior, assaults and other forms of violence are a way of life.

The workplace is often a hornet's nest of abusive and aggressive behavior and activity. Employees are targets of verbal, psychological, sexual and physical abuse by strangers, clients or colleagues, or they are themselves perpetrators. Employees either suffer physical and psychological injury because of other people's actions toward them, or they cause injury to others. Some people are even killed doing their jobs.

While such conditions do not occur in every workplace, many workplaces tolerate behaviors that can only be defined as violent. Despite the progress made over the past decade to bring the problem out into the open, a common attitude among decision-makers is that the problem exists, but "not in my organization." This "ostrich in the sand" phenomenon allows small incidents to quickly escalate.

Often when concerned senior managers want to correct the problem, they do not know how. As a result, they often fail to pick up on the cues, or deal adequately with abusive conduct or incidents. Without corrective action, the situation often deteriorates, to the point where employees can no longer cope, and performance and customer service is affected. Sometimes the situation deteriorates to such an extent that people are either severely hurt physically or killed.

Workplace violence is a critical problem. Doctors, lawyers, nurses, teachers, flight attendants, postal workers, cashiers, taxi and bus drivers, salespeople, secretaries and executives are occupations that are high risk. For many of these people, violence or the threat of violence is something they continually face on the job. When things get really out of hand and people are shot, stabbed or murdered, we hear about the incidents on the nightly news.

For some time now, people have been speaking out about the violence they face at work. Some tell horrible tales about what their work life is like for them. More people than ever before are reporting incidents to their unions and professional associations. They complain about the lack of security and management support. They anguish over the fact that they are not believed but rather punished, isolated and even labeled as troublemakers. They also complain about having to deal with violent or potentially explosive situations without guidance and support.

Since the mid-1990's statistics about workplace violence have emerged, supporting what employees have been reporting and complaining about for years. The data comes from a variety of sources: union and professional surveys, government research and statistics, the media, and occupational health and safety reports. While the most extensive and most frequently quoted statistics and studies come from the United States, increasingly international cooperation on occupational health and safety issues and the Internet point to a growing global trend. Violence has become a critical workplace problem and social problem. Its impact is being felt in the global workforce and on the global economy.

SCOPE OF THE PROBLEM

The earliest data about workplace violence came from the United States in the early 1990's, giving the impression that this was largely an American phenomenon. It was not. Britain began documenting protocols to deal with violence in social services, health care and transportation before this. Much less voluminous reports also came from Canada, Australia and France. While the United States has given us the most statistics, greatest understanding of the problem and disseminated a great deal of information about prevention and management strategies, in fact, just about every Western country is contributing to the growing body of documentation about workplace violence.

What brought this problem into the public domain was not the daily incidents of verbal abuse, harassment and physical assault that employees in health care and social services had been complaining about for years, but the extreme cases. The preponderance of shooting sprees and multiple homicides in all kinds of workplaces and schools in the early 1990's, occurring primarily in the United States, but in other countries as well, caught the media's attention. Although not at the same frequency, shooting sprees still take place. For example, OC Transpo in Ottawa, Ontario (1999), Xerox in Honolulu (1999), and Edgewater Technologies, in Wakefield, Massachusetts (2000) were more recent scenes of multiple homicides by disgruntled employees.[5] From 1980-1989, the U.S. Postal Service had been particularly hard hit with 35 work-related homicides of postal workers. Embittered co-workers or former co-workers committed 20 (57%) of them. Fourteen of the 20 occurred in a single incident.[6]

Workplace violence, including assaults and suicides, accounted for 15% of all work-related fatal occupational injuries in the United States in 2002. Violent acts are perennially among the leading causes of workplace fatalities for all workers, and a major cause of fatalities among taxicab drivers, police officers and sales workers.[7] According to the Bureau of Labor Statistics Census of Fatal Occupational Injuries (CJOI), there were 639 workplace homicides in the United States in 2001, excluding the fatalities resulting from the events of September 11. This made homicide the third-leading cause of fatal occupational injury on the United States.[8]

Homicides and shooting sprees are one form of extreme workplace violence capturing our attention, terrorist activities are another. September 11, 2001 with the horrific destruction of the World

Trade Center and the 2,749 deaths of people who were simply doing their jobs, made most people realize that the workplace was no safe haven from terrorism.[9] Anthrax, delivered to employees in innocuous white envelopes, heightened people's fears, panic and sense of vulnerability. Terrorism in all its forms—bioterrorism, suicide bombings and sniper attacks—has created a new wave of extreme forms of workplace violence.

Still, it is not large-scale terrorism or homicides that pose the biggest threat to employees and employers. It is the other forms of violence that occur daily. Hold-ups, assaults, harassment and bullying, sexual harassment and verbal abuse are a constant workplace reality. This reality strikes at workers in every conceivable industry and in every country. Data comes from the United States and the entire Western world, but it is also coming from developing and transition countries. This problem is well known and a headache for CEO's and security executives. A Pinkerton annual survey of Fortune 1000 companies rated workplace violence as the number one security threat in 2002, for the fourth straight year, placing it slightly ahead of terrorism and business interruption.[10]

Workplace violence represents a global workplace epidemic and occupational health and safety risk. Consider the following data:

Violent Crime

- In a 2001 report analyzing data from the National Crime Victimization Survey from 1993-99, the Bureau of Justice Statistics (BJS) estimated that an average of 1.7 million Americans become victims of violent crime while working. Workplace violence accounted for 18% of all violent crime during the seven-year period. These acts of non-fatal violence include rape and sexual assault, robbery, aggravated assault, and simple assault.[11] The British Crime Survey recorded almost 1.3 million violent incidents in 2000, 634,000 of which were physical assaults and 654,000 of which were threats.[12]
- In the area of education, students and teachers are no safer. According to a BJS report on Indicators of School Crime and

Safety, 2002, while crime in schools is declining, during 1999, students were victims of about 2.5 million crimes at school, 1.6 million thefts, 880,000 non-fatal violent crimes, including about 186,000 serious violent crimes (rape, sexual assault, robbery and aggravated assault). In 2001, the nonfatal violent crimes dropped to 764,000.[13] Over a 1995-1999 period, teachers were the victims of 1,708,000 nonfatal crimes at school, including 1,073,000 thefts and 635,000 violent crimes.[14]

Robberies

- Robberies present a major risk for employees who work in all commercial establishments, but especially for those who work in transportation, retail, banking, service stations and convenience stores. In the banking industry alone, the FBI reported 8,565 robberies of Federally Insured Financial Institutions in 2000.[15] The Chartered Banks in Canada reports 1,155 holdups for the same year.[16] While the robbery trend mainly involves a lone "note passer," there have also been occasions of violent "take-over" style robberies, where the robbers use force to control the employees and customers during a robbery.
- Banks represent a particular target for robberies, but not the only one. According to a United States BJS report, almost 4 of every 10 robberies occurring while the victim was at work or on duty were committed against persons in retail sales or transportation.[17]

Verbal, Psychological, Physical and Sexual Violence

- In the European Union, 2% (3 million) workers are subjected to physical violence from people belonging to their workplace; 4% (6 million) workers are subjected to physical violence from people outside their workplace; 2% (3 million) workers are subjected to sexual harassment; and 9% (13 million) workers are subjected to intimidation and bullying.[18]
- The International Labour Organization (ILO) revealed the results of an extensive worldwide workplace violence survey in

1998: France, Argentina, Romania, Canada and England had the highest rates of reported assaults and sexual harassment on the job out of 32 countries, placing them ahead of the United States.[19]

- Recent data from developing and transition countries, where data on this subject was previously either unavailable or scarce, shows that more than half of the health sector personnel surveyed had experienced at least one incident of physical or psychological violence. In South Africa that figure reached 61% and in Thailand 54%. Research was also conducted in Portugal where 60% of the 212 respondents from a large Urban Health Centre indicated that they had been subject to at least one incident of violence in the last 12 months.[20]

Gender and Occupation Specific Violence

- Except for rape and sexual assault, males experienced workplace violent crime at higher rates than females. The U.S. report places the violent crime victimization rate for working or on duty males at 54% higher than the female rate. About two-thirds of all robberies, aggravated assaults, and simple assaults in the workplace were committed against males.[21]
- In the United States, high-risk occupations include law enforcement, mental health, retail sales (especially late night outlets), teaching, transportation, and health care. In the transportation sector, taxi drivers were victimized at the highest rate. Within the retail sales field, bartenders were victimized at a rate similar to that of gas station attendants and somewhat higher than that of convenience store workers.[22] The ILO study reported similar findings, adding to the list of high-risk occupations, social workers and domestics working in foreign countries. [23]
- Whether in North America, the European Union or developing countries, women are generally more at risk for violence (other than crime) because so many are concentrated in high-risk sectors and occupations where violence is most prevalent, including nursing, teaching, social work, banking and retail. They also

experience sexual assault and are vulnerable to sexual harassment.[24]

- Certain tasks make workers especially vulnerable. These
include: a) handling money or valuables (cashiers, transportation workers, bank and post office staff, retail staff); b) providing care, advice, education and training (nurses, social workers,
ambulance staff, teachers); c) carrying out inspection or law
enforcement duties (police and traffic officers, ticket inspectors);
d) working with mentally disturbed, chemically impaired, or
potentially violent people (prison officers, mental health workers, bar staff); e) working alone (home visitors and domestics in
foreign countries, late night retail staff, taxi drivers, domestic
repair workers).[25]

Costs Associated with Violence

- The National Crime Victimization Survey reported that,
because of workplace violence, an estimated half a million
American employees miss 1.7 million days of work each year,
an average of 3.5 days per crime. The missed work days resulted in more than $55 million in lost wages annually, excluding
days covered by sick and annual leave. People who were victimized by a crime at work lost an estimated 876,000 workdays
annually, costing employees more than $16 million in wages,
excluding days covered by sick and annual leave.[26]
- In reality, because of large scale underreporting, differences in
definitions and data collection methods, it is difficult to put an
accurate dollar value on the impact that work-related violence
or fear associated with violence has on business and the economy. As a result, the correlation between violence and fear of
violence, increased medical and stress-related disability claims,
and salary replacement and benefits' costs are largely specula-
tive. Nor is the full impact known of all forms of work-related
violence on employee performance, turnover rates or organizational effectiveness. However, the Northwestern National
Insurance Company (NWNL) 1993 study on Fear and Violence

in the Workplace shed some light on this. It found that victims of workplace violence and harassment experienced twice the number of stress-related conditions as non-victims. This included depression, anger, headaches, insomnia and ulcers.[27] This has been supported by union surveys which for years have consistently cited their members reporting a rise in sick leave time, low morale, burn out, employee turnover, conflicts and a deterioration in patient and customer service. The unions suggest that these are all direct consequences of the abuse employees suffer. In fact, the Third European Survey on Working Conditions found that 35% of workers exposed to physical violence and 31% of workers exposed to sexual harassment had been absent from work over the last 12 months.[28] In Germany, the total cost of mobbing (ganging up) has been estimated at 2.5 billion marks per year.[29]

- Widespread differences in practices occur among Workers' Compensation Programs across North America related to the acceptance of violent work-related incidents as legitimate work accidents. As a result, employees who suffer physical injuries from work-related violence often do not file a claim or, they file the claim only to have it rejected. Many employees are unable to get compensation either for sick-leave coverage or medical treatment. The problem is even more acute when injuries involve psychological trauma or harassment. Without clear policies or guidelines, claims are often reviewed on a case-by-case basis. Claims involving psychological injury are received with even more skepticism and are often rejected. Still, claims have skyrocketed. For example, The Association of Workers' Compensation Boards of Canada reports that the number of fatalities and worker days lost due to acts of violence grew by more than 88 per cent from 1995 to 1997.[30] This represents a trend in other countries as well.

- Bullying, involving an estimated 1 in 6 or 16% of American workers[31] and cited as a major problem by the ILO study, is a health hazard to the targeted person: 47% of people bullied experience stress, and 34% of workers exposed to bullying have been absent from work over the last 12 months.[32] A calculation by Australian experts estimates that each case of bullying costs employers $16,977.[33]

- Negligent lawsuits are expensive. Legal fees, lost management time, and negative publicity alone are heavy costs. Add to this, the settlement costs. While figures are unsubstantiated, some people place the costs at an average of $500,000 for out of court settlements and $3 million for cases that go to trial.[34] The out of court settlement figure is not altogether unreasonable. In a 2002 ruling, punitive damages of $3.2 million was awarded a female stockbroker against her employer, Salomon Smith Barney for tolerating and failing to prevent a hostile work environment for women.[35]

- The New York based Insurance Information Institute (ILL), lists the following as costs that can result from a violent incident in the workplace. Tangible costs: medical bills (including lifesaving medical attention, dental repairs, cosmetic surgery and psychiatric counseling) attorneys' fees, lost wages, security costs, rehabilitation and property damage. Intangible costs: lost time, cost of temporary workers, staff replacement, training expenses, absentee wage costs, company liability, damage control and morale issues that affect productivity levels.[36] As a result, many insurance companies are now offering companies Workplace Violence Coverage.

NEVER-ENDING PROBLEM

No matter how much we would like to pretend that our workplaces are the sites of civility and harmony, the truth is that violence is a major occupational safety hazard for employees. The ILO concludes that this problem occurring in workplaces around the globe, suggests that this issue is truly one that transcends the boundaries of a particular country, work setting or occupational group.[37]

Not only strangers commit the violence. The people we try to help, those for whom we work, and those with whom we work also commit violence. Violence and fear of violence damage the culture of our workplaces, negatively impacting on customer service and the bottom line. Yet too often managers view incidents as unconnected, isolated events. They respond to the incident but fail to see how much the developing pattern of events and pervasiveness of incivility and hostility, resulting in such behaviors as verbal abuse, bullying and harassment, impact on the bottom line. These emerge as human resource costs, poor productivity and customer service, and employee apathy.

Why is this? Below are several possible reasons.

- The *real* causes of the violence may not be apparent or clear.
- Conceiving of employees as victims or offenders is difficult.
- Priority issues and activities related to the organization's business take precedent, and executives and managers have little time or energy left to handle "troublesome human resource issues or employee behavior problems."
- Violence has a negative connotation and is thus difficult for most senior managers to acknowledge.
- The organizational culture tolerates or supports uncivil behavior and does not respond well to internal conflicts, high levels of stress, expressions of discontent, hostility or low morale.
- Senior managers fail to see how ridding the organization of uncivil behavior can improve the bottom line, and therefore worth the investment of time and resources.
- Dealing with this issue is outside the realm of experience and competency of the average manager.

However, the biggest challenges in managing this problem adequately relate to the four following issues:

1. This is a complex problem requiring a thorough organizational analysis and a strategic plan that is rigorously followed.
2. "Fixing" a workplace violence problem involves a culture change impacting on the way people treat each other, work together, provide a service and conduct business.

3. Success is likely only if CEO's and their senior managers demonstrate their commitment by leading or actively supporting the process, and then requiring "buy in" from their employees.
4. Resolution can be time consuming, labor intensive and costly.

This is difficult work. As a result, most organizations are reactive, instead of proactive, using a band-aid to fix a problem, when radical treatment is the more appropriate intervention. Without an openness and commitment to supporting a zero tolerance policy and a culture of respect and collaboration, incidents of varying degrees of violence keep happening. Senior managers and employees often remain silent and underestimate the gravity of the situation or the scope of the problem, seeing incidents and complaints as unconnected and unimportant.

Often the cause and effect is minimized. Everyone wants to believe that abusive conduct or other acts of violence are random happenings causing minimal distress to victims. Since much of the time the violence is not fatal, and targeted employees suffer no life-threatening physical injury, people can downplay the consequences of the incident and reassure themselves that "little damage was done." However, consequences of violence are not always immediately apparent or visible. Moreover, despite the absence of physical injuries, victims of violence suffer some degree of psychological trauma. Since people want desperately to believe that the victim is unaffected by the experience, the absence of physical injury allows people to deny the impact of the incident on the organization. They can also minimize the negative effects on employees directly or indirectly touched by violence, on bystanders and others in the workforce, on clients, and on job performance.

More than anything, most people want to believe that violence is not a problem at work. Who can blame them? If employees were to acknowledge the pervasiveness of the problem and the risks, they would have to accept that they too are vulnerable, and could get hurt. Going to work would then become frightening and threatening. Moreover, people in leadership positions would have the additional burden of dealing with this problem.

Who wants to do this when there are so many other pressing issues to deal with?

Employees' invisible psychological wounds enable people to keep up the pretense that violence such as harassment, abuse of power, robberies and physical assault are innocuous incidents. Yet victims of harassment, who often suffer no apparent or outward signs of injuries, routinely claim the experience leaves them feeling highly stressed, burned-out or severely traumatized.

The effects of prolonged harassment can last weeks, months and even years. Sometimes employee-victims never recover. They are so deeply wounded, they go off on a sick leave or quit their jobs because they are unable to return to work and face their abuser again.

Robbery victims experience a similar plight. Despite the startling numbers of holdups committed, fortunately few people suffer physical injury or die. This enables us to consider holdups as a "safe crime." We mistakenly believe the business rather than the employee was robbed, since the money "belongs" to the business. We rationalize that if an injury were suffered, it would be to the business. Employees, serving only as agents for the business, cannot be emotionally scarred by the event.

This denial of employees' suffering or blaming the victim for the incident is widespread. The case of Barbara is one example.

While on night duty on a psychiatric ward, Barbara, a 33-year-old nurse, was kicked and screamed at by a patient who suddenly went out-of-control. Barbara escaped with only a couple of bruises. Weeks later, she was still having flashbacks of the patient suddenly lunging at her. Worse still, she kept hearing in her head the yelling, insults and swearing to which she had been subjected. Although Barbara "appeared" to be all right, she could not stop hearing the screaming, nor put the memory of that attack out of her mind. Barbara was not crazy, nor was she ill. She was suffering an acute, but normal stress reaction to a traumatic incident.

Typically, Barbara's supervisor and attending physicians showed her little sympathy. They believed that she was overreacting to the inci-

dent and that her fear and apprehension were signs of weakness. When she asked for a reassignment to day duty, so that she would feel safer because more staff would be around, Barbara's request was turned down. Everyone denied her injuries and the inherent risks in her job. Repeatedly they told her, "Patients act that way. It's part of the job. You should be used to it."

The example of the nurse and the plight of bank tellers and convenience store personnel show the problems employee-victims face. By downplaying the impact of robberies or patient assaults, we can deny the existence of employee distress and suffering. Our failure to see the problem as it really is enables us to perpetuate the myth that the only outcome of robbery is a loss of money, or that nurses should accept that getting hit by patients is part of their job.

By downplaying the incident and denying that employees' reactions and fears are legitimate and directly related to violence, responsibility and ownership for the problem can easily be shifted from the offender and the workplace, to the victimized employees. If employees become traumatized or fearful, or suffer ill effects from the violence, it is their own fault: they are not strong enough, tough enough, or skilled enough. Blaming the victim happens frequently, particularly in a helping profession such as nursing.

Nurses are *supposed* to be trained to handle violence, but they are trained to do nursing, not self-defence. Nurses are *supposed* to be prepared for violence. Nevertheless nurses, like all of us, want to believe nothing bad will happen to them and so are ill prepared when an incident does occur. Nurses are *supposed* to be able to handle the attack, but it is hard for them to believe someone they are helping or caring for would want to harm them.

When violence strikes, it is hard to be objective. It is *normal* for people to be disturbed after a violent act. It is *normal* to suffer psychological injury even in the absence of physical injury. It is *normal* to fear that something bad will happen again.

By minimizing the violence and denying the presence of normal emotional reactions, we alienate our employee-victims, re-injure them and make them believe they are sick, emotionally disturbed, or incompetent.

COST OF DENIAL

Our blasé acceptance of the violence around us, our refusal to fully acknowledge the problem of work-related violence and our disregard for the welfare of employee-victims is costly. Not only do employees suffer distress unnecessarily, they are also unable to do their jobs. In the end, the workplace pays the price.

On-the-job violence and the stress and fear associated with it claim many victims. While employees who are directly involved are the first people to suffer injury, they are not the only ones. The repercussions from a single violent incident reverberate throughout the organization. Many other employees, even those not at all involved, can suffer severe emotional distress by virtue of their having witnessed the incident, or their believing a similar thing could happen to them. When violence strikes too close to home, people feel vulnerable, frightened and become distressed.

Just one incident of violence in an organization can paralyze its entire workforce and change the organization forever. This is exactly what happened to an advertising agency.

Helen, a 54-year-old secretary, arrived and found her boss, a senior executive, dead. He had been shot at his desk. The police later established that the shooting occurred an hour earlier. Her boss, an early riser, was often at his desk working at 7:30 in the morning. The assailant was never found.

Helen and the three other executives, who had all seen the wounds to the body, suffered severe traumatic reactions. Yet most of the sixty people employed there also became afraid and experienced some degree of distress. A couple of employees quit soon after the incident. A few, including the secretary and one executive, went on sick leave. Others complained of insomnia and fear of walking on the street. No one wanted to work late or come in early. People's attitudes changed. Almost overnight morale dropped. Gone were the camaraderie and the "joie de vivre" this company had previously enjoyed. It was replaced by despondency and pessimism. People came to work and did their jobs, but they never recovered from the murder of one of their own.

The shooting destroyed the heart of this organization and took away something from just about everyone who worked there. Employees' sense of security was shattered. Their loss and their fear of the unknown assailant overwhelmed them. They worried they too could suffer a similar fate.

Reactions and feelings experienced by the people at this company are common. Whatever the nature of the incident, violence plays havoc with every work organization it touches. Singlehandedly it is destroying the fabric of our service industries and economy. In every work environment, be it in health care, education, social services, transportation, retail and in our biggest corporations, violence exacts a price. Morale declines, productivity decreases and employees go off on stress-related sick leaves or quit their jobs. Conflicts escalate, anger rages, and a cycle of violence takes root. While we deny, ignore and play down the problem, the fact remains that our workplaces are not immune from the violence that is ravaging our communities, cities and families.

Over the years we have seen a dramatic increase in the number of reported cases of psychological and physical injuries due to work-related violence, as even more people report abuse and demand help. On-the-job violence is becoming a leading category of Workers' Compensation and benefits claims in North America. If this trend continues, violence will become identified as the *leading* occupational hazard of our times.

This means violence will be the leading cause of work "accidents" resulting in death, and physical and psychological disability. As the number of employees requiring treatment and time off work to recover from their physical and psychological injuries increase, there will be an escalation of sick leave benefits and health care costs.

Skeptics or uninformed people may find it hard to believe that we are on the brink of a global workplace and economic crisis.

Yet just stop and think about the situation for a moment. Can you not remember at least one incident when you were put down by a boss in front of other people or ridiculed by a co-worker? Can you not recall getting into a heated argument with a colleague or client, with whom to this day you do not talk, because of the mean things said? Do you not recollect an employee becoming upset and abusive because you firmly stated the work was unacceptable? Can you not remember the time someone threatened you or your family? Do you not recall being punched, pushed or hit? Can you not remember the unwanted kiss, the quick caress or being told that you had better be nice if you wanted to keep your job? Can you ever forget the gun or knife being pulled on you or on a work colleague? Do you not know someone personally who was abused or attacked at work and kept silent about it?

When we think about it, most of us can recall being exposed to some form of violence during the course of our work lives or we know someone who has been at risk.

Sadly, some people have been killed at work or because of their jobs. Most people exposed to incidents luckily escape physical injury. Some people are minimally affected psychologically, and are able to push the event or series of events away, where they remain hidden in the far recesses of their minds. Many can get on with their lives, perceiving what happened to them as a minor inconvenience, even though they vividly remember the experience.

Yet many more employees are unable to forget the pain or hurt suffered because of an abusive event, even when the incident occurred months or years earlier. They struggle to push the incident away and ignore their fears so that they can function at work. Sometimes they can succeed for a time. However, if they allow themselves to recall the incident or if something triggers a memory, they relive the trauma and repeatedly feel the intense pain associated with it. The stimulus, which I call the *trigger effect*, arouses the memory and feelings associated with a past trauma or violent incident that the person has blocked or completely forgotten.

As much as employees want to ignore what happened to them, they do not easily forget the incident or the way their colleagues, employer, clients or strangers treat them. Nor can they disregard the fear and other effects the event had on them. As much as executives and senior managers would like to keep believing that violence has a minimal impact on the workforce, they should not too quickly dismiss the correlation between violence and job performance or organizational effectiveness. Victimized employees have become our *working wounded* and, sadly, there are many of them. People who are hurting have little energy to give to their jobs and no interest to devote themselves to the organization's goals. When too many people are preoccupied with violence or work wounded, their decreased productivity, lack of commitment to their work and preoccupation with safety and security issues severely affect the organization's ability to carry on with its business.

Despite the progress, we still do not handle the problem of work-related violence at all well. The disinterest in this issue by most senior administrators is surprising, since business is losing millions of dollars because of fear, employee abuse, harassment and other forms of violence. Health care costs alone have soared because of the associated stress-related illnesses. Employer liability is also clear. Moreover, the cost to people, in terms of the destruction of quality of life, is staggering.

Employees' stories of their experiences with violence are shocking. When people are willing to listen, employees readily talk about their hostile workplace environments, the traumatic events they have experienced and the extent to which their professional and personal lives have been ruined. They even admit to being apathetic or having difficulty doing their jobs, to questioning their professional competency and to a loss of positive feelings for their employer.

When senior administrators examine and understand the violence, they are not only able to deal with it, they can remove it from their organizations.

Unfortunately there is no quick fix or magical solution. Controlling violence is a matter of understanding the nature of the problem, knowing what actions to take, and taking the action.

When this is achieved, the organization will be transformed into a dynamic, respectful environment that will improve its performance and give it a competitive advantage.

- 2 -
The Workplace:
A Battlefield

Workplace violence is not a new phenomenon, although the number of incidents seems unprecedented. Perhaps it is because we are hearing and understanding more about the violence now. In the early 1980's bank tellers, nurses and social workers were frequent targets. However, because of society's ignorance and denial of the problem, we misunderstood and treated employee-victims poorly. Anne was one of these unfortunate people. Not only was she a victim of nine holdups, she also had to contend with some unresponsive health care professionals to whom she had gone for help.

Weeks after the holdup and still feeling anxious and fearful, Anne, a twenty-eight-year-old bank teller, went to a community health clinic for help. She complained of chest pain, insomnia, nausea, headaches and heart palpitations. She thought some medication would help calm her down. After the doctor had ruled out a physical problem, he asked Anne to talk with a counselor. She reluctantly agreed.

Anne explained to the counselor that, although she had returned to work the day after the holdup, going to work had become harder and harder and she felt she could no longer continue. Anne cried and sat wringing her hands as she related the details of this latest holdup. The robber had not displayed a weapon nor fired any shots. He simply passed her a note. It read: "This is a holdup, give me your money or I'll kill you." Anne complied, gave the robber the money in her cash drawer and watched him leave. The holdup was over in a couple of minutes.

After Anne regained her control, she talked more easily about the eight other times she had been robbed over the last four years. What was striking was her complete absence of emotion when she described the most severe incident. It had happened two years earlier and was her fifth robbery. While robbing the bank, two masked gun-

*men had fired several shots, luckily injuring no one. Anne just contin-
ued to work.*

*As for danger, the last holdup was uneventful. Anne could not
understand what was happening to her and why it was happening now.
She felt anxious, fearful and depressed. She also had nightmares and
flashbacks. Anne was upset and embarrassed that, of the five tellers
working in the bank, she was the only one having a rough time. She felt
guilty because of her inability to work. She was ashamed of her reaction, which she saw as a weakness. Haunted by the experience, Anne
believed she was going crazy.*

The multidisciplinary team consisting of a doctor, consulting
psychiatrist, nurse and social worker at a community clinic assessed
Anne, but they did not know how to help her. The psychiatrist
signed a sick leave certificate, gave her some medication and sent
her away with a referral to a psychiatric hospital for outpatient follow-up.

Unfortunately none of the professionals told Anne she was suffering from a traumatic stress reaction. While she needed help, her
reaction was perfectly understandable for someone who had suffered so many traumas. It would have eased her pain to know that
many holdup victims suffer similar reactions.

The medical team did not discuss this with Anne because they
were simply unaware of it. In the early 1980's, post-traumatic stress
disorder (PTSD) had only begun to be recognized as a condition by
the medical community.[1] So Anne left the clinic, the place where she
had gone to get help, feeling embarrassed and confused. Unable to
understand why she could not function, she believed she was having a nervous breakdown. Leaving the clinic with medication and a
referral to a psychiatric hospital reinforced this idea. How frightened she must have been.

Although their situations may be different, there are today
hundreds of thousands of people like Anne. While they vary in age
and work in many different work settings, these men and women
have one thing in common—they suffer from the effects of workplace violence. Often they do not know where to go for help. They

try to cope as best they can until one day their bodies show signs of accumulated stress. They show up in doctors' offices, clinics or psychiatric hospitals where they are often diagnosed as having anxiety reactions, panic attacks or depression. Doctors put them on minor tranquilizers or antidepressant medication to "help them cope." Even today doctors and counselors may not make the link between the violent episode and their symptoms. They may not correctly diagnose them as suffering from acute traumatic stress (or critical incident stress), an acute stress reaction from a sudden, overwhelming, life-threatening event. They may overlook a post-traumatic stress disorder, a more long-term intense stress reaction, with symptoms that include depression, anxiety, panic attacks and flashbacks.

If people are "lucky," holdup victims like Anne work in financial institutions. Most banks offer employees psychological help after a holdup, usually by way of a debriefing session. Help comes from either their employee assistance program counselor or an outside mental health professional. This kind of intervention effectively decreases the intensity of emotions, reduces the immediate impact of the trauma and provides information about normal reactions to trauma and coping strategies.

Not all employees are so fortunate. Many people who work in high risk occupations for robbery do not have immediate access to psychological help. Taxi drivers, employees and owners of convenience stores, fast-food restaurants and service stations rarely receive help after an incident. Others receive inadequate help. Although the health care community has become more experienced in treating people like Anne, holdup victims often see doctors and mental health practitioners who wrongly diagnose them or provide inadequate treatment. Even with proper care, many robbery victims still suffer severe and chronic stress reactions.

Most of the time, however, they suffer their pain in silence. They hide their hurt from colleagues, family and friends because they do not want to admit how much the holdup affected them. Often they themselves do not clearly make the connection between the holdup and their distress.

Instead they try to deaden their pain by using alcohol, drugs, over-the-counter medication, minor tranquilizers or sleeping pills. Despite their attempts to forget the incident, their stress intensifies, heightened by the knowledge that another robbery can take place anytime. Although security measures have improved over the years in banks, employees and owners of small businesses know they are open targets with little protection. When they cannot take the stress any longer, they go on sick leave, quit, or give up their business.

Although holdups are a major problem in the banking and retail industries, robbery represents only one aspect of the workplace violence issue. Hospital workers make up another large group of employees who continually encounter violence on the job. These caregivers, who want only to take care of their patients, are attacked by the very same people they help. Doctors, nurses, psychologists, psychiatrists, attendants, receptionists and technicians are hit, kicked, punched, bitten, scratched and stabbed by their patients. When attacked, they face tremendous peer pressure to take the incidents in their stride and are even encouraged to forget them. As professionals, they believe they should be able to cope with the violence and not let it get to them.

The severe stress reactions health care professionals suffer are not always the result of serious physical assaults. Minor incidents can also deeply affect employees for weeks or months on end, leading them to question their professional competence and suitability for their jobs. Helen's story typifies the complex problem of violence facing caregivers in health care institutions.

Helen, a 28-year-old nurse with four years' experience on a psychiatric unit, went to the staff health clinic in a daze. She had just been scratched, bitten and kicked by a patient. She had no physical injuries other than superficial scratches, teeth marks on her arm and redness on her leg where she had been kicked. When asked what had happened, she burst into tears. After calming down she told the staff health nurse that a patient suddenly and for no apparent reason lunged at her. She then said: "I must have done something to provoke him. But I tried so hard to calm him down. I don't know what I did wrong."

In the 1980's, nurses and other caregivers believed they must have done something to provoke an attack. Many still believe this. Employee-victims, like so many other victims of violence and crime, think that violence perpetrated against them is their fault. Caregivers in particular believe they are responsible for an attack by a patient, reasoning that they could and should have done something to prevent it.

Neither the type of incident nor Helen's reactions are unusual. In hospitals and other health care settings, caregivers are constant targets of minor assaults. Even if their patients do not physically hurt them or they suffer only a minor injury, most caregivers suffer some degree of psychological distress from patient abuse. This point underscores an important fact about the impact of violence on people's lives.

> There is no correlation between the extent of physical injury and the degree of psychological injury. People do not have to be physically injured to suffer psychological trauma from a violent episode.

The following story highlights this important point.

Jim, a 32-year-old hospital orderly, had his finger pulled back and broken by a patient. After four months Jim still refused to go back to work, coming up with a series of minor medical complaints to justify his continued absence.

Frustrated by Jim's attitude and unaware that fear and psychological trauma from the incident were the cause of his resistance to return to work, the staff health physician referred Jim for counseling. In his first meeting with the employee assistance program counselor, Jim revealed that he was still suffering from stress, anxiety and depression. He was not eating and had lost weight. He was using liquor as a way to deaden his pain. Jim's smoking increased from one to two packs of cigarettes a day. He had crying spells for no apparent reason. Jim was experiencing nightmares and flashbacks. He kept reliving the scene of the patient lunging at him, screaming, then grabbing and pulling back his finger.

Jim felt he could not return to his job as an orderly. Rather than go back to this job, he was prepared to quit. Unfortunately nobody had realized that for four months Jim had been suffering from acute emotional stress from the incident. His symptoms suggested he was suffering from post-traumatic stress disorder.

All this time Jim had hidden the real reason for his inability to work. No one suspected how much a "minor" incident of patient assault had traumatized this 6 foot, 210 pound man. The counselor asked him why he had not told anyone what he had gone through.

"Nobody would have understood how this little incident got to me," Jim said. "They would have laughed. Look at me. I'm a big guy and I'm strong. I'm supposed to be able to handle this. I feel like such a wimp."

Jim was experiencing common symptoms and reactions to a traumatic incident. Yet he could not believe such a minor thing could affect him so profoundly. He felt he did not have enough stamina to work with psychiatric patients.

A week later Jim told his counselor, "It's obvious I don't have what it takes to work here. I've decided to change jobs. I'm going to work in a store selling shoes or clothes, somewhere safe."

Jim's solution is a typical one for many victimized employees. Often people quit their jobs because of emotional distress, worry about safety and loss of enthusiasm for their work.

THE MYTH OF PROTECTION

Unless it personally affects us, we are oblivious to the damage violence causes. Until something happens to us, we tend to believe our workplaces are safe and that we are protected from harm. One incident can quickly shatter this faith in the employer as protector and leave victims feeling betrayed and vulnerable. Realizing there is no protection in the workplace, employee-victims become acutely aware of dangers and risks previously unseen or ignored.

After an incident, employees are shocked and hurt if their colleagues or manager seem indifferent to the incident and potential risks. They expect others to share their fears and sense of danger.

The sense of betrayal runs deep. They feel isolated and alone, believing no one really cares about them.

Erica, a 28-year-old child care worker kicked, bitten and scratched by an acting-out twelve-year-old, summed up the feelings so often expressed by others. "The only thing that matters is that we are there to do a job."

The violence that healthcare workers and bank tellers are exposed to is not unique. Violence and crime do not just happen on our streets. Most people are easy targets for work-related violence and they are not even aware of it.

> Violence is a critical occupational hazard. Many people are in danger because of the work they perform. They are at risk, not from just one, but from multiple incidents of violence during their working years. The violence ranges from verbal abuse, to bullying, sexual harassment, physical assault and even murder.

Employee-victims suffer distressing and debilitating reactions from these incidents, similar to those experienced by victims of conjugal violence, sexual assault and other crimes. To make matters worse, most employees and owners of small businesses have no escape. Without retraining, or lacking other job skills, they have no other place to go. Others—judges, lawyers, teachers and doctors have put in too many years educating themselves in their chosen profession to throw it all away.

After a violent incident, many people live with a daily malaise, not feeling good about their work and themselves, but not really understanding what is wrong. They are unable to talk about what has happened to them. Like all of us, they have learned that, as adults, they should be able to cope with whatever happens at work. So employees unfortunate enough to be victims of a holdup, death threat, sexual harassment, bullying or assault at work, keep quiet. They often pretend that they are unaffected by the ordeal. For if they were to acknowledge the pain they were really suffering, they would make themselves vulnerable. This is even more so when someone, a superior or co-worker, implies "you haven't got what it takes to do the job."

VIOLENCE DEFINED

What do we mean by the word *violence*? Although this may seem like a simple question, it is not. The commonly held definition of violence perpetuates a misconception about the nature of violence and who gets hurt.

To many people, violence means a physical attack on either a person or place. When someone is beaten up, the action is considered violent. When a home is broken into and vandalized, it is considered an act of violence.

Generally implicit in our definition of violence is some kind of *visible* evidence of damage either to a person or property. If an attack is perpetrated against a person, we expect to see evidence of this—a bloody nose, bruise, scratch, broken bones or open wound. The same is true of vandalism. Here we expect to see evidence of the property damaged or destroyed, such as broken furniture, busted walls or doors, or shattered windows. This is the understanding many people have of the word *violence*.

Random House Webster's College Dictionary, 2001defines violence as: "**violence** *n* **1.** swift and intense force **2.** rough or injurious physical force, action, or treatment **3.** an unjust or unwarranted exertion of force or. **4.** a violent act or proceeding. **5.** rough or immoderate vehemence, as of feeling or language. **6.** Damage, as through distortion of meaning or fact: *to do violence to a translation*".[2]

Although the words may differ, dictionary definitions describe violence foremost as *a physical force or attack with an intent to injure, damage or destroy*. While no one is likely to refute this definition, is the dictionary definition explicit enough in its description? Does the definition help people to understand that along with physical aggression, there is also sexual aggression as well as a vast range of verbal and psychological behavior that is violent?

The simple ditty we learned as children summarizes the socially accepted view of violence that many people carried over into adulthood. How often did we repeat and act out in game form the expression "sticks and stones will break my bones, but words will never hurt me?" What we learned from the time we were very young was that things injure us, but words do not.

Yet when we played this game as five and six year olds, we picked a child as "victim" and tauntingly hurled words at him. The words were meant to hurt and often they did. Yet this was make-believe and as children, most of us knew we were not supposed to feel or show our hurt. Thus the child-victim steeled himself against the words because the ditty said that he could not feel hurt. Even as children we were afraid of being perceived as weak and vulnerable by our friends. This idea carried over into adulthood. We learned that hiding our hurt as a sort of self-protection is best. Even when hurt, we often pretend that nothing bothers us. When something happens at the workplace, it is even more so.

Most of us learned the ditty well, though we knew the message was wrong. We all know that verbal and psychological abuse does hurt. From experience we know the pain we feel when someone yells, swears at us or belittles us. We know that words once spoken, cannot be taken back nor are they easily forgotten.

Far from being insulated from critical, hostile or demeaning comments, we feel attacked. The bite of the words and the meaning behind them wound us. Yet unlike physical violence, no one *sees* the injury. Pain suffered from verbal abuse results in internal emotional bleeding. Without blood or broken bones, we can perpetuate the myth that abusive words are harmless. People who display weakness or vulnerability are often chastised for feeling hurt or for being too sensitive. They quickly get the message that they are not tough enough to handle a little rough behavior.

Another issue compounds the definition of violence. It relates to the psychological effects of physical violence. Many people assume the only effect of a physical attack is injury to the body. When someone is scratched, we see an abrasion. A kick or slap leaves a bruise; a knife attack or a bullet leaves a gaping wound. Understanding pain coming from a physical injury is easy, but we often overlook the psychological injury from a physical attack. An assault does not only injure the body, it also injures the psyche. Usually the body heals faster than the mind.

Verbal and psychological abuse must be explicit in any definition of violence. So too must the emotional injury that results from physical, sexual and psychological abuse. Serious reflection must lead us to conclude that the standard definition of violence needs to be expanded upon, since it does not clearly reflect current knowledge about the effects of all forms of violence on people's lives. I therefore propose a broader, far more encompassing definition of violence, which forms the basis of the discussion on workplace violence in this book.

> Violence is an act or a continuum of behaviors that jeopardizes one's physical and/or psychological well-being. It is a threat or a perceived threat to one's life and/or a risk to one's safety, health or integrity. It is an act of verbal, psychological, sexual and/or physical abuse. It can be an attack on one's person or personal beliefs or an attack on one's property. The intent is to control or dominate, to injure or destroy, or to deprive a person of dignity. When the incident occurs at work or is in work-related circumstances, it is workplace violence.

This expanded definition of violence[3] consists of a wide range of physical, psychological, sexual and verbal behaviors that are abusive. Violence is not one behavior but a continuum of attitudes and actions. At one end is degrading or offensive conduct. In the middle is sexual harassment, bullying and abuse of power. At the extreme end is physical aggression displayed as sexual assault, physical abuse and murder, and finally, the ultimate act of violence—terrorism.

When we accept that violence is a range of destructive behaviors, we can appreciate more fully the extent of its damaging force.

Violence in any form is a way of controlling and assuming power over another person to further one's self-interest and goals. This is always done to the detriment of another person—the victim.

Abusive behavior relates to anger and the way it is expressed. At some time or another we are all guilty of abusive behavior towards another person. However the degree to which we are abusive varies: some people scream when they become frustrated and angry, others become physically and sexually aggressive.

How we act and treat others conveys messages about what we have learned about the world and how we view it. It reflects how we have been taught to handle our anger, disappointments and failures, and how we have learned to resolve our conflicts. It relates to how we feel about ourselves and our need to dominate or control others. It relates to how we view our rights, privileges and place in the world, the values we hold and the respect we have for other people and for ourselves. Whether our abusive actions are deliberate or unconscious, we are responsible for these actions and for their consequences. Every type of abusive action hurts another person. Whatever form it takes, violence hurts and the emotional wounds are often deep and long-lasting. As you will learn from the stories that follow, and as you know from your own experiences, the victim nearly always suffers some degree of psychological injury or trauma.

THE AGGRESSORS—GOOD GUYS AND BAD GUYS

At the workplace, who is a threat to our safety? While the answer is simple, unfortunately it is also frightening. Abusers can be co-workers, employers, subordinates (*internal violence*), clients or consumers of services and their families (*client-initiated violence*), or total strangers (*external or stranger-perpetrated violence*). Violence can also be perpetrated by staff toward clients or consumers of services (*client-directed violence*) or be part of a department's or organizational culture (*organizational violence*). Violence can be a physical assault or armed robbery. It can involve protest violence, random acts, and indiscriminate or gratuitous violence. It can also be expressed as verbal abuse, harassment and bullying behavior, or cyberstalking or e-bullying.

None of this should be surprising. At times we can all get into the act. How many of us are guilty of being abusive at work? Do we yell when we get angry? When we are upset about something or with someone, do we tell the person off? When we want something and someone gets in our way, do we backstab the person? Do we gossip and spread rumors? Do we pick on some people or ostracize others? Are we sometimes mean and vicious? How often do we go on the offensive because of feelings of insecurity, and a need to protect or further our own interests or goals?

In the height of our anger or hurt, we rarely think about what we are doing or the effect of our actions on our colleagues, manager, subordinates, clients or consumers of services. Most of us are unable to see our own abusive behavior as a form of violence. If asked to describe our conduct, many of us would excuse ourselves by saying we were having a bad day. While we may admit to being bad-tempered or even a little power-hungry, do we not usually find reasons to excuse away our abusive conduct?

Yet our attitude changes when we are on the receiving end of this kind of behavior. When a person, from whom we would not expect this kind of behavior, verbally abuses, sexually harasses, intimidates or physically attacks us, we are shocked and hurt. We want protection! We cannot understand how a superior, co-worker, subordinate, patient or client, that is, someone we trust and with whom we have a professional relationship, can be abusive toward us.

These aggressive men and women, whom we know and trust, are the *violent good guys*. We ourselves may even be one of them. We do not expect these people to be violent and we feel betrayed by their behavior and actions toward us. They may not even perceive themselves as violent. Compare them with the *violent bad guys* who are, for the most part, total strangers or people with whom we have no relationship.

A violent bad guy is a person who enters the neighborhood store and commits a holdup. We pray that he will just take the money and leave and not harm us physically. Even though he may be polite and in control, we perceive him to be bad. Why? Because we have learned that a robber is bad. We perceive him as dangerous because we have no way of predicting his behavior or knowing what he intends to do to us.

Anne, the holdup victim whose story was described earlier, became fearful of strangers. She could find comfort in the fact that she could still trust the men she knew and worked with—her colleagues, superiors and clients. However, what happens when someone known and trusted commits the violence? Who remains to be trusted? We fear and become cautious of strangers, because they commit violence and crime. When someone we know commits the violence, how can we trust anyone? Abusive actions by people we know totally shatter our sense of security. Not only do we feel hurt and betrayed, we also know we can rely on no one to help protect us. This is especially true when the violent good guy happens to be our superior or employer.

Robert, the marketing manager described in the first chapter, found this out. He had no one to go to with his problem. He knew no one would believe that his boss, highly respected for his competency and achievements, would treat him so badly. Even if someone did believe him, Robert knew it would be unlikely that anyone would intervene.

When something bad happens at work, we search for reasons to explain or justify what happened. Thinking about the event rationally, we know that during a holdup, for example, a robber is more interested in getting the money than in harming us personally. When we have recovered, we understand that he did not choose to attack us as a person, but picked the site for the money or goods he wanted. We were unfortunately in the wrong place at the wrong time.

On the other hand, how can we explain abusive behavior by a boss, colleague or client with whom we have developed a working and trusting relationship? We have to assume that the actions are deliberate and that the person wants to harm us. Or we blame ourselves for being at fault. This destroys our confidence, our ability to develop trust and heightens our perception of vulnerability and powerlessness.

Is it possible then, that the actions of violent good guys can be even more damaging to their victims than the violent bad guys? Do most people not have a little of the violent good guy in them? Finally, think about it: in what ways do you contribute to the escalation of violent behavior in your workplace?

COMMON FORMS OF WORKPLACE VIOLENCE

Workplace violence can be broadly grouped into eight categories as follows:

1. Verbal
2. Psychological
3. Sexual
4. Discrimination

5. Physical
6. Vandalism
7. Criminal acts
8. Terrorism

These broad categories are useful, but it is all the forms they include that really give a complete picture of the scope of work-related violence. In essence, workplace violence does not only consist of a single behavior or action but a continuum of threatening conduct and damaging actions. As shown on the following chart, there are many forms of violence, ranging from verbal abuse and harassment to physical assault and murder. Sometimes the violence can be a singular act, such as physical abuse or an assault. Other times the violence can be ongoing, such as psychological abuse in the form of harassment or bullying.

The *Workplace Violence Continuum* presented on the next page subdivides the above categories into the most frequent forms of violence. It is divided into two groupings of violence, *soft* and *extreme*. Although subjective in nature, there is a gradual progression within each grouping. While one may question the ranking of the various forms of violence, the chart is meant to show the existence of a range of behaviors and a division and progression between the soft and extreme forms of violence. Soft forms of violence, such as verbal abuse and threats do not always lead to extreme expressions. However, bullying and unresolved conflicts can, and often do, escalate into extreme expressions of violence, leading even at times to life-threatening situations. When many forms of violence exist, or when the violence escalates or becomes pervasive, a hostile or poisoned environment develops.

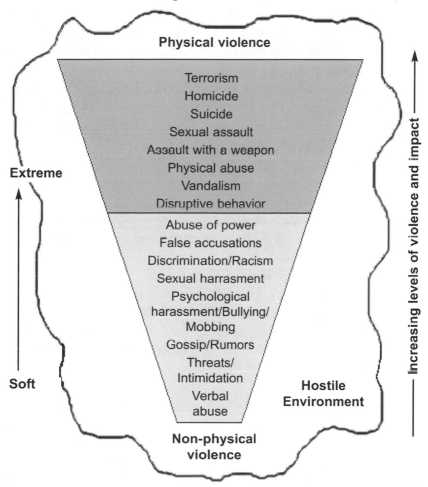

If we are to stop workplace violence and prevent it, we need to be able to identify the many kinds of violence and understand the damage each causes. Let us look at each type of violence that appears on the continuum in more detail.

Verbal Abuse

Verbal abuse is so common and we are so accustomed to it that we do not even view it as a form of violence. It consists of verbal maltreatment and negative comments that are aggressive and attacking in nature. The comments include criticisms, slurs, belittling, obscenities, threats, accusations and lies. Anger is often expressed by a raised voice or screaming. What makes these behaviors abusive is their repetitive nature and lack of respect. Since most people tolerate an abusive outburst, it is usually repeated.

Verbal abuse is rampant in our personal and work relationships. When we are in nasty moods, we say mean things to each other. When we are displeased, we criticize, lash out, or badmouth whomever is the convenient target.

It seems as if everyone is verbally abusive at some time or another. Instead of crediting employees' good work and helping them learn to do better, supervisors and managers too often only lash out at them for their mistakes. Clients, dissatisfied with a product or service, yell at and threaten employees. Employees badger supervisors because they cannot deal with change, especially when it affects their workload or work conditions.

While we do not see the injuries, wounds from verbal attacks are often deep-rooted and slow to heal. Verbal attacks create stress and anxiety, destroy self-confidence and affect job performance. They explain why many employees take extended sick leave due to "stress at work."

Mary, a 43-year-old credit officer, had been verbally abused by her boss for two years. Her boss constantly criticized, yelled at her whenever she made a mistake and belittled her. Life at work became unbearable. Mary could not defend herself because she was afraid. The constant abuse got to her. She began to suffer from colds and viruses and then from burnout. She became anxious, depressed and had trouble deciding even the most routine things.

Because of stress at work, Mary's doctor put her on sick leave. She was off work for nearly eight months. During that time she underwent therapy to help put her battered psyche back together again. Eventually she was well enough to work but she could not return to the job she had been doing for eighteen years. She was fortunate in that her company was able to place her in another position. All of Mary's suffering had been due to her manager's verbal abuse over a long period of time. However, nothing changed for the manager.

Threats/Intimidation

For many employees, the nature of their jobs means living with intimidation and threats. Jane, the bank teller described in Chapter 1, is one of them. The robber intimidated her by his behavior and the gun he held, and threatened her life in the note he showed her. His behavior and words had the desired effect. The gun proved he meant what he had written. Jane believed him. By taking him seriously and following his directions she reduced the risk to her life.

Threats and intimidation involve words, gestures or actions used to gain power over another person. It is meant to frighten the victim, often to the point of submission. Frequently both employees and management make light of intimidating acts and death threats, not taking them seriously. Employees who feel threatened or fear for their safety, usually end up coping with the situation on their own, as best they can. Often they are too ashamed to admit to their fears and too frightened to stand up to their abuser. Feeling trapped, they continue doing exactly what the abuser demands of them.

Anthony, a 53-year-old college professor, endured threats and intimidation on the job. He was in his office marking exam papers, when an angry student stormed in. Anthony had failed the student on his last assignment. After yelling and arguing with Anthony, the student suddenly lowered his voice. He delivered a clear and powerful message. "If you don't pass me, I'm going to kill you."

Anthony believed the student could harm him because of his belligerent attitude, his punk appearance and his way of intimidating stu-

dents in class. Not knowing what to do, he spent many sleepless nights worrying. He kept the problem to himself, because he could think of no one in authority who would take the matter seriously. He also did not want anyone to know he could not handle the situation. In the end, he did the only thing he could do to protect himself. He passed the student on the last assignment, although he should have failed him. Believing the student would carry out his threat, he was too frightened to consider doing anything else.

Threats are directly expressed or arrive in notes. They also appear through the Internet, arriving in e-mail messages or appearing in a chat room.

A threat can be overt or direct as in, "I'm going to harm your children." It can also be veiled or indirect as in, "Is this a picture of your children? They go to that primary school nearby, right? You should be careful, you never know what can happen to children these days."

Some people think that expressing a death threat is simply a way of venting anger or frustration over a situation or a person. How often has someone said in anger, "I'm going to kill you" and not been taken seriously. Only the person making the threat knows how far he or she is prepared to go. Yet at times the threat is a warning of real danger and of future events. Because of the volatile situation and our inability to control someone else's anger, we should take death threats and intimidating behaviors seriously and always act upon them.

Gossip/Rumors

Everyone wants information about what is going on in the organization and about the people who work there. Keeping informed helps people feel connected. Knowing what is happening is vital to employees' positions and careers.

News circulates in a variety of ways. Memos, policies, announcements, internal bulletins, e-mails and newsletters disperse official company news. Decisions are also transmitted verbally and in writing from the top down.

There are also unofficial channels for keeping abreast of who's who and what's what. Every organization has an unofficial information network. No matter how large or small an organization, a thriving grapevine allows employees to receive and pass on information on just about anyone and anything. Usually the grapevine is harmless and even helpful, enabling employees to keep abreast of what goes on inside and outside the organization.

The rumor mill or gossip can be useful to everyone in the organization. After the CEO of a major corporation announced his resignation to the board of directors, the news "leaked" through the organization. The media also reported it. Had the employees not had a well-functioning grapevine, they would have learned about it in the newspapers or would have waited days or weeks to hear the official announcement.

Yet grapevine chatter has a negative side, one that is malicious. People use the grapevine to spread nasty rumors, and malicious gossip, propagate smear campaigns, and pass on confidential information. Rumors can be a form of psychological violence that creates a hostile work climate and affects the victim's job, family, social life and emotional well-being.

Greg, an analyst in a federal department, was going through a separation. Not wanting it publicly known, he told only his closest friends. One of them told someone else in confidence and before long, the news about Greg's separation started getting around.

Kitty, a manager, returned to work after having been off sick for two months. She had undergone breast surgery for cancer. A private person, she did not want anyone to know about her illness. Within days though, almost everyone in the organization knew what had happened to her.

In both these cases the rumor mill flowed, going beyond idle gossip. When rumors transgress people's privacy or are done with malicious intent, there can be serious repercussions. When a disgruntled employee deliberately starts a rumor that is untrue to discredit a person or get a person fired, this is no longer idle talk but violence.

Rumor senders may deliberately start smear campaigns, usually about something nasty that victims have or have not done. By spreading disparaging information about their personal or family lives, culprits attempt to discredit their victims or tarnish their reputations. Unfortunately once a smear starts, refuting or stopping it is difficult. Marilyn found out just how hurtful and damaging the rumor mill can be.

A successful and ambitious MBA graduate, Marilyn was on the fast track in her organization. Within five years she had climbed the ranks of management to become the CEO's assistant. A senior level male employee had always held this position.

Her male colleagues whom Marilyn had beat out for the job started a rumor. They said she probably worked her way up the ladder by sleeping with her superiors. Before long, rumors were flying that Marilyn was sleeping with the CEO, since the position involved frequent business trips with him. Neither rumor was true. When her friends told her about the rumors, she was furious and hurt. They tried in vain to negate the rumor but the damage was done. No one wanted to believe that Marilyn had achieved her promotions on merit, and that she had became the CEO's assistant because of her intelligence, organizational capabilities and refreshing approach. No matter how hard she tried, she could not shake people's perception of her as "the woman who slept her way to the top." Unable to live down the reputation of getting promotions in exchange for sex, Marilyn eventually left the company.

Psychological Harassment/Bullying/Mobbing

In some countries people refer to a group of behaviors that target an individual as harassment, or psychological harassment. In other countries it is known as bullying. When many people join in, it is mobbing. These behaviors are unrelenting and mean-spirited; over time they wear down a person's defenses and resistance.

Jerry is a 52-year-old systems analyst. His supervisor constantly checked on him, belittling him and picking apart minute details of his work. He also assigned Jerry work outside his area of expertise with no explanation about what he wanted and with unrealistic deadlines to meet. Jerry's team members also made life miserable for him. They rarely talked to him, never invited him to lunch, and in meetings frequently ganged up on him. After months of enduring this, Jerry quit his job.

Like other victims of psychological harassment, Jerry coped with the behaviors—at the beginning. However, after a while the stress and pressure from persistent harassment became too much for him. Psychological harassment wears people down, tiring them out and making them feel insecure, anxious and depressed. It is another powerful, effective form of psychological violence.

Bullying and mobbing is harassment. Bullying has been described as deliberate repeated hurtful verbal or physical attacks, perpetrated by an individual or a group who have contempt for others they consider worthless or undeserving of respect. It is about power, intolerance and lack of empathy. The aim is to harm and belittle a person considered less powerful, less confident, shy and isolated. Bullying can also be racially motivated or gender-related.

While harassment generally connotes only psychological battering, bullying can go further. It can be direct, typically involving verbal, psychological and physical actions. It can also be indirect, often taking the form of gossip, malicious rumors, ostracism or exclusion. Bullying can take the form of physical violence, sometimes even resulting in death. It can also involve taunts, threats, intimidation, manipulation, emotional violence, extortion of money or goods. It involves a combination of abusive behaviors and acts.

Bullies may be or appear to be quite self-confident, but they are just the opposite. They feel threatened, have a sense of entitlement, and have little tolerance toward what is new or different. New immigrants, racial minorities, someone new or different, insecure, shy, socially, psychologically or physically challenged, may be the bully's target. Targets can also be high achievers whose competency upsets the complacency of the group and raises the barometer on performance.

Mobbing can involve bystanders who watch the attack and do nothing to stop it, or they join in the attack. They surround and taunt, intimidate or physically attack a victim, leaving no way out.

Commonly associated with children, and schools and the playground, bullying behavior and even mobbing are becoming increasingly associated with workplace abuse.

Tanya, a 32 year old nurse and recent immigrant from Russia was ostracized by her co-workers. Every time she entered the room they stopped talking. They made it clear she was not welcome in the staff room and even withheld information that she needed for her job.

Three male employees of a hospital's kitchen cornered a recently hired college student who was working his way through school, and told him to slow down: he was making his colleagues look bad. Weeks later, when he was walking through the hospital parking lot, these same colleagues surrounded him. They began pushing him around to make sure he got the message.

Marguerite had been student-teaching for only a couple of months when the e-bullying started. At first it was a message that threatened to have her killed. Then a note appeared on an Internet chat site.

The last example represents another form of bullying or harassment. It is a product of our technological evolution. E-bullying is the new millennium's form of bullying. While schoolteachers and students have become targets of cyberbullies, employees everywhere can find themselves discussed in someone's e-mail, which can get broad distribution with the hit of the "send" button.

Bullying, mobbing and psychological harassment cost organizations dearly: in lost productivity, low morale and high turnover. The impact on the target is fear, anxiety and depression. Sometimes out of desperation, a bullied person will suddenly quit. Or, when they cannot take the taunting, harassment, threats and intimidation anymore, sometimes suicide may seem like a way out. Finally, from the media reports of shooting rampages, we also know that targets of bullying and mobbing can snap and go on a shooting rampage.

Sexual Harassment

For close to four days in October 1991, millions of people across North America sat glued to their television sets, watching Professor Anita Hill accuse Judge Clarence Thomas of sexual harassment. The event raised questions about who had more credibility and who had the more convincing explanations about a series of events and conduct. In this case of sexual harassment, Anita Hill was bright, articulate, and professional. Even so, she had difficulty establishing her credibility. What does it take for victims to be believed?

Seldom does sexual harassment cause such public interest. Seldom does it result in such a spectacular hearing. What usually comes to mind when we talk about sexual harassment is a story similar to Gloria's.

One afternoon Gloria, a factory worker, stayed a little later to do some extra work. A single parent, she was pleased when Bob, the fore-man, offered her a chance for overtime because she needed the extra money. Soon after everyone left, Bob tried to kiss her and fondle her broasts. When she protested and pushed him away, he became angry. He told her he wanted to sleep with her. He also let her know that if she wanted to keep her job, she would have to keep him happy. Gloria got away that evening, but Bob was always after her. She was careful to make sure she was never alone with him and avoided him as much as possible. Soon he began complaining about her work. He picked on her and often yelled at her for no reason. She began to feel the pressure. She could not sleep, developed headaches, felt anxious and had begun slowing down at her machine. Finally one day she was fired because of her low performance. Deep down she knew Bob had pushed her out. It was her punishment for not sleeping with him.

Sexual harassment is unwanted sexual attention which may be a one-time event, repeated and persistent, or a combination of different forms of abusive actions. What Gloria went through was one form of sexual harassment. The harassment usually involves a wide range of unwanted sexual behaviors. These include suggestive remarks, verbal abuse, derogatory comments, degrading jokes, sexually explicit photos, unnecessary touching or patting, leering at a person's body and compromising invitations. It can also involve molestation and sexual assault.

Sexual harassment involves an abuse of power. A subtle or clearly stated promise of reward usually accompanies the request. Conversely, an implied threat to one's status or job can accompany the demand. Often the request for sexual favors involves harassment, threats, intimidation and psychological abuse. The harasser knows his actions are out of line and unwelcome, but he continues the behavior anyway.

Sexual harassment is violence and it is a pervasive global workplace problem. It is largely violence against women but men can also be victims. Victims lose no matter what happens. If the victim gives in to the sexual demand, she loses a part of her self-respect. On the other hand, if the victim does not submit to the demand, she stands to lose economically, with a demotion, blocking of career advancement or even loss of job. Always, the victim suffers some degree of psychological trauma from the episode. Fear, anxiety, distrust of men (or women if the harasser is female), degradation, loss of faith in authority figures, depression, stress and erosion of self-confidence are common reactions. Sexual harassment can be devastating to the victim. It can even lead to a post-traumatic stress disorder.

To make matters worse, even when the victim reports the behavior and management take action against the aggressor, the victim almost always loses. The ongoing stress takes its toll. While company harassment policies are meant to be protective, they also set up a process of hearings that are rigorous and demeaning. Going through an internal investigation or an arbitration or labor board hearing is not easy. The victory is shallow when your actions and credibility are scrutinized and attacked by the very offender who has made your life miserable and even terrorized you.

Discrimination/Racism

Many people in our society suffer emotional distress and psychological injury because they are members of a minority group and often face discrimination by the majority. Victims may be the "wrong" color, speak the "wrong" language, embrace the "wrong" religion, belong to the "wrong" sex or have a different sexual orientation. Instead of appreciating their differences, the majority frequently belittles or snubs them or treats them unfairly. Victims can be targets of cruel jokes, demeaning comments or slurs, or can be made to feel like outcasts. Despite their actions or how hard they try, they are somehow not accepted or welcomed.

Racism, sexism, ageism and many other forms of "isms" still raise their ugly heads. Despite human rights legislation, education and affirmative action programs, we remain an intolerant society. Intolerance of people whose color, sex, culture, language, ethnic background, sexual preference or politics are different from the majority, is one of the toughest problems to resolve in our workplaces.

Placing discrimination and racism in the *Workplace Violence Continuum* demonstrates the significance of this behavior. Discrimination or racism is not merely a snub against an individual or a group of people who happen to be different. This is an abusive act that is either overtly or covertly expressed in attitude, words, gestures or conduct. It is an act of power aimed at suppressing, marginalizing or the silencing of one group by another. Discrimination is a form of verbal and psychological abuse. Unless stopped, discrimination intensifies in its expression and increases in frequency, often leading to other forms of violence.

Discrimination targets one person or a group. A single employee can carry out prejudicial acts or the acts can represent a philosophy or culture of an entire organization. This intolerance is a subtle or overtly hostile form of violence. It is a manifestation of hatred and a way of propagating hatred. Not hiring or promoting people because they "do not fit or belong," is an act of exclusion and a way of keeping out unwanted people. It is also a way to ensure that power remains in the hands of the dominant person or majority group. The victim hits a glass ceiling and cannot move beyond a certain level in the organization.

George, a 44-year-old African-American lawyer, worked in the legal department of a transport company for seven years. His boss and colleagues always treated him "correctly." Yet for years he noticed that many other people at his level received promotions. His performance reviews were good and he was liked by everyone. He expressed interest in moving up the organizational ladder and even went on interviews, but he never got the job. George suspected the reluctance to give him a promotion was because he was African-American. While everyone's attitude seemed correct, he noticed people of color never reached higher than a middle management level at his workplace.

A similar experience happened to Carlos, an air traffic controller, who speaks English with a Spanish accent and to Mary, a nurse, who speaks French with an English accent. In the community clinic where Alan practiced medicine, two gay applicants for the position of staff doctor were passed over. The man hired was not as well qualified as the other two, but management thought he was a better "fit" with the rest of the team. In many corporations across the country, women never seem able to go beyond a low or middle management level. Nor do qualified women seem to make it onto corporate boards. Often for their own comfort and self-protection, people in power positions deliberately promote employees of their own gender or ethnic persuasion, to the exclusion of all others.

Discrimination is another soft form of violence that tends to be subtly expressed at our workplaces. Often minorities face a stone wall when they try to advance or gain power. The more employees are discriminated against, the more they realize that equal opportunity is a misnomer. They are left with the feeling that they were overlooked for a job opportunity or promotion because they are different from others. Resentment and bitterness builds, heightening emotions and conflicts between the parties.

False Accusations

To accuse someone of doing something wrong when there is some evidence of wrongdoing is deserved. Accusing someone willfully and intentionally, knowing the accusation is not true, is an expression of hostility and abuse. False accusation is spiteful and aggressive behavior and represents another soft form of violence. The effect on the victim's career and personal life can be devastating.

Accusations of wrongdoing insinuate improper conduct. The dynamics involve a power imbalance between the parties. It also involves malicious, vindictive behavior that is meant to discredit someone. In either case, one party lays a false charge against another to get even for a perceived slight or to avenge an action taken against them.

Timmy, a sixteen-year-old client of a social agency complained to his teacher that Jason, his caseworker, had made improper sexual advances toward him. In fact, Timmy was angry with Jason because of his upcoming court recommendation. Jason believed Timmy needed a closed residential center because of his stealing, lying and truancy at school. His single mother supported this because she could not control Timmy.

Jason was suspended for three weeks while the agency conducted its investigation. A highly skilled and dedicated social worker who only wanted to help people, he could not understand why this child would falsely accuse him. Worse were management's attitude and the reaction of some of Jason's colleagues.

Instead of the complaint being discussed with him, he was subjected to a hostile interrogation. To his amazement and hurt, his employer treated him as if he were guilty. His colleagues began to snub him. Jason seemed to have become a social outcast. He stayed home, becoming more and more depressed. He had no one to turn to for help. Petrified that no one would believe him, he became convinced he would be fired and would face criminal charges.

Weeks later, Jason was cleared of the wrongdoing. Timmy had retracted his accusation. Although his manager told Jason to return to work, he never received an apology from anyone in the organization for what they had put him through. His supervisor continued treating him as if he had done something wrong. Without even consulting him, Jason was taken off the case "for his own good." His supervisor never gave him the chance to face Timmy and demand an apology.

While everyone carried on as if the incident was over, it was not finished for Jason. He perceived the accusation as a deliberate attempt to injure him and ruin his career. While clearing himself, a part of him was destroyed. He had been under tremendous stress, felt victimized, betrayed and violated. At work, he could not pretend that everything was all right and that he had forgotten the incident. As for Timmy, he was transferred to another caseworker and his behavior was never dealt with.

When an employee is accused of wrongdoing, especially involving a breach of conduct, the organization must understandably take the complaint seriously and undertake a rigorous investigation. This creates a dilemma. When innocent, the employee can be victimized not once but twice. First the accuser victimizes the person, knowing the employee is innocent. Then the organization can victimize the employee again while it investigates the complaint. To protect itself, the organization often treats its own employee as if guilty until proven innocent. Sometimes, to make matters worse, the investigation takes too long; in Jason's case, it took three weeks.

The false accusation is one episode of violence. The manner in which the employer treats its employee while it conducts the investigation may signify another abusive action. Both represent different aspects of a violent act.

Abuse of Power

To find out what people are really like, give them authority and time and their true colors will soon emerge. Power has a magical

quality. It changes people. When used properly, power can be vital-
izing and positive. When used improperly, it can be dangerous and
damaging. Let us look at these situations.

*Walter, a Vice President of Accounting, was in charge of a depart-
ment of more than two hundred and fifty people. He was also a friend
of the company's President, over whom he had a lot of influence. His
attitude towards the President was helpful and charming, far different
from the way he was with his employees. Most of them disliked Walter
with good reason. Not only was he moody, he pitted people against
each other. He used them, taking credit for their work. He was quick to
criticize and degrade them, and often yelled when he became angry.
Walter's employees were afraid of him; he never let them forget he had
the power to fire them. They had no one to go to with their complaints
because of his closeness to the President.*

*Walter made life miserable for his staff. His concept of leadership
was that his workers were there to serve him. Because he misused his
power, his employees always had to be on guard. Not only did Walter
create a hostile work environment, he abused his position and victimized his employees.*

*Gladys was a shift supervisor for a public transit system before she
was promoted to division manager of two hundred drivers. Until her
appointment, grievances and strikes had dominated the division. While
her predecessor was autocratic, her management style was different.
She believed in teamwork and consensus-building. Gladys used a
"power by influence" approach. Within a short time, the number of
grievances dropped dramatically, people became cooperative and productivity went up. Gladys used her power and authority well.*

Abuse of power involves conduct that combines bullying,
manipulation and control. The power dynamic creates a hostile
work environment that builds a climate of fear in the workplace.

Disruptive Behavior

Twenty-seven-year-old Jimmy worked as a computer programmer for a federal department. He was competent at his job, but he was argumentative and difficult to get along with. Jimmy was a loner and since his co-workers found him eccentric, they maintained little contact with him. He ate his lunch alone and did not participate in any of the usual friendly bantering among employees.

At times Jimmy would become more argumentative than usual, take up everyone's time asking for advice, explanations and clarifications, and accuse his co-workers of sabotaging his work or spying on him. He would become extremely aggressive, was difficult to understand and pestered the women to go out with him. Usually at this point his co-workers began to be afraid of him. Then Jimmy would go off for four to six weeks on sick leave. When he returned, he would be his normal, eccentric self until about six months later, when the cycle would begin all over again.

While his boss and co-workers did not understand what was wrong with Jimmy, the medical department was aware that he was schizophrenic and had to be periodically hospitalized. His acting-out behavior and paranoia were manifestations of his inability to cope any longer with the stress. An adjustment of his medication and time away from work reduced his stress level. During the weeks preceding his absences, his co-workers and supervisor found him frightening to be with. He also made a pest of himself, kept people from doing their work and disrupted the department's operations. Yet when Jimmy returned from sick leave, although he was difficult to work with, he could do his job very well.

Paul was a 47-year-old Vice President of Operations. He was an excellent performer who surrounded himself with a loyal team. For months, Paul had been coming to work more often drunk than sober. Lately he became obnoxious, and began screaming, swearing and insulting everyone. His staff was fed up doing his work and having to correct the problems he caused.

Although people tried to cover for him, the stress of working around someone who was drinking took its toll. Even when he was sober, he was disruptive and abusive. People became afraid of him and tried to avoid him because of his unpredictability, nastiness and rudeness.

Paul was an alcoholic and was drinking on the job. Yet no one intervened because he was the boss. The CEO and the Executive Vice-President to whom he reported worked in another city and Paul was smart enough not to drink on days when they were in town. While they knew he abused liquor, they tolerated his drinking. They did not realize his disruptive behavior had been interfering with his employees' ability to do their jobs. They did not know his performance level was maintained because his staff covered for him. The CEO would have been furious to learn how much he embarrassed the employees and customers, and the extent to which he was giving the company a bad name.

These two examples exemplify disruptive behavior. The disruptive individual displays an unusual, unreasonable or unacceptable attitude or behavior that interferes with the organization's operations or with employees' ability to do their jobs. Disruptive behavior can include verbal abuse or threats, physical attacks, property damage, misconduct, incessant and unrealistic demands for time and attention, interference with the work environment, and excessive, inappropriate or bullying behaviors. What characterizes behavior as disruptive is that it continues. The conduct is not due to cultural differences. Nor does the disruptive individual necessarily have malice in mind. The person may suffer from an untreated or uncontrolled psychiatric problem or have a chemical dependence, poor social skills or simply be very manipulative. The behavior may pose a threat to the safety and welfare of other employees, negatively affect the business's operations and reflect poorly on the organization's image.

Disruptive behavior is hard to deal with because reasoning with the individual is difficult. Attempts to confront the employee's attitude or behavior often result in increased agitation or anger. Inattention to the problem allows for further deterioration. Everyone is under stress and concerned about safety. Employees have to work while being disturbed or harassed, correct mistakes of the disruptive co-worker and be constantly on guard.

Vandalism

Vandalism and destruction of property commonly occur in the workplace, yet few people consider this as a serious form of violence committed against people. Graffiti on buildings and broken furniture and equipment is a familiar scene. So is scribbling in toilet stalls—swear words, racist remarks or obscene messages. While people may find graffiti offensive, it does not "harm" anyone. However it wounds the collective, creating a negative and visually unpleasant work environment.

A community health clinic was beautiful when it opened, and the employees were excited to work there. Six months later, the waiting room looked dirty and shabby. The carpets had coffee stains all over them, chairs had cigarette burns, and a magazine rack had been ripped off the wall, leaving large gaping holes. The staff, who had worked so hard to create the right kind of environment in their clinic, found this destruction of their workplace demoralizing.

While graffiti and damage to furniture show a total lack of respect, employees can still work and business goes on as usual. Yet overnight, quiet workplaces can suddenly become pitched battlegrounds. Wilful destruction of property can be terrifying and psychologically damaging for employees. They feel violated because of the destruction of their property. The vandalism can also endanger their lives.

In the aftermath of sports victories, many celebrations turn into violence. Soccer matches in Europe and hockey championships in North America have been occasions for gratuitous violence. What happened following the 1993 National Hockey League Stanley Cup victory is one example.

Excited Montreal fans spilled out onto the streets of the city and paraded around, drinking beer and celebrating the win. The huge crowd was an invitation for gangs of vandals who roamed the downtown area, inciting a riot. They smashed store windows, looted merchandise and

destroyed the interiors of many stores. Some owners, fearing that excit-
ed fans during the victory celebration might damage their stores, had
locked themselves inside. They had hoped their presence would ward
off any potential vandalism. When hooligans attacked their premises,
they could only watch in horror. The size and maliciousness of the
crowds paralyzed them and they were powerless to stop the rampage.

Property damage caused by vandals can be terrifying. When an organization's own employees cause the property damage, the effects can even be worse. Employees fighting with each other create rifts between groups that are almost impossible to heal.

During a lengthy labor dispute at a post office, management per-
sonnel took on the work of the inside postal workers to try to reduce the
disruption to the public. The employees were unhappy with this and
with the slow progress of contract negotiations. One night a gang of
vandals, assumed to be postal workers, laid siege to the building where
managers were inside working. They broke windows and tried to set fire
to the building by throwing Molotov cocktails. While they were out to
destroy some property and frighten the managers, they ignored the fact
that they were endangering people's lives.

The union denied having anything to do with the incident. When the
dispute was over, the union members went back to work as if nothing
had happened. Since no one had been caught, nobody could be held
accountable for the actions and damages. Nor could anyone be held
responsible for the terror and risk to the managers. The vandals literal-
ly got away with attempted murder.

The managers, who could not forget the terror of that evening,
could not pretend everything was all right. Although they felt deceived
and enraged, they had to behave cordially with their subordinates. The
events of that night were never addressed.

Physical Abuse

While some people may find the idea of physical abuse surprising, incidents of physical abuse and assault in the workplace are widespread and increasing. Strangely, the abuse happens most often in service industries, involving helping relationships. Hospitals, social agencies, child treatment centers, psychiatric hospitals, nursing homes and residential centers are settings where employees are most vulnerable. Instead of being assaulted by strangers, employees in their role of helper or caregiver, are physically attacked by the very people they try to protect and help.

Susan, a 28-year-old social worker had to remove a child from the parents' care because they had been physically abusing their son. When she went to the child's home, the father screamed and threatened her and pushed her down the stairs.

Jennifer, a nurse on a geriatric unit, was attending to an Alzheimer patient when he suddenly kicked her several times in the stomach. Eight months pregnant, she went into premature labor. The attending physician and nursing administrator excused the patient's action, claiming that he was confused,

Lisa, a nurse on duty in a geriatric nursing home, was suddenly belted by a male patient whom she had taken care of for years. When asked why he had done it, he could not explain his behavior.

Carl, a hospital psychiatrist, was on duty when a male patient attacked a female patient. When Carl tried to intervene, the male patient turned on him and began punching and kicking. The patient got hold of Carl's tie and attempted to strangle him. It took three other staff members to release Carl.

In addition to being attacked by patients, employees can also be assaulted by frustrated or disgruntled individuals who are angry with the organization. The employee is seen as a conduit for settling a score with the organization.

Peter was a foreman in a manufacturing plant. Acting on a directive from management, he fired two people because they were not doing their jobs. One evening after his shift, two masked men beat him up in the company parking lot. He could not identify them, but strongly suspected the two people he had fired.

Physical assault can also occur at random. For no apparent reason, the aggressor attacks an employee. The employee is unfortunately in the wrong place at the wrong time. The aggressor may be high on drugs, drunk, or in a state of hallucination.

Tom, an orderly on duty in a hospital emergency ward, was jumped on and attacked from behind by a male patient whom the police had brought in. Before anyone could come to his rescue, Tom suffered blows to his head and kicks to his back. His assailant was under the influence of drugs and thought he was in danger of being attacked by a monster.

People in a helping profession, in education and others who work with the public are especially vulnerable to physical abuse. Dogs routinely attack letter carriers while their owners seem not to care and do not feel responsible. Angry drivers assault parking ticket agents, drugged robbers attack taxi drivers and intoxicated passengers attack airline agents. Physical assault is a common form of violence against workers.

Assault with a Weapon

All across the country, workers can find themselves suddenly and unexpectedly facing someone with a weapon. It can happen in an office, taxi, on an airplane or in a school. Offenders use weapons to rob, overpower, control or even commit murder. Conventional weapons are guns and knives; unconventional ones can include axes and hypodermic needles. Moreover, simple objects such as ashtrays, pens, forks and knives, tables, chairs and telephones can also be turned into deadly weapons.

Certain occupational groups, such as police and prison guards, are assumed to be at risk because of the nature of their jobs. They have been trained to anticipate sudden attacks, to defend themselves and disarm violent people. The average worker never even thinks about the possibility of being assaulted with a weapon, let alone being trained for it. While anyone can be exposed to a random attack, workers who deal with the public or handle money are more vulnerable. Holdups are an easy way to get money and are often committed with a weapon.

Phil worked nights in a neighborhood convenience store. A man walked in, pulled out a knife and demanded the money. Phil tried to reach for a steel bar that he kept under the counter. Before he could get it, the robber repeatedly stabbed him in the chest and stomach.

Hard as it is to imagine, doctors, nurses, physiotherapists, orderlies and teachers are among the professionals assaulted daily by the very people they are treating, helping or teaching.

Donald, a hospital x-ray technician, was slashed with a knife by a patient who was high on drugs.

Theresa, a nurse on the psychiatric ward, was hit in the eye by a patient who threw a glass at her.

Paula, a high school teacher, had a chair thrown at her by a student who lost his temper because he failed a project assignment.

Whether or not physical injury occurs, assault with a weapon usually leaves an indelible mark on the employee's memory. While the incident may be over in a matter of seconds, the effects do not easily go away.

Sexual Assault

Despite the public's growing awareness of sexual assault as a major form of violence against women, people still deny the reality about who gets raped and where. Working women are targets for sexual assault, either because the nature of their work places them at risk, or because the setting creates a convenient place for an assault to occur.

When sexual assault occurs in the workplace, it can take place as a single event or as part of other forms of violence. A total stranger or colleague, employer or client can commit sexual assault. The assault can take place during or after an office party, while on a business trip or at the office. Sexual assault can be the culmination of sexual harassment when the harasser's behavior is not stopped.

When a woman is sexually assaulted at her workplace, her suffering is compounded. Like all sexual assault victims, she will become traumatized. She must deal with her intense feelings and reactions and reconstruct her view of the world. Since the assault took place at her workplace, she will also have to cope with the added anxiety of risks in her job or profession. Even if she changes jobs, she will continue to associate the assault with her work.

Jean, a sales clerk, worked in a boutique. One evening just before closing, a man entered the store and held it up. He then took her into the back and raped her at gunpoint.

Rebecca, a real estate agent, was showing houses to a man who said he was from out of town and was planning to move to the city with his family. He raped her while she was showing him an empty house.

Heather, a child care worker at a reception center, was meeting with an adolescent to talk about his belligerent attitude toward the other kids and staff. He beat her up and raped her in her office.

None of these women had ever thought about the possibility of being sexually assaulted at work. Sexual assault in the workplace is not supposed to happen. Unfortunately women are just as vulnerable to the possibility of sexual assault at their workplaces as they are anywhere else.

Suicide

Ask doctors or nurses what is the worst thing they have to face, and they will probably answer, the death of a patient. Ask the same question of mental health professionals and the answer will be a patient's suicide. This is the one thing that caregivers dread and constantly worry about, to know that in spite of their efforts, sometimes their help is not enough. Their self-confidence can be shattered upon learning that their patient was in so much despair that he sought relief by ending his life. A patient's suicide makes caregivers question their professional capabilities and their sensitivity to another person's pain.

Suicide is a form of violence. Depending on one's view, suicide is either self-mutilation or a release from pain for the victim. It can also be perceived as an act of rage, and violence by the victim toward others.

Dick, a 33-year-old father of two, was hospitalized for depression. He had been receiving medication and therapy from several members of a multidisciplinary team of psychiatrists, nurses, social workers and psychologists. At a weekly case conference meeting, his treating professionals reported that his spirits were up and his outlook was improving. At six-thirty the next morning, he opened a window and jumped to his death.

Rhoda, a child care worker in a locked treatment facility, had accompanied an adolescent boy back to his room after having a long discussion with him about his behavior. It was time for lights out. When she returned twenty-five minutes later, she opened the door and found him hanging. With the help of three guards, they cut him down. He recovered after three days in a coma. He laughed off the staff's concern and seemed to enjoy all the attention he was getting. Ten days later Rhoda was still unable to return to work. She had nightmares, flashbacks and crying spells. She blamed herself for his suicide attempt.

A patient's suicide may affect the people directly involved. However a co-worker's suicide generally affects an entire organization. It is shocking to learn that a colleague took his or her own life, when just minutes or hours earlier someone had been talking with the person. The suicide brings up feelings of shock, grief and guilt.

Jerry, a 34-year-old computer analyst, committed suicide at his home on a Friday night. No one had noticed anything out of the ordinary, although that same week Jerry had seemed a little calmer and happier than usual. When his co-workers learned about his suicide, they were devastated. They felt guilty for not having noticed his unhappiness or that something had been wrong. While Jerry's death was not their fault, his co-workers felt responsible.

Suicide or attempted suicide affects many people's lives. Family, friends, co-workers, supervisors and helping professionals all feel violated, betrayed and abused by the victim's action. Dazed over what has happened, they may believe that the deceased comitted suicide because of something they did or did not do.

Not only is the act of suicide an expression of violence, but also of significance is the method chosen. It is shocking to find someone hanging, or with a bullet hole in the head or with slashed wrists. There is an expression of rage in the manner in which these suicides are committed.

Homicide

We want to believe murders are only committed on someone else's street, in someone else's home, in parking lots and in parks. However, people do get murdered at work. Although homicides have drawn attention to the problem of workplace violence, compared with other forms of violence, the homicide rate is low. Yet all over North America, and the world for that matter, employees go to work in the morning and never make it back at night.

Employees are murdered by co-workers, clients or total strangers. A workplace murder can take place while another crime is being committed. Sometimes it is politically motivated. More often than not though, the murderer holds a grudge, wants to settle a score, or get even for a perceived or actual offense committed by people in the organization. The victim may be the person who, according to the assailant, has wronged him. The murderer may also hold a grudge against the organization, and the victim or victims are in the wrong place at the wrong time.

What make the headlines are incidents of multiple murder. A disgruntled ex-employee, employee, student or stranger goes on a rampage. He enters the building with an arsenal of weapons and either seeks out specific people or shoots at random. Before taking his own life, he kills as many people as he can. Universities, schools and worksites have all been scenes of shooting rampages. The U.S. Postal Service was particularly hard hit with several shooting rampages in the 1980's. The many incidents in schools and universities include the shooting rampages at Columbine High School and University of Montreal's École Polytechnique. These are the murders that make television evening news and newspaper headlines around the world.

People rarely stop and consider that individual employees are murdered because of the type of work they do. Judges, lawyers, social workers, business executives, teachers, taxi drivers, bank tellers, doctors, peacekeepers and humanitarian aid workers have all lost their lives while doing their jobs.

Ronald, an adult-education teacher, was stabbed to death outside his classroom by a student who was upset that Ronald had failed him on his exam.

A man gunned down Jonathan, a family court judge because he resented the divorce settlement Jonathon had rendered in favor of the man's ex-wife.

Nadia, a pregnant teller, was shot to death during a holdup at her bank.

Cathy, a social worker was stabbed to death by a client whom she was counseling.

A robber shot and killed Norm, a taxi driver, for twenty dollars.

When an employee is murdered, the effects are staggering. Co-workers feel the impact, not only through the loss of a colleague, but also knowing it could have happened to them. Even people in the same occupation, but who work in other organizations or cities, feel like sitting ducks. When murder happens in the workplace, no one is ever the same again.

Terrorism

Far from being an anomaly, terrorism has become the most gruesome and deadliest kind of violence we have experienced. Terrorism has emerged as a workplace security threat. When terrorism occurs, the devastation is widespread. The bombing of the Oklahoma City Federal Building and the 9/11 devastation of the World Trade Center show just how vulnerable workplaces can be domestically. Suicide bombings on buses, in restaurants and other public places such as those incidents that occur in Africa, in the Middle East, Europe and Asia have been chosen to inflict the most damage. The bombings of the United Nations offices in Iraq, and the killings of peacekeepers, humanitarian aid workers and journalists all over the world, have shown that few occupations are safe.

Bioterrorism, in the form of anthrax, for example, followed September 11, 2001, arriving at select American workplaces in innocuous white envelopes.

Terrorist activities such as these examples cause rampant fear and curtail normal activity, destroy lives and property, destabilize law and order and play havoc on the economy. This emerging problem is new to the workplace violence issue. With each incident workplace security will heighten. How we will deal with this as a workplace violence issue will become clearer in the coming years.

THE BATTLEGROUND

While not every workplace has a problem with violence, every work setting is a potential target. While not every employee experiences violence on the job every employee is potentially at risk. While not every employee is abusive, abusive behavior is pervasive in our workplaces.

The abuse is not only directed at employees. Another side to this issue is the problem of violence by employees towards people in their care. This is an emerging problem and targets the most vulnerable in our society. Along with terrorism, client-directed violence will need our attention in the coming years.

In a long-term care facility, a family suspected their handicapped sister was being abused by the staff. They hid a tape recorder. Caught on tape were the voices of several patient care attendants who swore at their sister, threatened her and terrorized her into believing she would be sexually assaulted.

Whether violence is directed at a client or a staff member, the offender's actions hurt, injure or demean the targeted person. When violence occurs, the result is some form of injury.

We want to believe that after the violence ends, victims can forget the incident. We want to believe that the organization does not suffer any negative repercussions. However, most organizations exposed to violence suffer major economic consequences, no matter what form it takes. Most employee-victims cannot easily forget what happened to them. The following poignant testimonies come from employees during seminars I conducted on preventing workplace violence. The stories highlight the nature of workplace violence and the damage it causes.

"Several times a day he would find ways to say: 'You're stupid, you're no good, you're useless.' Everything I did seemed to be no good. After a while I started thinking he was right. I hated work and felt sick all the time. I know I shouldn't have stayed, but I needed the job, and

jobs aren't so easy to come by these days. Besides I didn't think anyone would want to hire me, because I believed what he said about me. After all, he was my boss."

"I believed him when he said, 'I'm going to kill you.' He said it so convincingly, I knew he could do it."

"He threatened my life, not directly, but he let me know that he was connected to the underworld. He told me to be very careful when I went home."

"She did not threaten me, but my children. I remember clearly what she said: 'I know where your children go to school. By the way, doesn't your daughter wear her hair in a ponytail?' How would she know this unless she saw me with my children?"

"The rape destroyed me. That my very own client, whom I was trying to help did this to me, I will never understand. Four years later, my life is a total mess. I can't go back to my job. Why did he do this to me?"

"They beat me up. I will never forget that knife. I saw them come at me and I could do nothing. The nightmares never end. For cigarettes and $150? I've lost everything—my store, my wife, my self-respect and my future. Look at me. I'm disgusted with myself. Five minutes, that's all it took to destroy my life."

THE IMPACT

Regardless of whether employees are targets of harassment, bullying or abusive behavior, or are victims of crime, the pain and disruption to their lives is always the same. They suffer degradation, distress and despair.

Victimized employees become someone else, a shadow of their former selves. They often become withdrawn, moody, depressed, anxious and frightened. Their self-esteem shatters. Often employees are so deeply scarred emotionally by the experience, they are unable to do their work. Violence robs employees of a future in their chosen career and wholesome relationships with colleagues, family and friends.

Workplaces change because of violence. Employers and employees display less and less trust, cooperation and civility. Tension rises. When employees feel they are going into a war zone every time they go to work, they divert their energies and attention from their jobs to ward off potential attacks. Sometimes colleagues clash with colleagues. Other times employers and employees are in continual conflict with one another. Often clients are hostile towards employees and employees are hostile towards clients. Occasionally total strangers wage war.

> When one considers the number of employees and the variety of occupational groups affected, it is clear that violence on the job portrays an occupational hazard of major proportions.

This occupational hazard has a major impact on employee turnover, extended sick leaves, increased health insurance claims, union grievances, bad judgments and errors. Violence affects morale. It leads employees to bicker with each other and with management over trivia. It creates conditions in which people become aggressive and lash out at other more vulnerable people—such as clients or patients in their care.

Violence erodes employee loyalty and leads to mediocrity at work. It reduces productivity and destroys teamwork and commitment, both essential ingredients for a successful operation. When employees have to worry more about their safety and security than about the quality of their work, the organization suffers. Violence in all its forms is costly to any public service or business endeavor.

Although workplace violence has become a globally recognized workplace problem, more often than not this problem is not tackled directly, or with much success. Employees are reluctant to speak out. Often managers seems to miss the early cues warning of trouble coming, wait too long to intervene, or apply a band aid solution when a more drastic intervention is needed.

Often employees will not discuss incidents because they are afraid no one will listen or believe them. They fear their manager and colleagues will ridicule, blame or reprimand them for speaking out. They believe the situation will get worse. Experience has shown that they face an uphill battle against this problem. So employees will often downplay the extent of the violence and the impact it has on them because they cannot cope with the pressure.

As a result, even today, despite widespread recognition, legislation, workplace policies, training and supportive counseling programs, many employees remain silent about verbal, psychological and sexual abuse

Workplace violence is a big headache for executives. This is understandable. This problem distracts from the organization's mission. It is difficult to know what to do about a disruptive employee who shows streaks of brilliance, or the screamer or bully who also runs the most efficient department or reaches the highest sales targets. For most managers, it is almost impossible to know where to begin when there are conflicts between departments, when team members do not get along, or passive-aggressive behavior creates tension and hostility.

Resolving these problems can be overwhelming for the leadership of an organization. In my experience, of all the aspects of workplace violence, dealing with internal violence is the most common problem and the hardest to deal with. When harassment, bullying, abuse of power and chronic conflicts become entrenched and part of the culture, resolution or change is a complex matter. It can also be labor-intensive and costly. Under these conditions, who can blame the leadership for wanting to ignore these problems? Moreover, knowing how to resolve these difficult problems requires skill and a well-thought out plan. Not easy for any CEO or a senior management team whose strengths are elsewhere.

Implementing a zero tolerance for violence policy is easy in principal but difficult in reality. Zero tolerance really involves implementing a culture change where civility rules. Zero tolerance means an absence of violence of any kind, by anyone—employee, manager, client, executive, CEO, and board of director.

While abusive conduct is not an easy problem to fix, it is fixable. How? By adopting a planned approach to deal with the problem and sticking to the plan. When the intervention involves a well thought out strategic plan to stop the violence and stop it for good, things change and get better.

FOUR R's of Violence Prevention

For more than a decade I have conducted training programs for employees and coached executives and senior managers in organizations of every size and complexity on how to get violence out of the workplace. How? By developing a strategic approach that includes early identification, analysis of the causes, determining change strategies and preventing it from happening again. The focus is always on identifying and managing behaviors and conflicts, and dealing with violence in all its manifestations.

Over the years I have developed and refined a model for managing and preventing violence. This four-step approach is simple to understand and work with. Employees who have to deal with client violence find it an easy model. Managers have found this to be a straightforward approach to dealing with internal violence. This model has proven effective in dealing with a single aggressive person, or a more complex problem involving whole departments or multiple work sites.

FOUR R's OF VIOLENCE PREVENTION

Recognition: Identify early warning signs
Roots: Understand the causes
Response: Know what action to take
Recurrence: Prevent a repetition

Stopping workplace violence requires a focused, planned, collaborative effort. It starts with *Recognition*, that is, being able to identify violence in all its forms, to pick up on trivial or so-called inoffensive behaviors, and to understand how abusive behavior escalates. The next step is to be aware of the *Roots*, that is, to understand the causes for the behavior, and the risk factors or triggers that provoke an angry outburst or hostility. The third and most critical phase is choosing the appropriate *Response*. This means knowing what action will effectively defuse the situation, will regain control, and restore calm. This may be easy to do with a single offender, much more complex and harder to do when it involves a whole department. Timing and follow through is critical to the success of this phase. Finally, it is important to close the loop by making sure there is no *Recurrence*. This means putting a strategy in place to prevent a repetition. Prevention strategies include ensuring everyone's collaboration and buy-in, promoting win-win conflict resolution and building a culture of respect and civility.

This model forms the basis for what follows in this book.

PART TWO

VIOLENCE AT WORK

- 3 -
Failure of the System: Violence in Organizations

Staff at a psychiatric unit had been under tension from a continual stream of violent incidents by its disturbed population. The primary targets were nurses, but patients had also attacked attendants, social workers, medical residents and occupational therapists. Minor incidents included swearing, screaming, kicking, scratching and punching. Employees also received death threats, were stalked and had chairs and other objects thrown at them. While covering a ward late one night, a nurse narrowly escaped serious injury when a patient tried to strangle her. Preoccupied by the number of patient attacks, employees talked about the incidents at lunch, around the coffee machine and behind closed doors. In spite of increasing numbers of incidents, they reported only the most serious ones. As one nurse said, "what's the use of reporting an incident when nobody does anything to stop it?"

The nurse, who had been the victim of the attempted strangulation, had come close to losing consciousness. Yet when she later described the event, she downplayed it, saying "the patient put his hands around my neck." While some staff made light of their experiences, the continual abuse they were subjected to overwhelmed many of them.

Management hardly reacted. They believed that incidents were isolated and unusual. They thought the assaults were due to the nurses' lack of skill in handling out-of-control patients.

Fearing for their lives, customs agents at border crossings protested to their superiors. They were expected to control drug smuggling and the illegal entry of people and goods into the country. Unarmed and without police backup, they reported frequent episodes of verbal abuse, scare tactics, physical assault and drive-through shootings. The division director did not respond to incident reports.

A television journalist who refused to return to a war zone was fired for insubordination. He had covered the same site a couple of years earlier and found the assignment too dangerous.

For years female prison guards were subjected to hazing activities at training events. Their male colleagues taunted and sexually harassed and assaulted them. Their superiors never answered the women's written complaints, and mysteriously, incident reports disappeared. Those who complained found themselves sidetracked, relegated to dead-end jobs, and ostracized. For years management covered up the problem, until it reached public attention.

An employee, suspended a week earlier for insubordination and fighting, returned to the sportswear factory where he had worked. He shot one of the co-owners in his office, then entered the plant floor and shot a seamstress. After chasing a cutting supervisor outside and gunning him down, he sped away in his car. The ex-employee was later arrested and charged with triple murder.

These five stories are examples of workplace violence and the way the matter is often dealt with. When management ignores the problem and is indifferent to the distress of employee-victims, it creates even more victims. When decision-makers do not perceive violence as a priority issue, they will ignore conflicts and organizational problems that foster violence, and do not control offenders.

Senior managers often fail to act because they do not know what to do. Sometimes they inadvertently blame, scapegoat and isolate employee-victims. It is hard to acknowledge a pattern of violence, and easier to perceive incidents as exceptional or isolated. Unfortunately inaction gives offenders permission to continue their abusive behavior. Within a short time, the problem becomes chronic and pervasive.

VIOLENCE AS A SOLUTION TO CONFLICT

We use complex reasoning to rationalize the prevalence of workplace violence. Yet the reasons are fairly simple. Most extreme incidents are not unprovoked acts by strangers or outsiders, such as the murders of sixteen four and five-year-olds and their teacher at Dunblane Primary School in Scotland in 1996. These incidents generally involve people known to the organization—disgruntled clients, patients, employees or ex-employees. Feeling unjustly treated, the person uses violence to get attention or to try to resolve a problem.

Workplace violence is due to a failure of the system. Violence occurs when an organization ignores cues that warn of a dangerous situation. Or, it occurs when the organization's response is inadequate and the problem is not resolved. Generally the system fails because cues are missed, problems are ignored, reactions are too slow, or responses are inappropriate.

Specific signals warn of a situation getting out of hand or reaching a dangerous level. Disgruntled individuals usually give out messages that tell of an inevitable explosion, long before they go over the edge. Situations involving escalating tension have the following features in common:

- The violence is usually not a single act but is a process that builds over time.
- The violence is often the result of a series of unresolved chronic problems and conflicts.
- A stimulus triggers a hostile reaction, almost like "the last straw."
- The disgruntled individual sees violence as the only solution to a difficult situation.
- The setting facilitates or permits the violence.

An analysis of many violent incidents in the workplace leads to one conclusion, especially incidents resulting in shooting sprees committed by disgruntled employees or clients.

> Most violent incidents can be prevented. Violence thrives in workplaces where employees and managers miss the cues, ignore or deny the problem, and do not take swift, firm action to stop it.

THE ISSUE OF TOLERANCE

Since violence has been clearly identified as a pervasive workplace concern, why does it continue to be such a problem? If this is an issue at your workplace, try to understand the causes by answering the following questions:

- Does the senior management group remain silent and uninvolved?
- Are victims' complaints ignored?
- Are offenders protected?
- Do employees tolerate abusive behavior from clients, colleagues, subordinates and bosses?
- Does the senior management group tolerate abusive behavior from clients, colleagues, subordinates and bosses?
- Do people view abusive conduct, such as verbal abuse and harassment, as normal?
- Do people ignore threats and other cues that warn of danger?
- Is attention paid to people's stress levels or emotional pain?

The answers to these questions give a fairly accurate picture of organizational tolerance for violence.

Our societies have a high tolerance for violence in general. Therefore it should not be surprising that we tolerate violence in the workplace, and the behavior of abusive people, since our workplaces are an intrinsic part of life. Our everyday exposure to violence has desensitized us.

The extent and complexity of the problem of work-related violence may come as a surprise to many because most people perceive workplaces as safe environments. Or, many people do not make the connection between violence and incivility and conflicts, viewing these issues as simply "irritants" for the organization. Yet far from being mere nuisances or isolated events, many people are discovering that the range of violent behavior described on the *Workplace Violence Continuum* in Chapter 2 is extensive and widely tolerated.

CORPORATE CULTURE SETS THE STAGE

What are the root causes of workplace violence, especially internal violence? For one thing, certain workplace cultures support and foster abusive behaviors. Abusive conduct flourishes in other organizations because of restrictive structures and practices. An analysis of work and business ethics, organizational behavior and human resource practices show how the stage is set for a lot of violence to occur in some organizations. Violence exists because many workplaces are tough, competitive environments with an organizational culture that condones or supports violence.

> ### Problem 1
> **The link between aggression and success**
> Abusive and aggressive behaviors are linked with success, power and money. Many role models and heroes are abusive people, giving the message that abusive conduct is normal and even a valued form of behavior.

While our society may abhor violence, it reveres success. Ambitious people are admired, even those who are ruthless. What is important is to reach the top. Abusive, aggressive, acting-out behaviors, mainly in the form of verbal or psychological abuse, are often equated with toughness, determination and power, all essential ingredients for success.

Equating abusive behavior with success makes this conduct acceptable and even respectable. Some of the worst proponents of violence are lauded as heroes because of their fame, fortune or power. These role models come from many sources—politicians, rags-to-riches businessmen, sports heroes and soap opera characters. The promotion and glamorization of war as a noble cause, and our adulation and identification with aggressive and violent television and movie characters, make heroes out of proponents of death and destruction.

Direct and subliminal messages from television programs and movies with their action-packed violent scenes bombard us. We are continually exposed to horrific and gory news reports, scenes of devastation from suicide bombers, terrorist activities and war.

This overexposure to violence has desensitized us. Moreover our acceptance of violence as a normal part of our lives and our admiration of people who are knowingly abusive distorts our outlook. We have become conditioned to believe that being abusive is normal for successful people. We think little of the meaning of their behavior and who they hurt in order to fulfill their goals.

It is widely perceived that nice people generally do not make it to the top. We receive the following message. "To be a successful person, you must be tough, aggressive and ruthless. You must be single-minded in your goal to make it. Do not allow people to get in the way of fulfilling your objectives and aspirations." In other words, the end justifies the means.

This type of distorted thinking about right and wrong leads us to tolerate and even reward offenders, and sacrifice innocent people who become their victims. The stakes for a work organization to deny the existence of abusive conduct or cover it up may be high. Confronting the problem may force management to discipline or fire a valued and successful employee who is abusive.

Problem 2
Survival of the fittest
Organizational success means survival of the fittest. Management value people who share their vision and can contribute the most to the organization's success.

Senior managers value employees who can transform the organization's goals and aspirations for success into reality. Leaders are chosen because they can surpass the competition and get the job done. Management must be single-minded in its purpose: ensure the survival, success and profitability of the business. While most CEO's want their organizations to be seen as good corporate citizens, survival can be a battle. Morality and ethics can easily be put aside.

Employees who can contribute most to the organization's success are valued and respected. Those who have little power, or present problems that divert it from its goals, are resented and sacrificed.

A survival or success-driven organization often does not have the time to address conflicts and underlying causes of abusive behavior. Resolving human resource problems is not seen as a money generating initiative.

The organization values people who have the stamina and the backbone to help it achieve its goals. That some of its brightest and best performers are abusive towards others is just simply an unfortunate by-product of the cost of survival or success.

Problem 3
The cultivation of violence
Workplace organizations are tribal societies. Power rests with an elite group that surrounds itself with people of similar values and conduct, and a shared view of how to do business and achieve success.

People who want to pursue a career rather than simply have a job quickly learn the importance of aligning with the power elite. Having a mentor or attracting the attention of the power elite is essential for advancement.

Employees who want to move up the organizational ladder must share their leaders' values, support their visions of success and model their behavior on them. They must also identify with the corporate culture, adopt the prevailing communication and behavior patterns, and conform to the rules.

The dominant group restricts entry to its inner circle by developing elaborate practices that tell people how to behave and what values to adopt. It closes ranks by promoting only similar-minded people who fit in with its culture.

Mentoring and fast-tracking allow for the continuity of tribal norms, values, behavior and leadership. Working for the good of the leader teaches team playing. Mentoring and role modeling ensure that new recruits learn to play by the established rules and fit in with the dominant culture. To separate the fit from the fittest, the elite encourages internal competition, rewarding those who come out on top.

Those who climb the ranks do so, in part because they have the skill, but also because they have learned to play the game. This means following the leaders' conduct and actions. In some organizations, aggression, intimidation, callousness and abusiveness become learned behaviors for which one gets rewarded. These behavior patterns become ingrained as the corporate culture, leadership conduct and management style.

The abuse does not stop there. Since few employees do in fact "make it," those who try to play by the rules and fail, end up feeling angry, resentful, disillusioned, alienated and powerless. These feelings foster intolerance, disrespect, abusive behavior, and thus even more violence.

> ### Problem 4
> **A closed patriarchy**
> Organizations are generally patriarchal societies. Male values and conduct that shape corporate thinking, behavior and attitudes dominate the culture.

Though women are significantly present in the workforce and have made impressive gains into male-dominated professions, most workplaces remain patriarchal societies that are gender-biased in favor of men. Men are at the helm and hold most senior and middle management positions. Competent women, for the most part, have little influence on shaping or defining corporate culture.

Defensive and offensive actions are central to the male-dominant workplace value system. Taunts, insults, aggression and infighting are normal behaviors for men accustomed to protecting what is theirs or seizing opportunities to enlarge their domain. They form alliances with like-minded people to ensure their self-preservation and the protection of their turf.

Rivalry is part of the game. However, when females advance their own particular value system, which may conflict with the existing patriarchal value system, they are rebuked. Resentment and hostility toward them rise. In a tribal environment, threats to the dominant culture and the way people behave and work need to be thwarted.

Restricting females' entry to senior management and executive positions ensures the protection of the dominant culture. Without a different value system to act as a balance, aggression, infighting and confrontation remain entrenched as the operating culture. Since there is no incentive for the group to alter their ways, a confrontational attitude becomes even more predominant and normalized.

Problem 5
Violence toward women
Social tolerance of violence against women spills over into the workplace.

Men commit a lot of the violence in our society and direct much of it toward women.[1] Men who are abusive in their personal relationships bring to work their same attitudes about women and how to treat them.

Women's complaints about men's abusive behavior at work often get ignored. Male managers who hear their complaints often do not react. They perceive the male's abusive behavior as normal, and the woman who complains as a whiner.

Many men and some women are more comfortable when women assume traditional roles and occupy support positions. The backlash and abuse against women escalate when females try to break down the barriers at work, either by moving into traditionally male-dominated positions or into the power-elite echelon. As women attain higher positions and open more of the once-closed doors, resentment and jealousy builds until a critical mass forms that forces a cultural change.

When women hold little real power and are not part of the power-elite, they can be an easy target for abuse. When no one is there to protect them, to insist that men stop their abusive behavior or to tell women how to deal with it when it occurs, they become easy targets.

When senior managers do not stop the abuse, act as exemplary role models in civility, and provide help for men to learn to control their anger, the behavior continues and tensions escalate. When abusive men have few role models to show them how to behave differently, tension, hostility and abuse toward women permeate the workplace.

Problem 6
The belief that toughness is good
Some workplaces operate with an authoritarian leadership. An aggressive, competitive climate and an attitude that "toughness is good" reflect the idea that violence comes with the territory.

The dominant culture promotes tough and aggressive leaders and an authoritarian management style. The chain of command is hierarchical and strictly enforced. Employees are paid to follow orders. They quickly learn that: the boss is always right; tough and aggressive leadership is in; always make your superior look good; play by the rules and you get ahead; never admit to weakness; and, take whatever is thrown at you like a man.

These attitudes place enormous stress on any employee who wants to fit in, become a team player and be successful. Moreover, the constant stress and pressure from the top and descending down the ranks make people more aggressive and intolerant. This process develops leaders who are tough, mean and often abusive, because only people with these attributes survive or succeed. In the wake of their success lie the casualties, those who did not have the "right" stuff, lost to the competition or got in the way.

Winners learn that toughness and meanness are valued charac-teristics that guarantee success. Losers, often those with the strongest sense of morality and fair play and who are the most respectful to others, learn that no one values these attributes. Their dreams of success vanish as they realize they do not fit in.

The power-elite become tougher and meaner and those left out become more resentful. The organization thinks it has won by selecting the best for the top. It really loses, because its selection process creates internal conditions ripe for even more tension, con-flict and abuse.

> ### Problem 7
> **Family violence breeds dysfunctional employees**
> Employees bring to the workplace their personal values, communication patterns and personal prob-lems that affect their relationships with co-work-ers, bosses and subordinates.

Employees are people with families, friends and life experi-ences. Many have been brought up in dysfunctional families where they either witnessed violence or were themselves victims of phys-ical, psychological or sexual abuse or neglect. Some people have had parents who were poor role models in relationships. They may not have learned how to handle anger well, either their own or someone else's, or how to handle conflicts in a non-aggressive way. Still others come from families or ethnic groups where screaming, name-calling, fighting and slapping is part of their learned behavior or cultural norm.

The cycle of aggression and hostility that comes from personal pain and experience also can play out at work. We repeat the pat-terns of behavior in our professional relationships that exist in our personal ones. People who are respectful at home are nice at work. Often those who are tyrants at home are tyrants at work. Moreover, people who do not heal from the wounds of personal victimization may become so enraged, they in turn may become aggressors, both at home and at work.

We also assume roles at work similar to those we assume at home. Sometimes these roles allow an employee to become violent. For example, colleagues, bosses and subordinates may become workplace "enablers" to an abusive person, as they have done in their own alcoholic or dysfunctional families. The enabling allows a boss, subordinate or colleague to act abusively toward them and others.

Employees who have been brought up or live in hostile family environments replicate at work what they live at home. People who have unresolved personal injuries or problems, who have not learned to act civilly, or who do not know how to deal with their anger constructively are problem employees.

> ### Problem 8
> **The role of the CEO**
> Executives who ignore workplace violence are either offenders themselves, believe violence is part of the job, are too far removed from the situation, or are insensitive to their staff's reality.

A CEO has the power to stop abusive conduct and decide how to treat offenders and help victims. However, many CEO's do not react to the situation despite employees' pleas for help. There are several explanations for their inaction. First, the CEO may be abusive himself. He may believe that abuse and violence are a normal part of the work culture. He may be used to treating others abusively and may not even be aware that he has been a negative role model or established a pattern of abuse throughout the organization. Bent on attaining his goals, he may not care how he treats people. He creates fear in the organization.

Another explanation is that the CEO believes violence is an integral part of the work and presumes that staff should be immune to it. Many administrators think violence comes with the territory. This is the prevailing attitude with respect to bank tellers, or caregivers who work in a nursing home facility, for example. Managers may not contribute to the abuse nor want it to continue. However, they view the violence as beyond their control and unmanageable. They believe staff know what the score is and should be able to cope with it.

A third explanation is that CEO's are so far removed from the line of fire, they do not believe the abuse actually takes place. Never having experienced it themselves, they may be unable to relate to the conditions under which their employees have to work. They have a distorted perception of the situation.

When executives and senior managers do not experience abuse themselves, forget what it was like, or accept abuse as normal, they may be uninterested in staff complaints. Caught up with their own priorities, these problems seem trivial. Violence is another problem to resolve, interfering with the "real" work. It can be perceived as a waste of time, energy and money, as well as a slur on their reputation.

Finally, the problem may seem irresolvable and overwhelming for people who do not have proper training. The priorities and skills of managers and CEO's are in operations, marketing and finance, but not necessarily in human relations or conflict management. Without training and proper counsel, they cannot detect or stop violence in their workplace.

> ### Problem 9
> ### The effects of restructuring
> Tough economic times resulting in company restructuring, layoffs and limited employment opportunities, create desperate people who have little hope for the future.

Downsizing and restructuring may be the only way organizations can survive tough economic times, but these actions cause tension, resentment and uncertainty for employees. With few employment prospects, workers facing layoffs become hopeless, disillusioned and desperate. It does not take much for people who are worried, angry and frightened to lose their cool and become violent.

Knowing that without a job they could lose their home, family and self-respect, employees can easily feel they have nothing to live for and nothing more to lose. Returning to a former workplace and gunning down the manager who laid him off, or murdering his own family and then committing suicide, may seem like the only reasonable action for a desperate person who feels he has lost everything.

One would hope that those lucky enough to retain a job after restructuring would be happy. However, working in a detested job with no chance for change or limited mobility within the organization or elsewhere, does not make for a happy workforce. When people feel trapped, they become resentful and abusive and when they are miserable, they can easily make everyone else's life miserable too.

Tough economic times can also set the stage for organizations to take advantage of their employees. Companies are pushing employees to do more with less. People will put up with increased workloads, more stress and abuse. They will complain less often out of fear that their grievances will cost them their job.

Difficult times give companies an excuse to get rid of unwanted employees, whom management feel are too costly or no longer useful. Firing a middle-aged employee who has given his best years to the organization, forcing people into early retirement, dismissing an employee without just cause, terminating someone just months before retirement, or harassing an employee so much that the person quits, are callous actions that sometimes provoke callous responses. These are often precipitating factors in cases where an ex-employee returns and murders his employer.

With tough economic times, many companies have to streamline their operations. When organizations do not handle this well, or do not provide proper help to enable their employees to deal with their emotions and the impact of a layoff, the potential for a lethal attack rises.

Problem 10
The strain of high stress environments
Chronic high stress environments create a vicious stress/violence cycle that is hard to untangle.

Work environments with chronic, high levels of stress are breeding grounds for abusive conduct. There is a high correlation between stress on the one hand, and frustration and anger on the other. While some people thrive in high pressure jobs or environments, eventually chronic stress will wear them down.

A high stress environment means that there is little or no reprieve: employees have to contend with one crisis after another. Without a chance to decompress and let go of their stress, they keep absorbing it until something snaps. Either people withdraw to get away from the constant pressure, or the stress builds within the unit creating more tension and thus more stress.

Chronic stress eventually triggers all kinds of reactions and problems that might otherwise have stayed in the background. Impatience, frustration, anger and hostility are often present in pressure environments, quickly leading to miscommunication and intolerance. This sets the stage for incivility, interpersonal conflicts, and abusive behavior.

> ### Problem 11
> #### The role of the hostile environment
> A combative workplace mentality pitches employees against each other and turns the workplace into a battleground.

Employees and employers enter a mutually beneficial relationship because one wants work and the other wants a worker. Yet the organization's structure, attitudes and expectations about work often polarize the parties and place them at odds with one another. A combative mentality develops almost naturally, pitching workers and management against each other because of their rights and obligations. Injustices occur on both sides. Labor and management have a lengthy history of conflict with each having acted against and taken advantage of the other. They are naturally suspicious and distrustful of each other, resulting in an entrenched "we-they" attitude.

Our "me-first" society has resulted in people being more preoccupied with themselves and acting less responsibly towards others.

Preoccupation with what we want coupled with rapid technological changes have weakened our attachments, bonds and allegiances. Family relationships and social connections have loosened. Employees are less involved and less willing to compromise to help management achieve their goals. At the same time, management feel less committed to their employees, who realize they have jobs only as long as it suits the organization.

The wider the gap in management-labor allegiance, the more entrenched the polarization becomes. This increases the likelihood for more misunderstanding and conflict.

Problem 12
Unfair treatment creates anger and hostility
An abusive climate stems from intolerance of people's differences, unfair labor practices, inattention to employee complaints and management teams unskilled in handling human resource problems.

Although racial and gender discrimination is illegal, informal discrimination exists in many workplaces. Intolerance of differences in people creates an unhealthy work climate. Intolerance leads to divisiveness, frustration, fear, anger, stress, resentment and powerlessness among employees. People who discriminate against others are abusive. Those who do not feel respected or who are under constant attack divert energy from their work to defend and protect themselves.

Many organizations do not appear to value their employees. Some do not base their labor practices on fairness, but as a way to further the interests of the leadership. Sometimes the leadership follows the barest minimum in labor standards. They may pressure employees to accept sacrifices, such as wage cutbacks or increased hours while employees do not see similar wage cutbacks for senior management. Or, employees might face the prospect of a near-bankrupted pension plan upon their retirement, after they have contributed for years in good faith and expected their employer to do the same.

Sometimes listening to employee complaints is not easy for managers because they feel employees complain a lot. Conflicts, which make up most of employee complaints, are easily ignored, put off or mishandled. Often managers do not deal properly with people problems and conflicts because they do have not the time, the desire or the ability to resolve them.

SPAWNING DISGRUNTLED EMPLOYEES

Organizations foster violence by creating disgruntled employees. This happens in many ways.

- They have formal or informal labor practices that discriminate against certain groups or classes of workers.
- They do not promote fair and equal advancement opportunities.
- They do not give employees credit for their work.
- They do not expect supervisors and managers to communicate effectively.
- They undertake biased performance evaluation exercises.
- They take advantage of their employees.
- They engage in unfair remuneration practices.
- They do not control autocratic leadership styles and empire-building.
- They pay no attention to chronic stress.
- They do not resolve employee complaints.
- They do not attend to irritating operations or systems problems.
- They ignore abusive or harassing behaviors.

People who feel unfairly treated put up with it until they can no longer tolerate the situation. They leave because they are financially able to do so, have found another job where they hope they will be treated better or because they can no longer cope. Others internalize the problem, become physically ill and go on sick leave. Some become so enraged at the injustice and the lack of protection, they lash out and attack either the cause of the problem or those weaker than themselves.

Victims of violence often learn to survive by becoming perpetrators themselves. This sets in motion a dangerous cycle of violence. Eventually, everyone learns what it takes to survive. Biased treatment, unfair labor practices and botched management interventions transmit a powerful message that abusive behavior is a way of life. Distrust, fear, resentment and anger build, setting the stage for more internal conflict, a cycle of repeated abuses and more violence.

HIGH COSTS OF VIOLENCE

Unresolved conflicts, psychological and verbal abuse and physical aggression create troubled or toxic environments. Apart from the human costs, violence causes workplaces to lose their competitive edge, and reduces organizational effectiveness. Workplace violence creates many difficulties for the organization:

- **Reduced morale** when no one protects or helps employees.
- **Decreased employee commitment** due to a perception that management does not care.
- **Decreased productivity** when employees worry more about safety and security issues and pay less attention to their work.
- **Increased performance problems** such as errors or accidents because of decreased concentration due to a preoccupation with violence.
- **Increased absenteeism** when employees can no longer tolerate the violence or become severely affected by it.
- **Increased health insurance costs** because of the associated stress-related physical and psychological illnesses.
- **Burnout** when employees suffer from violence overload.
- **Higher turnover rates** when employees quit because they can no longer take the violence. When abused employees remain on the job, it is more because of their economic situation, a restricted job market and commitment to their clients than loyalty to their employer.

- **Increased employee/management conflicts and union grievances** as employees hold management accountable for safety and security issues.
- **Deteriorated service and customer relations** because employees fear abusive customers or are preoccupied with their own safety, and because good people may go on sick leave or quit.
- **Increased legal costs** from dealing with union grievances and employee litigation.
- **Tarnished image** because the organization "permits" the violence and develops a reputation for not caring about its employees.
- **Stagnant climate** evolves because the best people leave, motivation and enthusiasm for work deteriorate and staff become alienated from the organization.
- **Increased losses in management time** as managers spend more time putting out brush fires than attending to their own work.

Workplace violence translates into lost dollars, loss of competitive edge and decreased market share. This is more than any organization can afford.

THE RIPPLE EFFECT

Most incidents do not impact solely on the employee directly involved. Every episode creates multiple victims. Physical and/or psychological abuse produces a *ripple effect* throughout the organization. While only one or two employees may be directly implicated, many others, even those far removed from the situation, suffer distress. Through the rumor mill and informal networks, employees talk about the incident and share their concerns. They worry about suffering a similar fate. They discuss their employer's sensitivity and response to the situation. Co-workers identify with the victim and worry about their own vulnerability and safety.

BATTERED WORKER SYNDROME

People who are victims of work-related violence suffer the same reactions as victims of violence in general. Sometimes the trauma is even more serious, because the violence affects their ability to earn a living and support themselves and their families. Eventually the violence takes its toll. For example, taxi drivers, shopkeepers and pharmacists, who are subjected to repeated armed robberies, may experience a complete breakdown of their psychological and physiological functioning and suffer from *holdup fatigue or holdup trauma.*

One does not have to face a gun to suffer from violence burnout. Repeated incidents of psychological battering can traumatize a worker or an entire department. Workers exposed to persistent incidents of verbal abuse, intimidation, harassment and psychological games develop a reaction similar to the battered wife syndrome. Repeated episodes of violence wear people down, regardless of whether the abuse occurs in a family or a workplace context. Reactions to these abuses, to which I apply the term *battered worker syndrome*, are more prevalent than we would like to believe.

Diane is a typical example of what happens to someone exposed to unrelenting psychological battering at work.

A secretary in the credit office of a major corporation, Diane had rarely missed a day's work in the fifteen years she had been there. She had been doing the same job for years and loved it. She was a team-player with above average performance and was used to working with a minimum of supervision.

Things changed with the arrival of a new supervisor. A highly nervous individual, Thomas was a stickler for detail. He was not well liked and had a reputation for being difficult to work with. Thomas routinely criticized Diane both in private and in front of others. He became angry easily and was always screaming at her. He never seemed satisfied with her work. At first she just took his criticism and harassment in her stride, hoping that he would soon change his attitude or get transferred.

As time went on, Diane's nervousness increased. So did her mistakes. The more he criticized and yelled at her, the less confident she became. She made mistakes and could not maintain her normal pace. Diane began to dread going to work. She had difficulty sleeping, became anxious and depressed, suffered memory loss. She had difficulty concentrating and became withdrawn.

As Diane's self-confidence waned, her boss's criticism and screaming increased. After nine months of this treatment, she got up the courage to complain to Human Resources. They could not transfer her because her last two performance appraisals had been poor, which meant she was not "sellable." Unable to function any more, she became acutely depressed and started having anxiety attacks. Her doctor put her on sick leave. He also sent her for a neurological investigation, since she complained of short-term memory loss. She was worried she was developing symptoms of early Alzheimer's.

Diane looked and sounded like a battered woman, only this time the battering occurred at work. She blamed herself for being unable to meet her boss's expectations and began to believe all the negative things he said about her. This abusive man had bruised her psyche so much that she became unable to make even the smallest decisions for herself. She began staying in bed, believing she was sick.

It took four months of twice-weekly psychotherapy sessions before she could even get out of the house and start socializing again. A year after she started her sick leave, she finally returned to her workplace. However she was unable to return to the job she had loved so much.

Her boss's abusiveness and harassment cost her a year's work, a demotion, the respect of her colleagues, her own self-respect and tremendous pain and suffering. Only after he retired and was out of the picture, could she really begin to pick up the pieces of her shattered life and completely heal.

Far from being an isolated case, many workers suffer from the battered worker syndrome because of unrelenting abuse from an employer, subordinate or co-worker.

BATTERED WORK UNIT

A group of five women who worked in the same college department had been victims of verbal and psychological abuse, intimidation and sexual harassment by their director over a five-year period. By the time administration acted upon the abuse, they had been emotionally worn out. They had became demoralized, suffered low self-esteem and were no longer able to deal with their work. Their bodies showed signs of the constant stress. They all suffered some type of stress-related condition that included headaches, gastrointestinal problems, high blood pressure and chest pain. Fear for their safety and for their families preoccupied them. They had insomnia and nightmares. They suffered flashbacks and were anxious and depressed. Believing the things he said about them, the women blamed themselves for the way their boss treated them.

Individually, the women had the profile of a victim of conjugal violence, and fit the description of the battered worker syndrome. Collectively, the whole work unit displayed symptoms of what I view as a *battered work unit*.

Before the battering, these women were independent, competent, satisfied people who liked their work and had active happy lives. Many questions come to mind about this case and the situation in which the women found themselves. How could these women, who held down demanding secretarial and administrative jobs, end up with such devastated psyches? How could they all suffer post-traumatic stress reactions? How could one person inflict so much pain on employees without anyone in the college being aware of what was going on? Why did they remain silent about the abuse? Why did it take so long for them to get together and do something about their situation?

While we could easily blame the women for their tolerance of the situation, the real answer lies in a failure of the system. They did not know whom to turn to. The culture of the college, the organizational structure and nature of the unit and its physical isolation made these employees vulnerable to violence.

Let us understand how the dynamics of battering evolve. There are many similarities between conjugal violence and kind of internal violence that these women suffered on the job. Victims of conjugal violence become isolated, economically trapped and suffer a gradual wearing down of their self-esteem from a constant barrage of belittling, derogatory comments and harassment. At first the abuser may be kind to the woman and may even be her savior. Gradually he becomes more and more abusive.

After several bouts of psychological battering, the woman believes she is worthless, just as he says she is. He has convinced her into thinking he treats her badly because she deserves it. He is all-powerful and persuades her she is nothing without him. At times he does nice things for her and even may be a loving, kind person. The woman develops ambivalent feelings about him. A cycle of violence develops, entrapping the victim because of her conflicting emotions about him, her worry about her future and because of his changing, unpredictable behavior and treatment towards her.

The five women in the story went through a similar evolution. They worked in a building that was separate and isolated from the main college campus. Their boss was a highly respected administrator, who developed a successful model program. He had total control over his department. No one at the college paid any attention to the way he administered the department since his program met the college's objectives and was lauded by its corporate partners.

At the beginning he was charming, personable and made his employees feel special. They felt privileged to have been chosen to work for him. A couple felt indebted to him because he had given them a chance. Although they were uncomfortable with his "good morning kisses" and other sexually harassing behavior, they accepted his explanations that this was just a friendly gesture and part of the workplace culture. Each of them felt the others thought it was all right. No one protested for fear of being considered a prude.

While their boss could be pleasant and seemed concerned about their personal problems, he also had a mean streak, yelling at them, belittling and humiliating them and threatening to fire them. Each woman rationalized his behavior to herself, thinking that he was a difficult man to work for. The women were not particularly close to each other, as he managed to alienate and set them against each other. As a result, they never discussed their problems with each other. Much of the abuse went on behind closed doors. He assured his control over the group by telling them individually he would know immediately if they talked to anyone in the organization, as he had friends in high places, which indeed he did. He let them know he had the power to hire and fire. He did not tell them about organizational policies and procedures, which would have informed them about their rights. They felt isolated and believed there was no one for them to turn to. They felt indebted to him, as they all needed their jobs.

In the end the college came through for them. Administration fired the department's director and defended the unjust dismissal claim he made against the college. The women received months of counseling and legal support. Eventually the arbitrator upheld the college's decision. Of the five women, three were placed in other positions, one remained in the unit under a new director, and one left.

In this situation the employees happened to be women. However men are also victims of battering and suffer the same debilitating effects of the battered worker syndrome.

Given the strong pressure in our workplaces to deny and remain silent about violence, it is not surprising that a cycle of violence occurs. The isolation factor, organizational denial, power and control of the abuser and an unresponsive system set the stage for the battering to take place. The victim's shattered ego, powerlessness, and fear of provoking further attacks and of losing a job, allow the cycle of violence to continue.

THE VIOLENCE CYCLE

Most of the time workplace violence is not an isolated event. It operates in cycles much the same way as conjugal violence occurs. Let us continue to use domestic violence as a way to better understand the cycle of workplace violence.

Family violence begins with a stress factor, causing the aggressor to become frustrated, unhappy, threatened, angry or insecure. This leads to an increase in tension, hostility and conflict, with blame for the stressor being projected onto the victim. If no one resolves the situation or defuses the aggressor's anger, then a blow-up occurs. This could be expressed through verbal, psychological, physical or sexual aggression. A period of calm or quiet follows.

The "honeymoon stage," giving a promise of hope, has the couple reconciling. The woman may try harder to please her partner or stay out of his way. He may be repentant, despondent over his actions and try to be extremely nice to her. This relief period for the woman, who hopes the violence will never happen again, is usually short-lived. The cycle will be repeated unless the aggressor finds other ways to release his tension, learns more appropriate ways to deal with his anger or someone stops him. It will never end, unless the victim receives support and protection and learns she does not have to accept such treatment.

A similar phenomenon takes place in the workplace. When no one attends to the events that provoke tension, anxiety and hostility, conflicts escalate. When no one addresses inappropriate and abusive behaviors by staff and clients, the offensive behaviors continue. When the leadership does not reprimand the offender quickly and decisively, the behaviors increase in frequency and severity.

Even when the violence is limited to a conflict between two people, its impact can be felt everywhere. When organizations experience repeated abusive incidents, they find themselves living in a dangerous cycle of violence. Left unchecked, the violence spreads, as even more people perceive that this is an acceptable way to behave. As presented in the *Workplace Violence Continuum*, a hostile environment develops.

Silence from the victim and inaction by management encourage the violence. Inaction allows for repetition and spreading of further abusive acts. The following situation clarifies how this works. Consider what happens when an employee complains to the Human Resource Department of bullying by a supervisor and nothing is done. The reasons may be that no one believes the victim, the offender is too powerful, the Human Resource Department has no clout, or nobody cares about these kinds of situations. The victim feels trapped, believing there is no protection. The perpetrator, knowing he or she can get away with the behavior, becomes bolder. The attacks increase, and the victim is punished even more for having dared to complain.

Learning not to go to the authorities because they will get no help and may even be blamed or suffer a backlash, employee-victims remain silent. The violence goes underground. It continues, and while everyone knows about it, they look the other way and no one talks about it. Senior and mid-level managers who can stop the abuse and change the culture assume a "see no evil, hear no evil, speak no evil" attitude.

This is a dangerous position. It is at this point that internal violence spins even more out of control. The longer an organization takes to respond, the more the abusive behaviors become ingrained as part of the culture. The longer the violence goes on, the harder it is to reverse the pattern.

TOXIC ENVIRONMENT

It is hard to believe that there are workplaces, where abuse is so ingrained in the culture, the whole environment is contaminated or toxic. This is not simply a case of isolated incidents of abuse but a continual stream of abuses affecting a unit, department or organization. Violence spreads and creates a dominant abusive culture, breeding unhealthy relationships and contaminating everyone.

What makes an environment poisoned is the widespread or systemic abuses against employees. The environment becomes hostile and toxic. The abuser's power and total control over employees silence and isolate them. They become focused on how to survive the attacks and avoid further abuse. Job performance takes second place for the abuser and the abused. This is an environment of survival of the fittest.

Abuse involves acts that range from abuse of power to manipulating and controlling employees. Abusers use fear, intimidation, blackmail and harassment to subdue anyone who gets in their way. They exploit people's weaknesses and manipulate their confidence to secure the loyalty of people who will then protect and help them achieve their goals. When the conduct and abuse spreads, hostility becomes part of the corporate culture. The perpetrators are dishonest, devious people. The more they get away with, the bolder they become.

Abuse can also involve financial malpractice such as fraud, manipulation of funds, stealing equipment or supplies, or using equipment, staff and premises for personal business. The aim of psychological abuse is to create a climate of fear in order to obtain absolute control and power. The more control and power abusive people have, the more they use harassment, intimidation and bullying to exploit people.

It is not difficult however to understand how the leadership of an organization could allow such people to have power. Often the people who create poisoned or hostile environments are valued employees who have contributed the most to the organization's success or financial health. Often they so skillfully control people and documents that discrepancies and wrongdoings do not become apparent until things begin to unravel. By then it is too late to change the culture. Since senior management generally do not challenge or control a valued employee's abusive behavior, they disregard complaints—until the situation becomes a major crisis and they have no choice.

ORGANIZATIONAL HEALTH

When we think about an organization's health, what immediately comes to mind is its financial health, marketplace viability and future prospects. Organizational health is most often linked to a management style that can capitalize on its personnel. However, organizational health can also be linked to its susceptibility and response to violence. This state of health is characterized by the position it takes on abusive conduct, its openness and ability to deal with violence, and the way it responds to employee-victims, and deals with offenders.

Organizations generally fall into one of four categories related to the issue of workplace violence:

- Violence-Prone Organizations
- Traumatized Organizations
- Toxic Organizations
- Healthy Organizations

Violence-Prone Organizations

Organizations prone to violence are usually organizations in a state of denial. Despite the repetition of incidents, management have difficulty acknowledging the existence of a problem and taking appropriate action. An intractable position of denying chronic stress and abuse makes these workplaces vulnerable to more incidents. Until management face the problem, the violence will not stop. Violence-prone organizations are governed by a management team which steadfastly refuses to accept "soft" incidents (described in Chapter 2) as violent. They cover up, ignore or downplay employee complaints. The management team of these organizations adopts several of the following attitudes, behaviors and reactions.

- Ignore employees' complaints and deny that violence is a problem.
- Trivialize incidents.
- Claim that violence is part of the job.
- Discredit employees.
- Blame victims.
- Discourage incident reporting.
- Believe frequent incidents make employees immune.
- Excuse aggressor's behavior.
- Find excuses for what happened.
- Condone or support abuse.

- Refuse to perceive employees as victims.
- Ignore organizational irritants and systems problems that increase negative stress and incite people to violence.

Each attitude, behavior and reaction by the senior management team to workplace violence has an impact on both employees and the organization's operations. Below is a closer look at what each response means and the effect that each has on employees and the organization. This analysis will help to clarify why workplace violence has become such a big problem and why controlling it is so difficult.

- **Ignore employees' complaints and deny that violence is a problem**. By doing this, management reject the consequences to direct and indirect victims and deny that incidents in any way affect the organization's operations. The denial can come from management, employees or both. The onus is placed on victimized workers themselves to handle problems of violence. The organization continues to go about its business as if nothing is wrong, thereby negating the importance of incidents on employees. When violence is pervasive and becomes part of the organizational culture, denial is more entrenched and even more devastating.
- **Trivialize incidents**. This diminishes the seriousness of events. By downplaying what really took place, negating the danger and effects on victims, the organization renders events meaningless. Employing "it was only" phrases reduces the gravity of incidents. For example: "Mr. X. only threatened the lawyer" (it is insignificant). "The patient only kicked and punched the nurse" (no one was injured). "It was only a note-passing incident" (no life-threat and therefore an inconsequential holdup). Relegating incidents to an insignificant status allows management to disregard victims' reactions and blame them for their inability to cope with difficult situations. This enables them to scapegoat and portray victims as having personal problems. Workplace violence, therefore, is not the issue.

- **Claim that violence is part of the job**. This normalizes abuse. Since many employees, particularly those working in health care and social services, are subjected to violence from patients or clients, the presumption is that violence comes with the job. However the only occupational groups that should have to deal with violence as a job requirement are law enforcement, correctional personnel or the military. Although other occupational groups may be exposed to it, no one should accept the notion that dealing with violence is "part of the job." Violence should be no more part of our jobs than our everyday lives. Such an attitude reinforces the myth that workplace violence is normal and acceptable and workers have to put up with abusive behavior. This position places the onus on employees and excuses abusers. Often the anger is directed towards employees when the person is really angry about an irritating problem in the organization's operations (e.g. patients in emergency departments who wait for hours in extreme pain). By adopting the position that violence is "part of the job," management do not need to analyze why their clients are angry. This position also eases management's responsibility to protect their employees.
- **Discredit employees**. This belittles events and consequences. Victims are questioned about what took place and whether incidents really happened the way employees reported them. By challenging the facts, management can reassure themselves that incidents were inconsequential. When employees are challenged, they receive the message that they have overtly or subtly provoked the incident and are therefore to blame. By questioning their employees' credibility or suggesting their perception of the events was exaggerated, victims become responsible. Worker safety therefore is not the issue.
- **Blame the victims**. This allows other people to avoid assuming their responsibility. Since everyone seeks to avoid liability, defenseless victims become convenient scapegoats. Management quickly transfer blame and responsibility for what happened to employees, as if they, and not the perpetrators, had committed the violence. Management often view employee-

victims as having provoked the incident, even when they could not possibly have shared in the responsibility. If management do not blame employees for the provocation, they blame them for doing unpopular things, such as: complaining too much, displaying atypical behavior or reactions, taking too much time to get over the incident, or making demands for protection, action or change. With responsibility taken away from the perpetrators, management avoid having to deal with the problem.

- **Discourage incident reporting**. This negates or covers up the violence. Employees quickly learn that filling out an incident report is a waste of time, since nothing will come of it. Often their supervisor discourages them from even filing a report. Their attempts to bring incidents out in the open and to draw attention to the problem is viewed negatively by managers who want to keep the problem hidden, so they do not have to deal with it. This conspiracy to stifle the truth allows management to maintain the stance of isolated incidents. With incomplete and inaccurate statistics, senior management can deny violence is a problem, though front-line employees know differently.

- **Believe frequent incidents make employees immune**. This discounts the impact of violence on employee well-being. Sticking to the principle that greater exposure makes people tougher, management can convince themselves that employees easily take the violence in their stride and can get on with the job. They liken the situation to a person who has fallen off a bike and can easily ride again, if only he or she would take the first step. Overcoming the stress from traumatic incidents is not that simple, nor is it only a case of learned behavior, which, with practice, becomes easier. Repeated incidents of violence wear people out.

- **Excuse aggressors' behavior**. This avoids having to confront perpetrators. Senior management *want* to find reasons to excuse perpetrators' abusive and violent conduct, because they fear the consequences of taking action. They may also make allowances for the behavior when offenders are a valued asset to the organization. Excusing the behavior negates the impact of incidents on victims, lets offenders believe the behavior is acceptable and gives permission for the abuse to continue. It also relieves the leadership of its responsibility to protect employees.

- **Find excuses for what happened**. This provides an easy explanation for the event. If management cannot excuse away offenders' behavior, then they must find a reason to explain why they acted so badly. By failing to assign responsibility to the offenders for their behavior or action and for the consequences, management can rationalize incidents. They were either due to the victims' negligence or were isolated incidents resulting from unfortunate circumstances. This position reduces the importance of an event and the circumstances leading up to it. In this way, possible organizational problems or a failure to respond adequately can also be ignored.

- **Condone or support abuse**. This allows violence to become part of the culture. Abusive behavior is perceived as a normal way of doing business. Abuse is a way of life. It encourages the position that those employees who cannot take the "heat" are weak. Organizational culture expects adults to be strong, in control and able to cope with tough situations. Those who are not able to withstand the pressure lose status, because their weakness or frailty becomes associated with incompetence. They lose the respect of peers and management, and become re-victimized. Abuse becomes even more ingrained in the corporate culture.

- **Refuse to perceive employees as victims**. This negates the severity and impact of the incident. This position frees the organization from its responsibilities and obligations to victims. When management deny the existence and consequences of violence, employee-victims receive little sympathy or assistance. Without compassion, encouragement or support, they have a more difficult time recovering from the trauma. Management view performance problems as employees' weakness of character or ineptness rather than linked to the trauma. Victims are sacrificed to uphold the organization's image. Without victims, senior management can dismiss incidents as having little importance and the organization can maintain its status quo.

- **Ignore organizational irritants and problems in the system that incite people to violence**. This allows the organization to maintain the status-quo. An organization's operations (e.g. long waiting periods in hospitals, lack of information about interruptions in essential services, etc) can provoke people and make them angry. False information, inadequate service, delays or postponements in resolving problems increase frustration. Even the meekest person in certain conditions can become agitated. A lack of sensitivity by staff can provoke violence. Irritating operational problems incite hostile reactions. Understaffing, rudeness, lack of respect, a cold or dirty physical environment and unresolved conflicts arouse anger in people, thus creating situations that are ripe for violent outbursts. This places the organization and everyone who works there at risk.

From the above, it is easy to see how violence can become a way of life in certain organizations. A violence-prone organization has a cold and unsympathetic culture. The CEO and management team lack empathy and have difficulty identifying with their employees have to deal with on a daily basis. When management acknowledges the violence and its effect on employees, the organization can and does change into a healthier workplace.

Traumatized Organizations

Dealing with crises created by violent acts can make or break a business just as much as its ability to sell a product or provide a service. Unprepared businesses or those unskilled in crisis management can reel from the effects of violence. Some never recover. A shooting, hostage-taking incident, terrorist attack or murder can thrust an organization into total chaos. An organization can also find itself subject to public scrutiny in a case of fraud, financial wrongdoing, sexual harassment or other offensive or illegal conduct.

Understanding how an employee can go into shock from a life-threatening incident is easy. Conceiving of an organization going into shock and becoming traumatized is harder. This is especially true when the incident involves murder or a fatal accident. At a time when the senior management team must be in top form and able to manage a crisis effectively, they may be unable to make competent decisions and to develop an effective response plan.

When the CEO and the senior management team are unable to function confidently in the crucial hours and days following a crisis, they often overlook important issues related to their employees. These include ensuring people's safety and security, keeping employees abreast of important information and dealing with the workforce's emotional collapse.

Time and proper assistance are crucial factors in helping people recover from the horrors of an accident, murder or disaster. When the management team is immobilized, people do not get the reassurance and care they need. The risk of their becoming traumatized increases. When too many of the workforce suffers debilitating stress reactions, the organization also becomes traumatized. Employees are unable to function and to carry out the organization's affairs.

Traumatized organizations, characterized by a dazed, overwhelmed, paralyzed leadership, go through reactions similar to those of traumatized individuals. As shock, disorientation, confusion and grief emerge, the organization is thrown into chaos. It appears leaderless and out-of-control. The sooner leadership can regain control and restore calm, the sooner the organization will get back on track. On the other hand, if senior management resume operations too quickly, more problems will arise. The leadership may be sensitive to employees' feelings and may try to respond kindly to them. However, in their haste to get on with normal business, they may underestimate the effects and push people to get back to work before they are emotionally ready.

Traumatized organizations remain that way, long after the crisis is over. The leadership may signal an end to the mourning period before staff have finished grieving. Still reeling from their experience, employees are unable to function. When hurt employees find no permission to complete the grieving process, they remain traumatized. Without its people in top shape, the organization may appear to be back to normal, but its workers are not psychologically present on their jobs. Months after the incident, staff are subdued and depressed, and the organization loses its "joie de vivre." On the surface things seem fine. Events continue, plans are made, business is resumed. Senior management assumes the incident has become part of the organization's history. For staff though, safety and security issues are foremost on their minds and they remain preoccupied with the incident. Their performance suffers because they have been unable to resolve the crisis and its effects.

Often CEO's and their executives do not even realize their organization is traumatized. They believe they have done all the right things after the crisis. They have kept staff informed and provided counseling and support in the days following the event. However, the impact of the incident on people's lives can be too intense and the help can be inadequate or too brief. People may give the appearance of functioning because they go to work. While the leadership assumes employees have recovered from the incident, the signs show differently. More and more people go on sick leave, take unpaid leaves of absence, quit, or are physically present but psychologically absent. Tempers flare, and conflicts between workers increase. Employees do their work and some even do it well. However, people's commitment to the organization's mission and goals weakens. Service delivery and profitability suffer from the impact of the trauma.

As months and even years go by, no one recognizes the pattern in the absenteeism, poor performance and internal conflicts, or connects it to the event that happened so long ago. Despite the good intentions of its leaders, the organization remains traumatized and suffers negative effects from a fatal incident, until their personnel are able to resolve their tumultuous feelings and put the incident to rest.

Toxic Organizations

Toxic organizations are abusive organizations. Just as poisonous gases can make the air toxic, incivility, hostility, conflict and abuse can poison a workplace atmosphere. An organization becomes toxic because the leadership allows it to. Employees' complaints about high levels of stress and abuse are ignored. Abusive behavior is part of the prevailing organizational culture.

Two different leadership styles, or a combination of the two, characterize a toxic organization. The first is a strong, authoritarian, repressive leadership that is itself abusive and keeps everyone in line by abuse of power, harassment and intimidation. Good people are afraid to show kindness, to confront the CEO or executive team, or step in to stop the abuse, because they know they can be the next target. Everyone's goal is to keep a low profile, stay out of the line of fire and do what needs to be done to survive. Employees feel powerless and hopeless about their work, and angry that they have no one to protect them. The abusive administrators are cunning and manipulative. They use people to advance their own positions. They have absolute control over the organization and total power over people. They surround themselves with like-minded people and rid themselves of any opposition. They create the toxicity.

The second is a weak leadership, which is ineffective, immobilized and powerless. The CEO or senior managers, who could have the power to end the abusive conduct and sanction the offenders, insulate themselves from people contact, refuse to "see" the abuse, or to get involved. Powerful, abusive advisors, whom those executives respect for their work and accomplishments and even in some ways fear, often influence and manipulate them. They believe they need their advisors to achieve success. When incidents filter up to them, executives refuse to believe the complaints. When they actually witness abuse, they do not take action. They lack self-confidence, are afraid to get involved or do not give the impression that they care enough about what is going on.

Although these leaders could have the power to stop the abuse, their silence permits the behavior. Inadvertently they give offenders permission to continue, and even reward their conduct. They allow the toxicity to take place. Although these leaders may be good people, their refusal or inability to see the reality and stop the violence creates intolerable working conditions for employees.

Fear is the predominant emotion in these organizations. Fear of reprisal keeps abusive people or bullies in power and the abused powerless. There is little chance that those who want change will do anything, as they lack the energy. They have even less power to overcome systemic abuses and to challenge and subdue the abusers. When people do complain or try to change things, they are singled out and penalized, pushed aside, or silenced. They may even be fired or forced to quit.

Violence and tyranny are a way of life in toxic organizations. The environment is poisoned, but the organization carries on as if nothing is wrong. Abuse takes its toll on the personnel. There is little respect for people's rights, and a lack of sensitivity to employees' suffering and pain. The stress is enormous. Abuse also takes its toll on the organization's performance. At best, it becomes a mediocre organization because it drains the energy from its people. With no relief or protection, employees have little left to give to their jobs. They are so battered that they work wounded.

In a toxic organization, the CEO rarely condemns the violence. Victims are blamed or their concerns are disregarded. People who try to do something are stonewalled and scapegoated, or they become disillusioned and burn out.

Little changes unless there is a change in top management. This may mean parachuting in a strong external administrator who is not contaminated by the climate or culture. To transform it into a healthy organization, a new administration may have to clean house. They will certainly demand changes in behavior from the old guard. The CEO will need to gain control of the organization and create a management team that is tough but fair, human, approachable, responsive, excellent role models and beyond reproach. The senior management team will need to develop a strategic plan to deal with the poisoned environment. The leadership must undertake a massive job of role modeling and educating themselves and employees about expectations for behavior and conducting business. To transform the organization successfully, the new leadership will have to work on a culture change that will instill respect within the organization and among the workforce.

Healthy Organizations

These organizations shine. Senior managers deal with internal abuses quickly and effectively. They do not tolerate abuse and harassment, from anyone. They properly investigate employee complaints and discipline offenders. They investigate consumer complaints and use the feedback as a way to improve the quality of the organization's service. They take action when either a client or a stranger is violent toward staff. They take swift measures to protect their employees, are sensitive and supportive of staff's emotional and physical needs and do what they can to help them recover if there is abuse. They resolve the crisis rapidly and take the necessary steps to restore the organization's well-being. In a healthy organization, even when the executives are traumatized, they can mobilize themselves. They quickly and effectively carry out a predetermined, thoughtful and thorough plan to manage the crisis.

Healthy organizations are proactive, with a flexible leadership style. Senior managers display self-confidence and a strong, progressive, friendly and open leadership. They treat employees and customers respectfully. Employees' ideas are welcomed and decision-making are more by consensus than by dictate. The organization values its people and creates the type of climate where employees look forward to coming to work. It offers such benefits as day care, employee assistance programs and flexible work schedules. Customer complaints are handled quickly and positively.

The management team works well together. Even though the management group may be viewed as demanding, employees respect them. Team building is encouraged. Employees feel a strong sense of community and caring and have a strong emotional attachment to the organization's work.

Often a healthy organization has considered its vulnerability to violence and has developed a crisis response plan. It can mobilize quickly and learn from its experiences in managing smaller crises. The senior management team is a take-charge group. It quickly pulls together its resources and uses everyone's skill to help the organization pull through the ordeal. It seeks advice from experts or from organizations who have suffered a similar fate. Because of its openness, it uses the most effective strategies to help employees deal with the trauma. The leadership is able to control the process of managing the crisis, thereby quickly restoring calm and order.

Healthy organizations are open organizations. Senior managers are willing to divulge information and to accept their responsibilities. They inform employees about the event in a way which is planned to reduce the trauma. They provide information briefings for employees. Displays of emotions are considered normal in the aftermath of the traumatic event and the leadership is sensitive to taking care of the needs of its community. Management address safety and security issues and encourage employees to use available psychological help. Senior managers also recognize and address their own emotional needs.

A healthy organization encourages its employees to work, but allows for continued open expression of sentiment and thought about the event and its impact on employee and organizational life. Management are patient with, and sensitive to, vulnerable staff, providing support, care and adequate time to recover.

Healthy organizations bounce back from a devastating incident, because the leadership is open, understanding and flexible. These organizations are willing to keep staff informed, give employees immediate and longer-term psychological help and allow people to mourn their losses. Because of this, these organizations are able to move through the normal grieving process. As a result, the organi zation can put the event behind it, regain its equilibrium and get on with its business. Management hold an operational debriefing to learn how well they responded to the crisis, the effectiveness of their actions and the impact the event had on employees and clients.

Healthy organizations also examine how they could have prevented the incident and their level of responsibility for it. The management team is open to change. Managers listen to employee and customer complaints and do something about them. They become more alert to their vulnerability to violence. Managers learn from their mistakes and make appropriate changes to their crisis plan, security arrangements, the way they conduct business and the way they deal with clients and employees.

BREAKING THE VIOLENCE CYCLE

The cycle of violence can be broken, allowing organizations to evolve into healthy work settings. This involves interventions in the following five key areas:

- Deal quickly with the systemic problems that cause interpersonal difficulties, frustration and anger.
- Support, help and empower victims.
- Sanction offenders.
- Resolve conflicts quickly and employ alternative dispute resolution methods and mediation to create win-win situations.
- Change the dynamics and culture from a violence-prone to a violence-free organization.

Senior managers, who take a step-by-step approach to violence control, as outlined in Chapter 12, will be able to create an organizational culture of zero tolerance for violence.

WORKPLACE VIOLENCE IS EVERYONE'S BUSINESS

Resolving the problem of workplace violence should not rest with the victim. Nor is it the responsibility of management alone. Combating abuse, disruptive behavior and aggression at the workplace is everyone's business.

It takes a joint effort to develop the kind of workplace culture that accepts and fosters disruptive and violent behavior. It will take a community effort to break the silence and speak out against it. The workforce needs a strong committed leadership to mobilize it. Everyone must believe in their right to safety at work. People must proclaim:

> "I have the right to work in an environment free from harassment, abuse and aggression."

There are no easy answers to this problem. This is not a gender-related issue, nor is it a labor or management problem alone. We cannot expect one group to fix something that affects us all. Workplace violence happens mainly because it is allowed to happen. While it seems to be more widespread than ever before, it will get worse unless something is done about it. If we refer to the *Workplace Violence Continuum* which explains the different forms violence can take and how they fit together, we will be better able to understand and identify violent behavior at the workplace. Until we understand it and the culture in which it is allowed to continue, it will remain a serious problem.

Violence is damaging our economy because it is damaging our workplaces. Its negative effects will continue unless we stop it. Only when workplaces are free of violence can people give their full attention to their jobs. It begins with a simple declaration:

> "I will not tolerate aggressive, abusive, disruptive and violent behavior of any kind at my workplace."

- 4 -

White-Collar Conflicts: Violence in Corporations

They go to work in business suits and carry attaché cases. They work at oak or teak desks with computers, charts and papers in modern, air-conditioned offices or at tiny workstations. Among the men and women employed in white-collar jobs are lawyers, accountants, salespeople, computer programmers, managers, executives and the legions of people who assist them—receptionists, secretaries, customer service reps, IT technicians, and other technical and administrative support staff. They are the people of the corporate world.

Ask them to talk about violence in their workplaces and an uncomfortable silence ensues. This subject is taboo. Corporations and large companies are not supposed to have this problem. Often employees are too embarrassed or afraid to talk openly about what really goes on behind closed doors or in the corridors at the office.

Violent crime or shooting sprees by a disgruntled employee or client may happen, but not in a corporate setting. However corporate executives are preoccupied about extreme violence, especially if they do business globally. According to a Pinkerton report on Top Security Threats and Management Issues Facing Corporate America, Western multinational or international companies face the challenge of global terrorism and the huge responsibility of protecting their facilities and their employees when they travel or work globally.[1]

A 1990 report published in *Fortune Magazine* revealed how much American companies worry about this kind of violence. They spend $1 billion a year protecting top executives and their families both domestically and internationally. Concern for safety and protection is so high; many Fortune 500 companies have kidnap and ransom insurance for their CEO's. They also hire bodyguards, maintain security departments run by ex-Secret Service or FBI agents, or retired police officers, and have a fleet of armored cars and drivers skilled in evasive driving.[2]

This is a sign of the times and one of the downsides of becoming a successful CEO or executive of multinational and international companies. Concern for security extends beyond the physical safety of these senior executives and employees. Big business has had to take measures to protect itself from attacks to its property. Embezzlement, financial misrepresentation, credit card and accounting fraud, computer viruses and hackers, and employee theft present major threats for business. According to the results of a survey of 1000 companies in 50 countries undertaken by PricewaterhouseCoopers, the figure of $2.2 million is the tip of the iceberg for companies affected by economic crime, such as accounting fraud, financial misrepresentation, asset thefts, or corruption and bribery.[3] Loss of money and financial mayhem are not the only damage caused by these crimes. Highly respected employees, who commit the crimes, break a sacred trust. The employer, or the shareholders and employees, if the leadership is the culprit, suffer lost revenues and deep emotional pain from having been robbed and betrayed by a trusted employee.

Just consider the impact of the corporate financial wrongdoings that occurred at Enron and WorldCom and the cover-up by accounting firm Arthur Anderson. Thousands of people were affected: employees lost their jobs and their retirement funds, and investors lost a lot of their savings. Compound these financial losses with the impact on families, careers, quality of life and psychological wellbeing, these wrongdoings had a much greater impact than just the loss of billions of dollars. While not "violent" per se, these events cause major suffering and are an abuse of social and economic rights.

Still this is not the biggest concern for most people working in the corporate world. They are more concerned about the high stress environments they work in and the way they are treated by their superiors, subordinates, colleagues and clients. For the most part, this treatment is expressed in incidents of sexual harassment, intolerance and discrimination, outbursts of anger and screaming, hostility and bullying.

Despite the hard work and efforts to rid the workplace of sexual harassment, this problem has not gone away. Media reports on current cases and magazine articles on the subject reveal the degree to which sexual harassment is still a major problem in the business world. In spite of legislation, corporate policies and extensive training programs, attitudes and behavior in many organizations have not changed much. Sexual harassment remains a major preoccupation for many working women in the workplace all over the world.

Moreover, despite legislation and equity programs, there are still complaints about racial and sexual discrimination, and intolerance. A lot of the discrimination is systemic. In many companies, the scarcity of highly qualified women and visible minorities in higher paying management and executive positions or as directors of company boards shows that they have not shattered the glass ceiling, despite proclamations that equal opportunity programs are working.

The corporate workforce consists of people with diverse attitudes, cultures, religions and sexual orientations. While people proclaim that diversity programs work, complaints about harassment, discrimination or exclusion suggest that it is not so easy for people who are culturally or visibly different to work together effectively. Putting aside differences and conflicts that come from bias, ignorance and intolerance is a challenge because most people have prejudiced attitudes. Being part of a diverse workforce does not necessarily make the office immune from narrow-mindedness, intolerance and discomfort of working side-by-side with people who are "different."

Verbal abuse, harassment, bullying behavior is flourishing in many workplaces in the corporate world. Too often yelling, insults, threats and rudeness are tolerated in collegial and management-employee relationships. At times anger and discontent are expressed loudly, furiously and with little regard for civility or self-control. Supervisors yell at, criticize, belittle, bully and harass employees under the guise of supervision. Employees challenge, block or sabotage unpopular management decisions, and taunt, ridicule and make life miserable for colleagues whom they dislike. This type of behavior can bring business to a standstill.

Stress buildup from heavy workloads, long hours, unrelenting pressure, too many e-mails and voicemails, and being accessible 24/7 exacts a heavy price. There's a popular caricature that captures the predicament many people find themselves in at one time or another. A man, wearing a white shirt and tie, becomes so frustrated at work, that he gets up, grabs his computer screen, ripping the cables out of the wall, and throws it across the room. What is more realistic is that this man, or woman, gets so frustrated, that he gets up from his desk and starts screaming at a colleague, subordinate or superior. The term coined to describe this high level of frustration is *Desk Rage*.

Aggression and bullying at the office is increasingly receiving attention as a global white-collar problem. How big a problem is bullying at the office? One just has to surf the Internet and the many websites hosting information, conducting informal surveys and giving tips on how to handle the bully boss, colleague or subordinate. In Japan, the Labour Ministry's dispute resolution system handled more than 6,000 complaints about bullying in 2002.[4]

WELCOME TO THE JUNGLE

The image of well-dressed business people sitting in large modern office buildings is one of irreproachable conduct and the essence of civility. While many professional and business people do behave with impeccable courtesy and treat their colleagues, subordinates and clients with great respect, much of the white-collar world is not so civil or genteel.

This abusive conduct is not necessarily the result of a colleague, boss or subordinate having a bad day or becoming occasionally enraged. Often the abuse involves a daily and persistent behavior pattern of screaming, swearing, lying, character assassinations, bullying, rumor campaigns, discrimination or sexual harassment.

Sandra, aged 29, worked as an administrative assistant for a computer software company. For over a year she had been subjected to the sexually harassing behavior of Jack, a male manager in another department. First he made sexual comments about her appearance and told her lewd jokes. Then he made insinuations about her sexual behavior and finally Jack propositioned her outright. Sandra was not interested in going out with Jack and told him so. However, she kept quiet about the harassment. She did not want to chance complaining because she knew Jack was a powerful manager and she felt no one would believe her. The comments worsened. Finding her alone one day, he grabbed her and attempted to kiss her. She evaded him but was angry, humiliated, embarrassed and shaken. Finally when she could no longer cope with the harassment, she went to Human Resources, and in accordance with their policy, they conducted an investigation. The investigation revealed that in addition to sexually harassing Sandra, Jack had been behaving similarly with four other women as well. One of them was so terrified that when she saw him coming one day, she hid under her desk.

Although Jack was fired because of his conduct, the company later had to defend itself against an unjust dismissal charge in court. It eventually won.

The above case is one example of sexual harassment. The following examples show a different side of the issue. In these cases the companies inadvertently set their employees up as targets of anger and harassment by clients. Mary and Nancy are examples of employees who have to deal with an angry public, without backup and support.

Mary, a 39-year-old customer service agent for an automobile company, handled customer complaints. Although she knew she should not take callers' comments to heart, sometimes they attacked her as if she owned the company or was responsible for the problems they had with their cars. While Mary was used to angry calls, too often she had to put up with people screaming at her, calling her names such as a "stupid idiot," and shouting obscenities. When the company announced a recall due to a possible brake-related defect, consumer anger and insults increased in number and intensity. To her disbelief and shock, several customers threatened her life. No one had prepared Mary to deal with abusive calls. She often had to listen to angry people who did not want to listen to reason.

Worried and frustrated customers took their anger out on Nancy, a 35-year-old ticket agent who worked for a major international airline. Each time a flight was delayed or canceled, Nancy knew she was in for trouble. The longer the delay, the more the anger directed at her intensified. When the delay lasted hours or the flight ended up being canceled, passenger behavior got even worse. They blamed Nancy as though she personally caused the problems or was conspiring to ruin their plans. Irate passengers would scream and swear at her, or would bang their fists on the counter. No one helped Nancy deal with the deluge of anger. With postponements and cancellations normal occurrences in the airline industry, Nancy was exposed to abuse on a daily basis.

The three cases represent abuse of power, intimidation, harassment and threats. In these examples a co-worker and client were the perpetrators. Sometimes verbal abuse, harassment and bullying can be used deliberately by a boss in an attempt to get an employee to resign. This happened to Henry, a 58-year-old credit officer.

Henry did not mind criticism of his work or being told how he could improve. However he did object to being criticized and belittled in meetings in front of his subordinates, by his boss Carl. Carl had a very short fuse and was constantly yelling. Henry knew that if something went wrong, he would end up the target of his boss's anger. He had no one to tell him how to handle Carl, who was known to be "difficult." No one attempted to stop the behavior. The abuse continued for months, intensifying until Henry became so anxious and distraught he could not sleep, experienced a loss of appetite and had trouble concentrating and functioning. Henry thought about quitting, believing that this was what Carl wanted him to do. The rumor mill confirmed that Carl disliked Henry and wanted him out of his department. Having lost confidence, Henry could not even think of looking for another job. The stress even-

tually caused him to take two weeks sick leave. When the company doctor refused to accept his claim, a defeated Henry returned to work. He tried to cope with the continual badgering, until finally he could no longer take it. Without consulting a lawyer, Henry quit with just under eighteen years of service and sixteen months away from early retirement.

All these cases are examples of white-collar violence involving individual employees. The following is an example of a bullying boss whose behavior set a pattern and had a devastating effect on the workforce, even though in this particular case the organization made money.

The board of directors of a large financial institution hired a new CEO and gave him a mandate to lead the corporation out of its financial doldrums and make it highly profitable. The CEO launched a reign of terror in the organization: so much so that the senior executives and the rank and file quivered every time they met him.

Recognized as a brilliant strategist and known for his ability to get the job done, he had carte blanche. To the delight of the directors and shareholders, he quickly began turning the corporation around. So pleased were the directors with the results, they ignored his angry outbursts, belittling comments and rudeness, even when it was directed toward them. They also chose to ignore reports about the impact of his conduct on the staff.

With no one to stop him, he became increasingly tyrannical. He was known for pitting one senior manager against another and then sitting back and watching the struggle develop. During an executive meeting he tore into several of his most senior advisors. These men simply sat and listened to the yelling, swearing and insults. Despite their positions and their own accomplishments, no one spoke out, took a stand against the abuse or told him to stop.

Not surprisingly the abuse permeated the organizational ranks. The abused executives had learned that this was the way their CEO expected them to conduct business and that aggression and ruthlessness would help them to survive. Over time, a couple of executives and senior managers left the company Others were silenced. Some of them became abusive toward their own staff, modeling the same behavior they suffered from the CEO. Abuse became part of the organization's culture.

Allowing oneself to be abused by a boss is common for employees, even for those in senior management or executive levels. Whatever their rank, people who are abused psychologically suffer a gradual wearing down of their self-esteem. Employees dare not challenge the powerful abusive boss because such a challenge could result in dismissal. The executives at this corporation had already seen the results of the CEO's ruthless behavior. No one wanted to be his next victim.

The CEO accomplished what he had set out to do. However, during his ten-year tenure, many excellent and highly competent people quit and others were dismissed. Morale plunged and hundreds of employees developed stress-related physical and psychological illnesses from the accumulated stress of working in such an intimidating and hostile environment. The corporation also paid out hefty severance packages.

The board of directors was pleased with the CEO's results. Profits increased and stock prices rose. Still, one might question the means of achieving the end and the board's responsibility in tolerating the abusive climate their CEO created. Surely this bullying CEO, who seemed to derive pleasure in destroying people, could have achieved his goals while preserving the dignity and integrity of the people who worked for him. Surely the directors shared some responsibility for the pain and stress of their workforce and for allowing their CEO to be the corporate bully.

BURNOUT FROM THE STRESS OF ABUSE

Employees in just about every occupational setting complain about job stress. Most claim that stress at the office is too much and they cannot handle it. Absenteeism rates and medical records show the effects of stress. Increasingly people use their health care benefits, go on sick leave, suffer work accidents, make costly errors, or quit.

Given the tremendous pressure on businesses to survive, demands placed on employees are greater than ever before. Increased workloads and tight deadlines are unlikely to subside. Burnout, stress-related absences and illnesses are often associated with hostility or protracted conflicts at work, impossible workloads, lack of job satisfaction and difficult family or personal situations.

Work-related violence and fear of violence correlates strongly with acute stress, burnout and illness. Unrelenting conflicts and persistent violence of any kind take their toll. Self-confidence erodes. Stress increases as employees try to avoid further nasty episodes or find ways to protect themselves. Bullied employees often become angry and abusive themselves when no one comes to their defense or supports them. Going on the offensive and becoming aggressive may seem like the only means of survival. When this happens, a cycle of violence quickly develops permeating whole departments or even the entire organization.

Abuse saps energy of employees at every level of the organization and diverts them from their jobs. Inordinate amounts of time are lost as employees think about incidents and talk with supporters about what happened to them. They also spend time and energy planning how to avoid further attacks. When colleagues and support staff are called upon to listen, give moral support, or try to help resolve the problem, they too lose valuable work time. As a result, productivity plunges. With so much energy spent avoiding or dealing with unbearable situations, employees have less time and energy to carry out the jobs they were hired to do.

CORPORATE JEKYLLS AND HYDES

Behind the facade of an educated, well-dressed person lurks a potential untamed beast. Push far enough and people have the capacity to turn into bitter, spiteful and attacking animals. We flex our muscles when we feel threatened, become frustrated, do not get what we want, or feel pushed to protect our turf.

Although people dress in attractive suits, some of them experience personality changes like Dr. Jekyll and Mr. Hyde. They are the
corporate beasts whom everyone detests, yet are allowed to roam
free. Sometimes these employees *adapt* to the culture. They become
aggressive and hostile. They change because of a consuming drive
to succeed. They are usually mentored and protected by achieve-
ment-driven executives who overlook how they achieve their
objectives and behave with other people. Their achievements are
rewarded.

Sometimes these employees *drive* the culture. Unhappy with
themselves and the direction their lives have taken, they create tension and unhappiness in everyone around them. They are moody,
angry, bitter people who take out their frustration and disappointments on colleagues, subordinates and even their bosses, by harassing, bullying or intimidating them. When managers ignore their
behavior, they tacitly give these bullies permission to continue to
misbehave.

While there are many variations of these corporate brutes, most
evolve from these two personality types. Although they work in
many different settings, their presence and behavior are particularly noticeable in the business world. They become the beasts who
need to be tamed. They create a tension filled environment and
make life miserable for everyone who works with them. Some of
them are, in many ways, like the gorilla. When relaxed and not
threatened, the gorilla can be loving and gentle. However, when
aroused and feeling insecure, he can be aggressive and domineer-
ing. He gains power through intimidation.

Human *gorillas* are the people at the office who feel threatened.
They are bosses who look for faults in everyone, who are rude and
never utter a kind word. They are moody employees who resent
taking orders. They are temperamental co-workers who argue constantly, who criticize and attack everything and everyone. Yet
despite an overbearing personality, at times the human gorilla can
be helpful, friendly and cooperative—when it suits his purpose.

The second animal prototype is the *chameleon*. Having the ability to blend in with the existing environment, chameleons appear to

be non-threatening. They alter their appearance when they perceive a danger. Human chameleons start by being unobtrusive, but when the opportunity occurs they make themselves noticed. Always on the alert, they are people who get caught up in their career ambitions, drive for success and hunger for power.

Human chameleons are in a hurry to get where they want to go. They yearn for control, power and money. Since they fit in well, they are often selected by senior staff, who act as their mentors. They feel tremendous personal and social pressure to succeed. They learn by example. Although their consciences twinge the first couple of times they stab someone in the back or steal another person's ideas, they quickly forget this in their haste to achieve their goals. They learn to lie, cheat and achieve their aspirations by taking the shortest route possible. They become politically skilled manipulators. While they may not intentionally start out being abusive, they learn to disregard or exploit colleagues who obstruct their paths or who are unimportant to them. They become tough, calculating and aggressive. On their climb up the organizational ladder, they leave many hurt and angry colleagues on the sidelines. People resent their attitude, success and the fact that they were "chosen." Chameleons may be opportunists, but they are chosen to be the system's heroes.

While I do not want to suggest that all fast-trackers behave like beasts, sometimes people who are not mean-spirited become so because the organizational culture changes them. Under pressure to perform, some employees become so goal-oriented, competitive and aggressive that they forget about civility, values and respect.

BEHOLD THE REAL CORPORATE CULTURE

It is easy to overlook what life is really like for the millions of people who work in white-collar jobs. The popular movies, *Nine to Five* (1980) and *Working Girl* (1988) portray offensive behavior, dysfunctional relationships and office politics at their worst. Backstabbing, lying, covering one's tracks, nastiness, bullying, outbursts of rage, sexual impropriety, gossip, and conflictual relationships are common in highly competitive, highly pressured office or department environments. This creates a hostile climate for everyone.

Many organizations have turned to re-engineering efforts to improve profitability. If organizations did not get the boost they hoped for, they may have overlooked a crucial element in the restructuring process—the typical negative reaction to change, the trauma reaction of the survivors, increased workloads and changed job functions of the workforce. When people are unhappy, they usually act out. Incivility, conflict and abusive behavior are often the result.

When an organization is plagued by such behaviors as outbursts of rage, intolerance, discrimination and harassment, it becomes toxic and dysfunctional. A superb product or service, a unique idea, creative marketing or a strategic plan might help a business become a leader in its field, make lots of money and keep its shareholders happy. But ultimately all the efforts and work may be in vain. Even an excellent business can suffer terrible consequences and irreparable damage when abuse is allowed to flourish within it.

A stressed workforce preoccupied with violence cannot give its best to its employer. When management do not promote respect and civility, employees become distracted from their work. They become alienated from the goals and mission of the company that pays their salary. When they feel the company does not care enough about them to ensure they are respected, treated fairly and with dignity, employees stop giving their best. After all, why should they care about people who do not care about them?

STRIVING FOR EXCELLENCE IN CONDUCT

Confronting the issue of violence in our largest corporations is an important challenge and, in fact, not difficult to overcome. It involves frank and open discussion about how the company wants to conduct its business, pursue its goals and have people behave.

To succeed in difficult economic times, companies must strive for excellence of their products and operations. The business world spends billions of dollars to improve employee communication, build high performance work teams, provide training, and offer assistance to employees to address personal problems. Senior managers understand how much these initiatives increase the organization's chance for success. It is therefore surprising how few business leaders pay attention, and place energy and resources into addressing problems associated with disruptive behavior, chronic conflicts, psychological and sexual harassment, intolerance and verbal abuse.

Good manners and conduct bring out the positive in people. They improve customer and employee relations. For these reasons, treating consumers and workers with dignity and respect should be an integral part of any organization's mission statement.

Many good companies have become trendsetters in streamlining operations. If companies were to set high standards for conduct and refuse to allow any employee to be abusive or to be abused, what a difference this would make to the overall productivity of employees and, therefore, to the bottom line. Ensuring that civility, respect and dignity become an integral part of the corporate culture makes sound business sense because these attributes are the cornerstones of a healthy and prosperous future.

How can this be done? Below are five recommendations to help an organization develop a violence-free culture.

- Establish a code of conduct for all employees, including the board of directors, based on the principles of respect, dignity and tolerance.
- Ensure that the entire leadership sets the tone by acting as role models in civility.
- Insist on and support courtesy and respect in all operations and interactions between customers and employees.
- Focus attention on resolving problems that produce hostility, anger, frustration, stress and burnout.
- Harness the wealth in employee diversity by creating a team that capitalizes on people's different backgrounds, opinions and experiences.

HALTING THE DECAY OF THE CORPORATE WORLD

Business has set standards for employees' appearance at the office. Dressing tastefully and looking one's best is a forceful, unspoken expectation. Yet by allowing any form of violence to permeate our workplaces, we have allowed a breach in business etiquette. White-collar violence happens because for the most part, management condones it. Just as most business executives would frown on an employee wearing a T-shirt and jeans for an important business meeting, they should not allow people to act in ways that demean them and the people around them.

Behavior and attitude are as important to success as education, skill and opportunity. Violence promotes violence. While not all companies condone or practice abuse, many retain staff who are abusive in some way or another. Abusive behavior of any kind has no place in the corporate world. Tame the beasts, value civility and celebrate diversity—then watch the synergy build. This is how a company can excel and even surpass its competition.

- 5 -
"Your Money or Your Life": Violence in Retail and Banking

We send them off to work but in a sense they really go off to war. This war is not fought in faraway places but in our cities and neighborhoods. The people who handle financial transactions are continually under attack.

These workers are part of a special workforce. Their jobs are routine. A customer buys a piece of clothing, food, a record or gas for the car, pays admission to a movie, takes out a video, or makes a deposit or withdrawal at a bank. The employee's job is to collect the money and give out the change. Cashiers as well as salespersons are the cornerstone of the retail industry. Women hold most of the cashier positions, particularly in banks, stores and supermarkets. The jobs are low paying, with little chance for mobility or advancement and limited access to other opportunities.

Strange though it may seem, cashiers and soldiers have a lot in common. Soldiers go off to war and risk their lives, cashiers also go off to work and risk their lives. Soldiers are trained for danger and knowingly put their lives on the line. Cashiers suffer from exposure to repeated and sudden danger. For soldiers this attack comes from enemy artillery, an ambush or a sniper's bullet. For cashiers the attack comes from someone toting a gun or knife during a holdup. Living with continuous life-threatening danger places a tremendous stress on both soldiers and cashiers.

Most people are aware of the consequences of putting soldiers under this kind of stress. We know about battle fatigue or post-traumatic stress disorder because of our exposure to television programs and movies about the wars (Korea, Vietnam, Iraq and Afghanistan) or even through personal experience. Many of these movies depict the hero suffering from post-traumatic stress disorder or PTSD years after the events. Soldiers, exposed to constant physical danger, human atrocities and the threat of death, want only to forget the horrors of war. Instead they find themselves continually reliving the events and suffering from the stress months or years after returning home to take up their civilian lives. Depression, flashbacks, nightmares, anxiety, fear, guilt and sometimes uncharacteristically explosive or violent behavior plague the veterans. Their marriages deteriorate and often end in shambles, their careers and jobs are wrecked, and they no longer fit in to society.

A holdup at work, even a supposedly innocuous note-passing incident, is not just an unpleasant event. Employee-victims of holdups are victims of violent crimes. Like other crime victims, they may suffer invisible, deep-rooted wounds that are slow to heal. Employee-victims often try to keep their pain hidden and therefore injuries suffered from holdups may not be evident. Sometimes they put the incident out of their minds and pretend nothing has happened to them. More often than not, they suffer severe reactions. Their suffering increases when their employer disregards their pain.

After a holdup, management's priority is to return the store or bank to normal operations as quickly as possible. Employees may be asked how they feel, but they are encouraged or even pressured to begin working again. Employees want to put the incident behind them and get on with their lives. Responding to subtle messages, they intuitively know they will cause the least trouble if they say they are all right. Everyone is relieved with their reassurance and business begins again as usual.

EASY TARGETS

The retail industry is a prime target for armed robbery as are taxis drivers and delivery people. Almost 4 of every 10 robberies, occurring while the victim was at work or on duty, are committed against people in retails sales or transportation.[1] This is a global trend. A study by the ILO found that taxis drivers in Australia, for example, ran 28 times the risk of non-sexual assault and almost 67 times the rate of robbery compared to the community at large.[2]

A holdup is simple to commit. It is also an effective and easy way to acquire money. Every retail business is a potential mark. Businesses of every size and description, banks, movie theaters, supermarkets, video stores, pharmacies and service stations, and in fact, any place where money is collected, are targets. The average holdup takes less than five minutes to commit. Most of the time the robbers are successful: the take though is often a couple of hundred dollars or less. With so many armed robberies, retailers and bankers are getting smarter. Less money is kept in the cash drawer. As soon as money accumulates, it is moved to a safer place or off the premises.

A typical bank holdup scenario begins with a lone male entering the establishment to check out the place. He will return another time, mingle with the customers and appear ready to buy something. Then, when the customers have left or the time is convenient, he goes into action. He may cover his face with a mask. He passes a threatening note, pulls a knife or gun out of a pocket and demands the money from the cash drawer. Feeling at risk, cashiers usually comply. They instinctively know that cooperating is safer than refusing. They have been repeatedly told not to jeopardize their lives. They have been warned to hand over the money. Fortunately most heed the warning. Because of this, the fatality rate and physical injuries from holdups are low.

Although some people believe holdups a "safe" crime, there are definitely risks. Some people do die because of a robbery and others suffer physical injury. Yet, while the vast majority may escape physical injury, they are not so lucky when it comes to psychological injury.

Store personnel, bank tellers and other cashiers work under unique pressure, knowing that a holdup can take place any time, as do taxi and delivery drivers. They never know whether he will be alone or part of a gang. They do not know whether the robber will remain calm or lose control. The robber might look like any other client or be masked. He may talk quietly and pass a note, or be aggressive and openly display a knife or gun.

During a holdup, employees are powerless. The robber has control over their lives and their safety. Not knowing what the robber will do to them, they are terrified. They just want him to take the money and leave. However, there is always the nagging fear that he will do more, perhaps physically or sexually assault them, take hostages, or shoot, stab or murder them. They worry that something might go wrong and they will not come out of it alive.

Although a holdup is short-lived, for most people the incident is horrifying, overwhelming and seems to go on forever. People are never sufficiently prepared even though they are aware that the type of business they work in makes them an ideal target for robbers. Employees do not really want to believe they could be involved in a robbery, nor are they sure how they will react if a gun is pointed at them. Will they stay calm and be able to follow the instructions or will they panic or freeze?

HOLDUP FABLES

We need to dispel the many myths about holdups, and the effects they have on people's lives if we wish to truly understand what life is like for taxi drivers, and people working in financial services, retail outlets and other commercial establishments where money is collected and dispersed. Wherever money is handled, robberies will be committed. It is by far the most frequent and easiest crime to commit.

Many myths relate to the dangers holdup-victims face. Others relate to the impression the public has that holdups are minor inconveniences, easily forgotten. Debunking the myths is important because they contribute to the problem of workplace violence.

> ### Myth # 1
> ### Holdups are not violent.

There is no such thing as a non-violent holdup. The majority of homicides in the United States, are not crimes of passion committed by disgruntled co-workers and spouses, but rather a result from robberies.[3] Moreover, of all occupational groups, taxi and delivery drivers are the most at risk for workplace homicide. They are also among those with the highest rates of non-fatal assault.[4]

Newspapers on a daily basis all over the world inform us about innocent employees who have been shot, knifed or murdered while on duty in convenience stores and service stations or taxi drivers and others in transportation occupations who have died on the job. Most of these happen during a robbery involving a few hundred dollars, a couple of cartons of cigarettes or a few bottles of alcohol.

Fortunately most holdups do not involve shootings and in the retail or financial industries, most cashiers do escape physical injury. However, employees usually suffer some degree of psychological injury. No matter how much employees are aware of the risks for violence on the job, few people really believe it will happen to them. When a robber enters the store, pulls a knife or gun or even pretends to be armed, the victim is ill-prepared psychologically and reacts to the unexpected attack. The victim recoils in shock, as the prospect of death becomes a frightening reality. Holdup victims suddenly realize they are totally vulnerable and powerless to protect themselves or the property for which they are responsible.

Besides having to contend with the constant threat of a holdup, employees face another difficult plight. Since a holdup is unforeseen, the cashier either denies a holdup is a prospect or lives with dreaded anticipation of the day it will occur. More often than not, it occurs when least expected. Employees face even more stress, for they never know who will commit the robbery. Which customer is trustworthy? The robber, most likely a male, can belong to any race or ethnic group or speak any language. He may wear a black leather jacket or be dressed in a business suit. He may cover his hair with a cap, his face with a mask or nylon stocking or reveal himself clearly. He may talk calmly and quietly or be belligerent, scream and swear. He may appear to be a typical customer or a tough guy. He may really be armed or pretend to be armed.

Since there are so many unknowns about who the robber could be or when a holdup will occur, most of the time the person is caught completely off guard. After a robbery, trusting anyone is hard, because every male customer who enters the establishment represents a potential threat.

Many holdup victims report having had a premonition of danger or feeling uneasy, either the day or weeks before the incident. People who expect something to happen are not necessarily better prepared emotionally when the incident does take place. Many are even more shaken because they thought something was going to happen but ignored their intuition. In any case, they would have been powerless to prevent the incident.

Whatever the robber's behavior or actions, his tone of voice, appearance and mere presence presents a threat of violence. Even note-passing robberies that occur in banks, and are shrugged off as minor, are violent. Referring back to the *Workplace Violence Continuum* in Chapter 2 will help to clarify that threats are a form of violence, even if they are not carried out. In the case of a holdup, a note's implicit threat to life for non-compliance is an act of violence. The following examples highlight these issues.

Sylvia, the owner of a small jewelry store, was robbed late one afternoon by two men. They had entered the store at separate times, but waited until a female customer left before going into action. When one man pointed a gun and demanded money, Sylvia assumed the other man, who had been looking at some jewelry and whom she thought was a real customer, would assist her. Instead he too turned on her. She tried to resist but he struck her on the head. As she lay on the floor, the robbers grabbed two trays of jewelry and the cash and rapidly left.

Besides suffering physical injury, Sylvia later reported feeling anxious, depressed and nervous. She suffered from flashbacks, nightmares, sleeplessness and felt in constant danger. She could not stay alone in the store, as she kept expecting the robbers to return. Her symptoms developed into a severe case of PTSD.

Diane, a travel agent working at a university campus agency, was robbed by a man pretending to be a customer. He never uttered a word. Like all the other customers, he wore jeans and a jacket. When he approached the counter, he passed a note. It read: "Holdup. I have a gun. Don't make a sound. Give me your money." She did as she was told and he was gone in a matter of minutes. The robber did not reveal a weapon or speak. The other agents, serving customers on either side of her, never even knew a holdup was taking place. After it was over, Diane began to shake. When the others found out that she had been robbed, they too became distraught. For days Diane and her co-workers suffered from severe stress. They were easily startled, nervous, fearful and anxious. Only after a lengthy debriefing session several days later were they able to calm down.

Andrew, the owner of a small men's clothing boutique, was locking the door at the end of the day when a man dressed in a business suit and carrying a briefcase convinced him to let him in. He said he needed a pair of black socks and it would only take a minute. He quickly chose a pair. While Andrew was punching in the amount at the cash, the man opened his briefcase. He pulled out a gun and demanded the money from the cash drawer. He took it and left quickly. Andrew was thoroughly shaken. Weeks later he was still uncomfortable being in his store. He was suspicious of every customer who came in and jumped at every little noise. At closing time, Andrew became nervous and anxious. It was months before he lost the feeling that someone was going to attack and harm him.

In each of the above situations, the robber took the victim by surprise. None of them could anticipate the outcome. While only Sylvia suffered physical injury, all the victims suffered some degree of psychological trauma. All felt threatened and believed they were in great danger. Months later, many of them were still stressed and frightened. Being alone in the store and walking in the streets unnerved several of them. They feared new customers and worried about another holdup and whether they would be hurt or killed.

While the location and robbers' behavior, physical appearance and dress may differ, the experience provokes similar feelings and reactions. No matter how courteous or mild-mannered robbers may be, when they present victims with a note, utter verbal threats or display a weapon, they deliver a clear message: A holdup is in progress, the robbers are in control and they have the power to hurt people. Employees hand over the money, jewelry or other goods, hoping the incident will end. It is only after the robber leaves the premises and they lock the door that they can breathe a sigh of relief. For the victim, even a so-called innocuous holdup, like a note-passing incident, represents a sudden and unexpected attack, a danger or life-threat.

> ## Myth # 2
> ## A holdup is a robbery of money. No one gets hurt.

Holdups are reported regularly in the media, taking on a pattern similar to the following story.

One day a radio broadcaster reported that two men had entered a bank brandishing sawed-off shotguns. He described in detail the way one robber jumped over the Plexiglas barrier and grabbed money from the three tellers. He reported that they got away with $2,400. "They left quickly," he said, "and no one was hurt."

Of course what the broadcaster meant was that no one was physically hurt. Yet one has to wonder whether the tellers would have agreed with him. Holdups are not just a crime against property but a crime against people. Although the theft is for money, the most victimized are not banks or stores but the people standing behind a wicket or in front of a cash register. What victims experience, perhaps for the first time in their lives, is a close brush with death. This often leaves them wounded psychologically.

When the gravity of the incidents is not acknowledged or when their ordeal is ignored, the suffering of employee-victims increases. When they are told that they have not been injured, they become confused. They know how traumatic the experience was for them. Nevertheless, a negation of their injuries causes them to question the legitimacy of their emotional pain and the extent and severity of their reactions. When others negate the relevance of the incident, they have a difficult time facing the reality of what they went through. As a result, many holdup victims try to suppress their fears or other reactions and block the incidents from their minds. This obstructs the healing process. Often employee-victims appear to be unfazed by the incident, even those who play the hero role. However, when someone does not properly deal with a traumatic event at the time of the incident, it can come back to haunt them. After having been repressed, this can play havoc with a person's life.

By downplaying the dangers of holdups, an injustice is done to employees. The police and company security officers repeatedly assure cashiers and tellers that robbers only want money. If they hand it over, the robber will not injure them. Most of the time this is true. The robbers run in, scoop up the money and make a quick getaway before the police arrive on the scene. Unfortunately this is not what happened to Daniel.

Daniel, a 24-year-old convenience store employee, was forced to lay face down on the floor while robbers proceeded to take several cartons of cigarettes and money from the cash drawer. Before they left, one of them came up to him and shot him. Daniel was lucky to survive. He now functions with only limited restrictions. The bullet is still lodged in his head because removing it is too risky. To this day, he cannot understand why he was shot when he did as he had been told. Daniel's way of dealing with his trauma is by denying the incident has made any difference in his life or that he is a walking time bomb. He pushes himself to carry on as if nothing had happened to him. Yet at times his emotional pain and fear overwhelm him. "I keep myself under total control and do not think about it," he said. "If I did, I would fall apart."

Myth # 3
Employees know and accept the risks.

When cashiers, tellers or convenience store owners read a report about a holdup that took place in an establishment similar to their own, they feel relieved. Instinctively the thought comes to mind, "it does not concern me. It happened in another part of town, in another city or at a competitor's outlet." They do not want to think about the possibility that such an event could ever happen to them.

Denying the possibility of danger is a natural impulse. Employees handle the prospect of exposure to danger at work by denying such a possibility. This is an instinctive protective mechanism. Although intellectually they acknowledge the risk factor, the idea of something bad *really* happening is simply inconceivable and too frightening. They distance themselves from the risks. They believe their work area is safe because somehow they assume they are protected. By denying danger, they feel comfort in the fact that a holdup may happen to someone else, but never to them.

This protective mechanism is so strong that even when employees only witness a robbery, they still believe "it will never happen to me." They breathe a sigh of relief, cheering inwardly that their invisible shield protected them. However when their turn comes, they suddenly have to confront the fact that there is no magical protection. For the first time, they come face to face with their own vulnerability, powerlessness and mortality.

> ## Myth # 4
> **When something goes wrong, it is the victim's fault.**

Often victims are blamed for their misfortune even when it could not possibly be their fault. The following event illustrates this point.

Three men wielding sawed-off shotguns entered a bank to commit a holdup. They yelled at the staff and told them not to move except to open their cash drawers. They were high on drugs and agitated. Marie, a 28-year-old teller who was seven months pregnant with her first child, was visibly nervous during the robbery and became panicky. When she moved, one of the robbers shot her. She died instantly.

After the robbery, Marie's colleagues tried to make sense of what had happened. They kept saying that if only she had not moved, she would not have died. The media picked up on this idea, and reported that because she had moved, one of the robbers shot her. The cause of death was a gunshot wound. Instead of laying responsibility for her death on the robbers' actions, which caused her to panic and move, her colleagues and the media implied that she was partly responsible for her own death.

This example illustrates many people's reaction to a holdup that ends in violence. Everyone searches for reasons why the robber injures or kills the victim. Eventually it comes back to the same question. What did the victim do to warrant being shot or knifed to death? This attitude goes back to the first myth about holdups, that they are not violent and no one gets hurt.

The need to justify violence and senseless injury or death leads people to search for explanations beyond the obvious. In a holdup, the perpetrator alone must accept responsibility—for whatever happens. The victim does not bear responsibility for the outcome, the robber does. The victim did nothing wrong, except to be in the wrong place at the wrong time. The robber must take full responsibility for what happens as well as for all the consequences of his actions.

Myth # 5
Once the holdup is over, the trauma ends.

The robber aims a gun or draws a knife, grabs the money and is out of the store in a matter of minutes. And it is over! While one might believe the trauma is over, it is just the opposite. During the crime, employees function in a state of shock or frozen fright. It is like being on automatic pilot. Adrenalin speeds up, the heart pounds and thinking becomes suspended. Feelings and reactions are frozen as body and mind concentrate solely on survival.

After the robber leaves and victims begin "to thaw out," reaction sets in. First the body responds to the shock and the stress in the following ways: rubbery legs, nausea, vomiting, loss of bodily functions, heart palpitations, trembling or shaking, fainting, screaming and crying. These are normal physical reactions to intense stress caused by a life-threatening incident.

Very quickly emotions take over as the psyche starts to absorb what really happened. When employees begin to grasp what happened, the realization of their exposure to danger hits. For many, the holdup is a first-time encounter with a weapon or threat to life. They feel fortunate in having escaped from a close brush with death. As the psyche continues processing more of the details of the incident over the days and weeks that follow, the realization of their vulnerability haunts them. If an incident could happen once, it could happen again. Danger lurks everywhere: they feel vulnerable and at risk. Fear intensifies as strangers become suspect and the chance of other life-threatening events take on a new meaning.

With this realization of vulnerability, emotions become overwhelming and intense. Emotional turmoil or upheaval, normal after a frightening and highly-charged incident, may begin immediately after the event. Victims may also experience a delayed reaction that surfaces days or weeks later. This reaction can last a few hours, a couple of days or may stretch on for months. It diminishes only when victims accept what happened and begin to find ways to cope with the threat to their lives. In addition to having to deal with the incident, many employees also suffer *secondary injury*. The crime per se does not cause this; it is caused by the way other people treat them in the hours, days and weeks that follow. Many people inadvertently hurt victims by their insensitivity and lack of appreciation for the victims' fragile state. Police officers called to the scene may try to lighten up the situation and calm employees down by cracking jokes. Employees often perceive this attitude to be insensitive and hurtful. Management may ask the employees to begin working shortly after the incident. Employees conclude the company is only interested in money and does not care about them. Customers ask for details about the holdup and may even relate their own worst experiences. Employees feel they are inconsiderate. Family and friends encourage employees to forget the incident and carry on as if nothing had happened. Victims feel misunderstood, rejected and unsupported. In addition, victims feel alone with new emotions that are frightening and overpowering. The aftermath of robbery is often more overwhelming than the robbery itself. It is then that the trauma really begins.

Myth # 6
Only employees directly robbed are affected.

On a busy Thursday evening, a man walked into a supermarket, picked up a can of juice and waited his turn in the checkout line. When he reached Susan, the cashier, he opened his jacket, quietly pulled out a gun and demanded the money from the cash drawer. She complied and the robber was out of the door in less than a minute. Only Jim, a packer who was bagging food for another customer a few feet away, noticed what had happened. Since there was no ruckus, the other cashiers were not even aware that Susan had been robbed. As the robber left the store, Susan yelled to her colleagues, "I've just been held up."

The manager quickly called the police, emptied the store of customers and locked the doors. Susan, who by this time was shaking and in shock, could hardly believe what had happened. Jim felt lucky that the robber had not seen him watching the incident. The other cashiers seemed equally upset—they had never believed they would be robbed. When Susan and Jim described the robber, several of them remembered having seen him during the previous couple of weeks.

Three days after the incident several cashiers, in addition to Susan, were experiencing difficulties. Two of them could not work at all, and the majority complained of insomnia. During a debriefing session one week later, they talked about their different reactions—anxiety, crying spells, nervousness, sleeplessness, nightmares, nausea and headaches. It was not only Susan who experienced symptoms of acute stress. What bothered all of them most was the shattering of their sense of security. That one incident made them realize that they were vulnerable. They were convinced that something terrible could have happened, and they were lucky to have escaped unscathed. They felt uneasy working late at night and refused to leave the store alone. For weeks they were on edge, easily startled, constantly watching the door and waiting for

*another robbery to take place. It was several weeks before they calmed
down and could work properly again.*

*Pedestrians watched in amazement as three armed robbers ran
from a bank screaming at people to get out of the way. Having seen one
robber raise his gun and shoot a man who was chasing him, several
onlookers ran into a nearby restaurant and hid. When the commotion
had died down, some of them began crying but gradually calmed down.
Gladys, who was still recovering from a holdup three years earlier,
began shaking and crying uncontrollably. No one could calm her down,
and the emergency medics took her to the hospital. The incident had
stirred up old wounds from which she had been slowly recovering. This
had been Gladys' first venture into a shopping mall. As she later said,
"there is no place where I am safe. Violence is all around me. It's almost
as if I attract it. Why did it have to happen when I was there? Now there
is another place where I can no longer go."*

These two scenarios are not unusual. They illustrate the impact
holdups can have on people other than the direct victim—colleagues, witnesses, people employed in similar positions and even
family.

Not only are bystanders vulnerable, but absent co-workers also
can suffer from stress and anxiety. Even employees working in similar types of settings in the same neighborhood can be affected. Fear
sets in as people begin identifying with the victim, and realize that
it could have happened to them. Or, as with Gladys, the incident
could trigger memories of a past trauma. Employees' security shatters when, for the first time, it dawns on them that they are neither
safe nor immune. They suddenly feel vulnerable, at risk and unprotected. The holdup brings out a shocking reality. This time they
were lucky, but there is always a next time, when they could be targets.

Family members of direct victims can also experience all kinds
of difficult reactions. They become fearful and anxious when they
see their parent, spouse or child traumatized. Their concern over
safety issues heightens. Their fear and sense of powerlessness

increase when their loved one has no alternative but to work in a potentially dangerous situation. This is the only available job and the family needs the money.

Myth #7
After several holdups employees become immune.

One would expect that the more holdups experienced, the easier they are to deal with. The opposite is true. If someone does not experience an intense stress reaction after the first, accumulated stress from repeated incidents eventually takes its toll. After a holdup one of three things may happen. Firstly, the person may be perfectly fine, or signs of nervousness, anxiety and fear may last for days. Sometimes the person develops a more acute stress reaction lasting several weeks.

Secondly, the more holdups experienced the greater the possibility of a long-term reaction. Eventually the stress becomes too much. Employees, who appear to cope, often put incidents out of their minds and suppress their normal fears and anxieties. They try to bury the incidents and for a time may even succeed. They carry on until the bubble bursts. This often happens because of repeated exposure to life-threatening incidents and when invisible wounds do not have time to heal.

Rather than becoming immune, people exposed to high levels of stress over time or who have been in too many holdups, may suffer from *holdup fatigue or holdup burnout*. Like job burnout or battle fatigue, the overloaded victim suffers from physical and emotional exhaustion and is unable to function, or, as one holdup victim described himself, "a regular basket case."

Myth # 8
Everyone reacts the same way to traumatic events.

As difficult as it is for people to understand employees' reactions to a holdup, it is even harder for employees to understand their own reactions. This is particularly difficult when several people have been involved in the same incident. Severely affected employees despair over their poor functioning and become even more discouraged if they seem to have a harder time than their colleagues in overcoming the trauma. Understandably, management also find the situation confusing when one employee suffers no ill-effects at all, another experiences short-term distress, and a third cannot work at all for a short period after the incident. When a fourth employee develops a phobic reaction and other symptoms of PTSD and is unable to return to work at all, everyone wonders what is wrong with the individual for reacting so severely—or for over-reacting.

While mental health professionals now understand the huge impact that life-threatening crises have, there is much that is still unclear. For example, why do some people become severely traumatized by an incident and others, experiencing the same situation, seemingly suffer no ill-effects at all? The following factors increase a person's susceptibility to more severe or long-term reactions following a trauma.

- Individual's perception of danger and risk.
- Amount of life stress before the incident.
- Presence of a previous traumatic injury.
- How well the person recovered from a previous trauma.
- Understanding and support the individual receives immediately after and during the days that follow.
- Individual's personality make-up and psychological state.

While these factors influence a person's ability to ward off a serious reaction, there is no right or wrong way to react to a holdup. One cannot be upset by an event that has no particular personal significance. On the other hand, when one is severely affected, it is not because of an overreaction but because the event had tremendous relevance for the victim. Until the person can integrate the event into his life experience, the incident will continue to disrupt the employee's life, sometimes tragically.

Myth #9
Recovering means returning to work and forgetting the incident.

A common belief is that the best way to handle trauma is either to forget what happened or to return immediately to the scene of the crime to confront one's fears and anxieties. However, overcoming trauma from holdups or other violent incidents is not as simple as getting back on the bicycle after a fall. While this may be the right formula for some people, it is not the right approach for those too traumatized to face the situation.

The question of sick leave or time off work is a tricky one. When people suffer minimal reactions, resuming work quickly lessens the chance of a work phobia developing. This is different when employees suffer such severe reactions that they cannot function. Forcing them to return to their jobs before they feel able to do so is counterproductive and even detrimental to their psychological health. Responding to pressure from colleagues, supervisors and even family, employee-victims sometimes try to return to their jobs as though nothing had happened, while they are silently screaming in pain. This is what happened to Cathy, a victim of a holdup and hostage-taking incident, whose previous therapist had pushed her to return to work prematurely. Unable to cope with the anxiety and her fears, her condition developed into a severe case of PTSD. A year later, in treatment with another therapist, she talked about what it had been like to go back to work before she was ready.

"I really wanted to go back to work. I loved working with the public. My work gave me so much freedom and pleasure. I was still on medication and pushed myself to do as I was told, because my psychologist and psychiatrist felt it would be good for me. It was so hard even to get myself to the store. The first couple of hours were not bad, although I did not feel ready to be there and was terrified. Then a customer raised his voice at another employee and I thought he was going to rob us. I became hysterical. They had to call 9-1-1 and take me to the hos-

pital. I never recovered. It's four years now and I'm still in this pitiful state. Look at me. I can't go out alone and I can't stay at home alone. I finally accepted that I will probably never go back to work. Now I just want to be able to relax and enjoy my life a little."

The case of Cathy shows how careful one must be in adopting the "get back on the bicycle" attitude. While most victims have to deal with jitters the day after a holdup, they also need to listen to their inner voices and judge when they are ready to return to work. Often family, co-workers, supervisors and even the medical community pressure the person to resume a normal life. While encouraging someone is beneficial, confronting the situation before the person is psychologically healed and prepared may cause a secondary injury. In Cathy's case, this resulted in her never being able to return to the store and having to live with severe limitations.

Myth # 10
Victims are to blame for their slow recovery.

Holdup victims suffering ill-effects from the incident want only to be able to put the event behind them, get back to work and get on with their lives. There is an inner pressure to return to their previous state of well-being. They mastered the message, "I'm an adult, I should be able to cope with this and not let it bother me." They also face pressure from almost everyone they meet. This may start with their initial contact with the police, for whom holdups are an everyday occurrence. Sometimes the police transmit this nonchalance to the staff, who are upset because the holdup is the most dramatic event of their lives.

Employees who suffer more lengthy reactions, who have trouble functioning and are unable to return to work with their co-workers, feel additional pressure. They wonder why they are taking so long to recover. Inadvertently society blames victims who in turn see themselves at fault for taking too much time to get back to normal. The longer they take to pick up the pieces of their lives, the more guilt they feel. Besides having to deal with their inadequacies, they often feel tremendous pressure from colleagues, supervisors, family and friends to put the incident behind them and carry on as usual.

This "blame the victim" attitude serves only to place more stress on innocent people who, through no fault of their own, suffer a trauma. Their pain increases when they receive the message that they are overreacting to an incident. They believe their intense reactions and their inability to be as they were before is due to a weakness in their personality. This increases their disappointment and anger with themselves. Blaming the victim for an overreaction or slow recovery is a common response to violence. This attitude shifts the blame from the criminals who caused the injuries onto the shoulders of victims who may be forever scarred.

Employees who suffer severe reactions need help. Their recovery depends on the type of help, the timing of the start of treatment and the social support they receive. With immediate, appropriate treatment, patience, time and a supportive environment, PTSD victims do recover and can work again. On the other hand, when holdup victims do not recover, it is not necessarily due to a personality weakness. Inadequate treatment, too little support from the people around them, too much stress in their lives, and the secondary effects all impede their recovery.

REACTIONS TO HOLDUPS

Experiencing an armed robbery is usually overwhelming. It causes a variety of stress reactions. These reactions may vary in intensity and duration. Physical reactions, psychological distress and behavior changes are normal responses to a frightening event. While some people suffer no ill-effects, others can experience troublesome reactions lasting days or months. These disappear only after the shock and impact is dealt with.

Since robberies are such a common event for many people, it is important to understand their impact. While a robbery may seem like an inconsequential event, anyone who has had a near miss when driving can relate to the shock of a sudden confrontation with danger. The experience causes us to modify our driving habits. We become more cautious, anxious and tentative in our driving. In the same way, holdup victims generally experience overwhelming reactions and drastic changes in their personality, behavior and lifestyle.

Common Reactions

Physical Reactions (Occurring directly after the holdup)
- No physical reaction
- Silence
- Incessant talking/babbling
- Crying
- Trembling/ rubbery limbs
- Vomiting
- Hot/cold accompanied by sweating/shivering
- Intestinal reactions, i.e., diarrhea, stomach cramps, frequent urination
- Headaches, neck or back pain
- Fatigue

Feelings (Occurring days, weeks and even months later)
- **Fear**. High level of fear, sometimes feeling highly suspicious or distrustful. Fear of being harmed by either the robber or another person.
- **Emotional numbness**. Feeling numb, in shock, unable to "thaw out."
- **Depression**. Feeling apathetic and discouraged, having nothing to look forward to, no interest in life, using sleep as an escape.
- **Anxiety**. Feeling apprehensive or stressed even over insignificant things, in a state of constant high-level tension.
- **Anger**. With everyone—the robber for what he did, the employer for lack of protection, the supervisor, police, co-workers and even family and friends for not understanding the effect of the incident. Lastly, self-directed anger for having

been "weak," for having lost control and for being unable to forget the incident.

- **Distrust**. Of everyone, but especially suspicion of strangers who represent a potential threat.
- **Revengeful**. Wanting to get even for what the robber did, the problems he caused and the loss of enjoyment of life.
- **Insecure**. Feeling unsafe and threatened. The workplace, public places and even home may represent unforeseen dangers.
- **Powerlessness**. Inability to regain control of one's body, thoughts and feelings undermine self-confidence and judgment, increasing feelings of powerlessness.
- **Becoming withdrawn**. Becoming anti-social and introverted or isolated because others have not shared the experience.
- **Decreased self-esteem**. Continued disequilibrium and inability to regain control and return to one's normal functioning and "persona" shatters one's self-confidence.
- **Loss of enjoyment of life**. Disinterest in and apathy to normal daily activities or in being with co-workers, family and friends.

Thought Processes (Occurring days, weeks and even months later)

- **Memories or flashbacks**. Repeated uncontrollable thoughts and memories of the event or reliving certain scenes.
- **Nightmares**. Recurring bad dreams and nightmares with graphic themes of being chased, trapped and harmed.
- **Sensory awareness**. A person, piece of clothing or object, a certain sound or smell can all act as a reminder and trigger a flashback along with anxiety or panic attacks, causing a continual reliving of the event.
- **Decreased concentration**. Difficulty concentrating on anything. Reading, watching television or talking with people become too difficult and stressful.
- **Memory loss**. Inability to remember things in the present or recent past, including routine or simple activities, conversations or plans.

- **Self-doubt**. Questioning one's spiritual beliefs, priorities, values, ideas about justice and one's ability to recover.
- **Loss of control**. Loss of mastery over one's body, mind, emotions, events and environment.
- **Discouragement**. Feeling depressed and disillusioned over the loss of self-confidence and changes in personality and behavior.
- **Belief that changes signify a mental illness**. Feeling reactions are abnormal and a sign of mental illness. The pressure to recover reinforces this feeling, as do messages from well-meaning people to forget the holdup and get on with life, and the medical profession who treat the trauma as pathological.

Behaviors (Occurring days, weeks and even months later)

- **Looking over one's shoulder** all the time because of a sensation of danger or in anticipation of another attack.
- **Increased startle reaction** such as being startled by sudden noises, always being on the alert for danger and never being able to let one's guard down.
- **Avoiding sleep** to avoid frightening nightmares, having sleepless nights or experiencing very early morning awakening. Feeling constantly exhausted.
- **Inability to stay alone** even in the comfort of home. Needing a continual family presence because of the constant fear of danger.
- **Losing oneself** in tasks and responsibilities to avoid thinking about the incident.
- **Sudden crying spells** or intense crying for no apparent reason.
- **Sudden or gradual change in temperament and behavior** that is totally out of character, e.g. fighting with people or overreacting to trivial situations or comments.
- **Change in eating patterns** resulting in substantial weight gain or loss.
- **Increased use of chemicals** such as cigarettes, alcohol, drugs, minor tranquillizers, or over-the-counter medication (e.g., aspirin and sleeping pills) to alleviate physical symptoms of distress or deaden emotional pain.

- **Avoiding family and friends** due to an inability to deal with the incident, feelings, reactions and changes in behavior and life.
- **Avoiding activities** that are reminders of the event (e.g., not going into a store or a bank because of fear of approaching the cash counter).
- **Avoiding people and unknown places** especially crowds or unfamiliar places.
- **Becoming withdrawn** because of a lack of interest in normal activities or embarrassment at being unable to cope.

RECOVERING FROM THE TRAUMA

When their world is suddenly turned upside down and intense reactions do not go away, it is hard for holdup victims to feel positive and hopeful about their chances for a complete recovery. While time alone does help diminish the intensity of trauma from an armed robbery, the presence of many of the reactions previously cited may suggest PTSD. In such cases, time alone is not enough to heal the injury.

Holdup victims have been through a life-threatening incident that affects how they feel, think and behave. Reactions they experience are *normal* reactions to an abnormal situation. They need time to grieve about what has happened to them, to deal with their physical or emotional injury and the loss of their sense of security. They also need to be allowed to heal at their own pace. Recovering involves healing an invisible psychological wound.

Experiencing a traumatic stress reaction is somewhat similar to catching a cold or the flu. We cannot altogether prevent the virus from invading our bodies, but once we become ill we can do many things to alleviate our symptoms and make sure they do not get worse. In the same way, holdup victims cannot will away a stress reaction. However, given understanding, support and appropriate help, most can recover.

Mental health professionals recognize that people exposed to sudden, life-threatening incidents suffer a traumatic reaction and need special help. It is becoming increasingly clear that the more quickly help is received, the less chance there is for long-term reactions.

More than ever before, employers are now calling upon social workers or psychologists to meet with staff and conduct a *group debriefing* session soon after a holdup. This intervention allows people to talk about the incident, deal with their overwhelming emotions, learn about normal reactions to crises, and stress management techniques. The session also ensures that anyone needing further help gets it. Individual employees can benefit from confidential professional counseling through the organization's *employee assistance program.* If the company does not provide these services, employees can obtain counseling at a community victim's assistance center or mental health center, or through referral from a family physician. Arranging for further treatment is important if the employee appears unable to function or is unable to work.

Holdups are not easy experiences to face. People need a chance to pull themselves together after the incident. Those who appear traumatized need time, encouragement, treatment, and support if they are to heal. There is no right or wrong way to react after a robbery and, unfortunately, no quick fix for getting over the traumatic incident.

NO LAUGHING MATTER

Armed robbery is a serious threat to the life, health and security of employees in the banking and retail industries, and in transportation. Yet our general attitude is to dismiss this as an inconsequential experience. Since holdups are a daily event, it is easy to ignore the real impact of this form of violence on people's lives. In comparison to the number of robberies carried out, there are relatively few people actually killed or physically injured. The devastation they wreak on so many people's lives is, therefore, easily ignored.

Armed robbery is not just a form of violence committed against a commercial establishment. It is violence against people. Employees who work in the retail and banking industries, as well as taxi drivers, know that robberies are a daily happening. However few believe it will ever happen to them. When it does, employee-victims need to be treated kindly. It relieves them of a tremendous burden when others acknowledge their pain and when they are reassured that their reactions are normal. They are grateful when their colleagues and managers encourage them in their efforts to recover and make their return to the workplace as easy as possible.

- 6 -
School Daze:
Violence in Education

Upset that he had not won the coveted annual $2500 prize for the most outstanding doctoral thesis, a Ph.D. graduate in Physics from Beijing, China, shot six people, killing five of them and then himself. Within fifteen minutes this student had murdered two professors, the Chair of the Department of Physics and Astronomy, the prizewinning Physics graduate student and the Associate Vice President of Academic Affairs to whom he had appealed the decision for the prize. He also permanently disabled a temporary secretary in the Office of Academic Affairs.

A 48-year-old high school teacher told her twenty-two senior English students to read their assigned novels. She began correcting papers when another of her students, a shy 17-year-old honors student, who had moved to the area five months earlier, walked into the classroom, drew a revolver and fired at his teacher. The first shot missed her and he squeezed the trigger a second time, sending a .38 caliber bullet into her right temple and killing her. He also shot to death a 51-year-old custodian, who had responded to the gunshots. As he removed the empty shells and replaced them with bullets, he told his classmates that he had one for each of them. A few minutes later, he offered to let go those who wanted to leave, but his hostages were too scared to move. After a few of them finally left, he gave the rest of his hostages their freedom. Just twenty minutes after he murdered his teacher, he surrendered to police officers who were waiting in the hall-way with drawn guns.

These murders at the university and high school in Iowa and Kentucky are not isolated cases and could have happened any-where. They are part of a wave of violence, including homicide, which has swept across the North American education system since the 1990's. Rather than being isolated acts by deranged people; for the most part, young people assault, shoot, stab and murder others because they have a gripe.

An analysis of several homicide cases points out how easily hurt feelings, slights and unresolved conflicts can end in extreme violence. A 1993 *USA WEEKEND* survey of 65,193 students from grades 10-12 across the U.S. reported that 79% of the students surveyed said that violence is caused by "stupid things like bumping into someone," followed by boyfriend/girlfriend disputes, outsiders, racism and gangs.[1]

A troubled youth or disgruntled person may perceive a school or university like enemy territory. For many teachers and students, schools are hostile and even dangerous places.

Children in elementary and secondary schools and young adults in colleges and universities often carry more than books to school. Children as young as seven years old go to school armed with knives, brass knuckles, pipes, ice picks, blackjacks, hammers, spiked jewelry, razor blades, wire and guns.

During the 1990's and up to the present time primary and secondary schools, colleges and universities have been besieged with security problems. Firearms and other weapons have turned many schoolyards and campuses into battlegrounds. When students take guns, knives and drugs into the premises, schools become war zones. Children, young adults and teachers are drawn into the mayhem.

Despite enormous efforts to curtail the violence, completely safe schools are a rarity. Most teachers and school administrators can list some of the following among the problems they routinely have to deal with: disruptive behavior, lying, cheating, vandalism, robbery, drug dealing, protection or taxing activities, brawls, gang warfare, assault, sexual harassment and assault, bullying, shootings, stabbings, suicides and at times murder.

In addition to learning, studying and passing exams, many elementary and high school students have to acquire a highly developed sixth sense. They must learn to be streetwise and able to hone their wits to survive the jungle-like school environment. They are vulnerable to sudden and unprovoked attacks by their peers or strangers.

In addition to the "expected" workload of yesteryear; course preparation, research, marking and teaching, there is today the added burden of lack of discipline and respect, and indeed, violence. Teaching has become highly dangerous because teachers are open targets. Many teachers work in fear, preoccupied with safety and security concerns. They are on the alert for premeditated or sudden attacks from students who may not like their grades, feel slighted or simply do not like their teacher.

Forty years ago school principals were preoccupied by problems such as students "talking out of turn," chewing gum, running in the halls, dress code infractions, littering and fighting; all these problems pale into insignificance compared to the present reality.

There are many reasons for this change: the breakdown of the family, family violence, the lack of respect for authority, the ease with which children gain access to firearms and the gratuitous and repetitive violence they view on television, in music videos and in movies. There is another important reason though. Although much progress has been made to curb school violence, those still living with the problem have trouble identifying, assessing and responding appropriately to warning signs and cues.

Many of the offenders are students with no diagnosed psychiatric problems, yet they display patterns of aggression, despair, frustration or anger long before they act it out. The school system has difficulty in identifying these students and dealing with their emotional distress, acting out behavior or demands. Inattention to complaints and poor problem resolution escalates the anger of people who already feel slighted and misunderstood.

Embittered or distressed people usually send out signals. In most situations where violence escalates to the point of murder, the signals have been misread, disregarded or mishandled. In the cases of the Ph.D. graduate and the high school student cited at the beginning of this chapter, both were above average students who expressed frustration and anger about a perceived injustice. The

Ph.D. graduate had appealed the decision about the prize to the Vice President of Academic Affairs and had voiced his disappointment and anger to others. He selected the people he killed. They were the people he believed had deprived him of what was his due. The high school student had become increasingly isolated and his preoccupation with violence, death and dying had been expressed in his writings and assignments. He was angry about the low grade he received and became even more furious when his teacher refused to change it. He talked to other students about killing his teacher. Although she expressed concern about his behavior to a school administrator, the latter was hesitant to take action and indecisive about what action to take.

Throughout this chapter a case will be made that despite the efforts and there have been many—violence exists in education because of a failure of the system to properly manage and prevent it. Despite zero tolerance policies, greater attention to the problem by school administrators and teachers, heightened security measures, peer mediation and violence prevention programs, violence is nevertheless entrenched in the school's culture. While attention is focused on preventing incidents, the root causes are often overlooked. A code of silence, unresolved grievances and conflicts and a tolerance for such "innocuous incidents" as verbal abuse, bullying, sexual harassment and hazing create a hostile environment. Alcohol, drugs, and weapons, messages received from violent movies and television programming, the pressure to succeed, personal and family problems and low self-esteem add to the volatility. Students who do not get the help they need to deal with those problems feel worthless. If they believe they cannot succeed, they give up. Their expressions of despair and acting out behavior turn inward or outward. They either harm themselves or harm other people.

On the organizational side, mismanagement stems from many sources: a) an oversimplified view of the problem b) the absence of strong leadership and positive role models for students c) uncoordinated responses that fail to address the root causes of conflict, alienation and despair, and d) a permissive or dysfunctional organizational culture that allows soft forms of violence to flourish.

An in-depth discussion about violence in education will demonstrate the extent to which violence is part of the school culture and, despite people's best efforts, remedial strategies have not gone far enough. The discussion will focus on three specific areas:

- Violence in Elementary and High Schools
- Violence in Colleges and Universities
- Transforming the Education System

VIOLENCE IN ELEMENTARY AND HIGH SCHOOLS

Topics to be discussed:
- Survival of the Fittest
- School Stress
- Creating Armed Fortresses
- Responses

Survival of the Fittest

Violence in North American elementary and high schools peaked in the mid 1990's. Although surveys and reports affirm that school violence has been decreasing, it is still a major problem. Moreover, according to the ILO, violence in education is a global problem. Some countries are experiencing an upswing in violence, (e.g. sexual violence against girls in South Africa) while others (e.g. U.S.) are experiencing a downswing.[2]

If we were to equate the number of incidents of school violence with SARS, or one of the other emerging contagious diseases, we would have long ago viewed this as an epidemic. Neither teachers nor students are immune. Parents can not send their children to school with the assurance that they will be safe and protected. Teachers cannot be guaranteed that they end the day unscathed. Safe schools are rare.

Many teachers and students dread going to school. In New York, Montreal, Los Angeles, Miami, Toronto, and many other cities across North America and around the world, teachers work in

fear of violence from their students. They worry about being physically or sexually assaulted or even about being shot. Many students
also go to school frightened. They worry about being beaten up,
stabbed or murdered by their peers.

There is good reason to be worried. Despite the decrease
in school violence in the United States, youth crime and school
violence remains a problem. A Bureau of Justice Statistics report
revealed that in 2001 American youths between the ages of 12 and
18 were victims of 1.2 million crimes of theft overall, and at school
victim of 764,000 non-fatal crimes of violence or theft. Between July
1, 1999 and June 30, 2000 there were 32 school-associated violent
deaths in the U.S., which included 24 homicides: 16 of these
involved school-age children.[3] A report from a nationally administered 2000 survey revealed that a majority of U.S. teens (70 % of the
boys and 60% of the girls) said they resorted to violence in the past
year because they were angry.[4] These statistics underscore the
depth of the problem. The presence of weapons in school and the
easy accessibility to firearms contributes to the problem. The same
study noted that one in five high school-age boys and fifteen percent of middle-school boys took a weapon to school at least once in
the past year. Sixty percent of high school boys and 31 per cent of
middle school boys said they could get a gun if they wanted to.[5]

Guns are not the only problem. In school corridors, at dances, in
the courtyard and outside school property, students use knives to
settle disputes, bully others into submission or to defend themselves.

Bullying and taxing is a huge problem. In a first study in 2000
to document the prevalence of school bullying in the U.S., nearly
30% of students reported having been involved in bullying, either
as a target or as a perpetrator. More than 16% said they had been
bullied at least occasionally during the current school term and 8%
reported bullying or being bullied at least once weekly. The survey
found that children who said they were bullied reported more loneliness and difficulty making friends while those who did the bullying were more likely to have poor grades, and to smoke and drink.[6]
Sometimes bullied students commit suicide because they can no
longer take the abuse, or tired of being targeted, they lash out at

their tormentor or towards others who remain silent or do not come to their rescue.

At an early age, students learn that violence is a way of life. They learn that "it is a jungle out there" and it is both "cool" and essential to have the protection of a weapon. They learn to settle disputes through violence. They learn that the toughest and meanest not only survive but hold the power and control others.

In addition to the factors previously raised, there are two others to consider. One is the code of silence: students learn to protect themselves by keeping quiet about what they witness or experience. The stronger the code of silence, the greater the reign of terror.

The other issue is more generalized. Desensitization to violence is the result of overexposure to violent movies and in television at an early age. According to a 1992 report by the American Psychological Association on television's role in American Society, by the time average children leave elementary school, they will have witnessed at least 8,000 murders and more than 100,000 other violent acts on television. Moreover a substantial proportion of young adolescents are exposed to extremely violent movies, including those that depict sexualized violence.[7] This desensitization to violence influences how they react to what they see and experience at school. Verbal abuse, harassment and bullying means little to children who are exposed to violence on the screen, or who have witnessed or been the victim of family violence or who, at a young age witnessed a shooting or stabbing incident.

The glorification of violence on television results in a lack of respect for the sanctity of human life. It leads to a troubling code of conduct that says "it's okay to pull the trigger on someone if you feel like it." Add to this an active drug trade in schools, fear of other violent youths and the inability of adults to create a safe environment. Some young people, who are not predisposed to violence, may resort to arming themselves for their protection or joining a gang to ensure their survival.

Violence makes no distinction between urban and rural settings, public and private schools, wealthy and poor neighborhoods. Nor are ethnic communities necessarily more vulnerable. Almost every school seems to have its share of problems with either intruder or student-provoked violence.

Most offenders are not outsiders to the school. They are troubled, belligerent or hostile students, from diverse social and family backgrounds. Some children have learning disabilities or emotional and behavioral problems. Many come from single parent or dysfunctional families. At school they sometimes assume a Rambo-like attitude, having no respect for authority or for the rights of their peers. With no one to stop them, they take control of the schools. They terrorize other students and even their teachers through their bullying, intimidation, and ready-to-wage-war mentality. Added to this is the ease with which they use conventional and self-made weapons: the situation is like a ticking time bomb.

Behind the statistics are the real stories that show what life is like for schoolchildren.

A furious argument over a school bag led a 14-year-old to whip out a 9-mm semi-automatic pistol and fire wildly down a crowded high school hallway. He killed a 16-year-old student and wounded a teacher in the neck.

A 16-year-old was shot at a school dance by another boy who wanted to cut in on his date. He later died of his injuries.

A 9th grade student opened fire in a crowded high school cafeteria, killing another 9th grader and wounding a 10th grade student. The previous day the murdered student had had a fist fight with the suspected killer, outside of school grounds.

Two students beat and stabbed a 15-year-old after he accidentally bumped into them in a school corridor.

After months of sexually harassing and stalking a classmate, a 14-year-old boy, armed with a knife, held a 13-year-old girl hostage in her home overnight because he could not accept the fact that she did not want to go out with him.

A gang of five youths, who accused an 18-year-old of scratching their car, accosted him while he was visiting his girlfriend during a lunch break. Although the principal intervened three times to break up the fight and protect him in school and on school property, the youths later beat him up when he was walking home with his girlfriend.

In a quiet suburban school a male intruder sexually assaulted a 7-year-old in the girls' washroom.

A gang of elementary school youths hounded an 11-year-old boy who they thought had squealed on their drug activities. After three terrifying weeks, he feigned sickness and refused to go to school. His parents learned what was happening when they discovered a hammer in his school bag and questioned him. Although the parents took turns walking their son to and from school, the threats continued. He was forced to change schools.

These events took place between 1993 and 1996 in schools in the United States and Canada. They reflect the fear and reality of many students. Violence is entrenched in our schools as a way of life, creating a violent culture and a "survival of the fittest" mentality.

School Stress

High-school children face tremendous pressures. Besides age-appropriate issues of self-image, peer acceptance and dating, they agonize over what clothes to wear, courses to take, their exam results and prospects for jobs. They also worry about their safety. Figuring out how to get through the day without being bullied, sexually harassed or assaulted, robbed, attacked or beaten up is a major preoccupation for many high-school students. Having to devise ways to avoid involvement with gangs, being taxed or saying no to drugs is stressful and frightening. Those who do not have the inner strength and strong family support to cope with the pressure and to stay out of trouble join the crowd and become one of the troublemakers.

The continual exposure to violence at a young age takes its toll. The psychological and social development of young people is certainly affected by the violence they witness and experience.

Violence poisons the environment. It is difficult for teachers to teach and for students to learn in an atmosphere of fear, intimidation and danger. Sometimes frightened students, trying to escape from the hostile environment, invent reasons to stay home. They develop imaginary or stress-related illnesses or develop mental illnesses. At times, children in high stress situations see suicide as the only way out. Finally children, even those as young as nine and ten, arm themselves in self-protection.

The impact of violence in schools has major consequences as follows:

- School violence jeopardizes children's lives and those of their teachers.
- Violence interferes with the educational process and undermines students' chances for a decent education.
- Violence psychologically affects children who experience or witness it.
- Constant exposure causes children to become desensitized to violence and to accept it as normal behavior.
- Violence becomes a natural response to resolving conflicts for those conditioned to it.
- Violence produces enormous stress on students and teachers, affecting their ability to study and work and damaging their personal lives.

How does this affect the educational system? Many experienced teachers leave their profession because of an attack, the threat of violence or fear. Others go on sick leave because of the stress of working in a hostile environment or as a result of physical and/or psychological injury from an attack or witnessing the impact of violence on their students.

Over the last ten years, teachers' unions in every major city across North America reported high numbers of incidents of threats, harassment and assault against teachers by students. In addition to tracking violence experienced by their members, they have been trying to draw attention to the problem for years. In New York City, the United Federation of Teachers (UFT) observed a steady increase in violent acts committed against teachers since they began keeping records in 1973. When incidents soared in the 1990's they decided to do something about it. They initiated violence prevention training for staff and collaborated with the school board on a victim support program. As a result, during the 1995-96 school year, they reported that the rate of student violence toward teachers had reduced by 1.5% over a two-year period.[8]

While 2002-2003 academic school year rates of violent incidents do not come close to the 1995-96 figures (4,712 reported incidents of violence, with 3,212 of these involving assault and harassment; and 1,574 teachers injured from an incident),[9] once again violence is on the rise. During the 2002-2003 academic year, the UFT reported a 38.9 percent increase of incidents against teachers over the previous year at all school levels. In the elementary schools this represented a 51.6 percent increase, 38.5 percent in middle schools and 29.7 percent in high schools. Special education schools followed the trend with a 13.2 percent rise in reported incidents against staff. This represents 3,151 reported incidents involving staff as compared to 2,268 the year before. While sex offenses declined by 16.7 percent, assaults rose 43.8 percent to 994 incidents. Of these, there were 501 reports of physical harassment, 642 incidents of verbal harassment and 783 reports of reckless endangerment. Students were responsible for 86 percent of the incidents, and 33 percent of the perpetrators were special education students. Staff injuries were at 1,648, up 38.4 percent from the year before. Special education staff accounted for 14.1 percent of the injuries. On an average day, between 6-7 staff members were injured.[10]

The situation in New York City is not unique. In Britain statistics show that school violence and threatening behavior has risen steadily since it first began to be collected in 1999. In 2002-2003 nearly 7,000 incidents were reported. Of the incidents, 35% occurred in primary schools. Incidents of physical attack, threatening behavior and verbal abuse accounted for 25% of all reported incidents.[11] The media reports suggest that teachers' views about the seriousness of the problem and solutions are at odds with those of government officials and elected representatives. As people debate the reliability of data gathering methods and appropriate responses, teachers are getting injured, suffer from stress and burnout and leave the profession.

Creating Armed Fortresses

It is hard to acknowledge that schools are besieged by so much abusive, disruptive behavior, drug trafficking, roving student gangs of students and stabbing and shooting incidents. A natural reaction is to deny it is happening. Despite the fact that school violence is widespread, many school boards, school administrators and government officials downplay the seriousness of the situation. Parents and school administrators waste energy and time quibbling over the extent of the problem, the reliability of statistics and the impact of incidents on students, staff and the academic process. Furthermore, it is hard to know what to do. When action is taken, the initial response usually involves an increased police or security presence and creating protective enclaves. As a result, the face of schools has changed. Once open and free, many schools are now fortresses. Armed guards patrol the halls, metal detectors in entrances screen for weapons, locked doors protect against intruders and cameras register the first sign of trouble. Undercover police roam the school infiltrating youth gangs and drug operations. Schools watch and even test students for signs of chemical abuse.

The amount of money spent on school security is astounding. In New York City, for example, many schools receive an enhanced safety and security budget for protection services. The safety and security budget for the public school system in New York City alone totaled more than $100 million for the 1992-93 school year, and an additional security package in 41 high schools cost another $28 million. The 3,000 member security force in these schools was among the ten largest police forces in the United States. Putting police in schools costs money. One high school in the enhanced program had an annual security payroll of more than three quarters of a million dollars. This major law enforcement effort is funded out of scarce education dollars.[12]

Schools across North America are facing a situation similar to that of New York City. Many schools have become closed and protected environments, with fenced-in campuses, metal detectors, locker searches, student shakedowns and armed security officers patrolling the halls. Yet even with all of this, the increased security measures are not enough to stop the mayhem in our schools and the harm to our young people and to our teachers.

Responses

All across North America attempts are being made to curb the tide of violence in schools and they are producing results. These include:

- Increased security.
- Zero tolerance policies for violence.
- Stricter discipline.
- Suspension or expulsion of violent offenders or moving them to special schools.
- Conflict resolution training and peer mediation programs.
- Drug and alcoholism awareness programs.
- Counseling services and rehabilitation programs.
- Violence prevention programs.
- Social skills training (e.g. saying no to drugs, anger management).
- Collaboration between schools and community.

Despite these initiatives, violence in schools is still a problem. Why is this? A couple of things appear to be hindering the progress.

There is a different reality between teachers, principals and students who experience the violence and government officials who oversee policy decisions from afar and administer funds. They disagree about the extent of the problem, the reliability of the data and data collection methods. Unfortunately this delays resolving the problem.

In order to tackle the root causes of school violence and to change the culture, everyone must work together. This requires collaboration and a broad-based approach, including representation from all school constituencies, in planning and in implementing strategies. If violence is to be stopped everyone must work together with a "school-family-community" approach; one that is comprehensive, collaborative and strategically planned. This is far different from band-aid solutions quickly put into place after a violent incident. This model integrates a variety of responses and goes much further because it changes attitudes and behavior. Shortcuts will not change the culture.

A strategically planned, integrated approach takes time, energy and money. It requires time, energy and commitment to make it a success.

The model calls for a collaborative, inclusive effort—well-behaved as well as disruptive students, teachers and administrators, government officials, parents and community members—who will work in partnership.

To achieve permanent change within the schools, the adults must initiate and direct the course, but the students must define the problems and drive the change. Adults must learn from students what needs to be done to change the culture and how this should happen. However, students must embrace the change and drive it. This means adults and children listening and talking to each other and working together.

There are also other things to do. Money must be found to ensure safe staff-student ratios. Curricula have to excite students and motivate them. Teachers and administrators have to be trained to identify the early warning signs of volatile students and develop appropriate response strategies. Isolated and troubled youth should be engaged in activities that will improve their self-esteem. Teachers need to be able to control student anger as well as their own. They must model conflict resolution strategies that make all parties winners and encourage students to use these to settle disputes with their peers. The complex problems related to family breakdown must be tackled so that children feel less alienated, angry, hurt and isolated.

More focus needs to be on creative initiatives that allow students to celebrate ethnic diversity and to enjoy multiculturalism. Ways must be found to break down barriers and bring adverse students closer together. Children need better programs to help them learn to value ethnic and cultural differences and importantly, their commonalities.

We also need better ways to deal with children coming to school. Making meals available to students who would not otherwise eat is important if they are to learn. Children who come from broken homes, or who have been neglected or abused, may take out their anger and hostility on others. It is therefore important for teachers to be able to identify these children and quickly refer them to school counselors.

The zero tolerance solution has to be looked at more closely because this is a double-edged sword. To restore law and order in the schools, school administrators must be explicit in their messages about the unacceptability of abusive conduct and violence. Zero tolerance creates a new set of social problems. Stricter discipline is critical to controlling violence in the schools. However, this has led to a trend to remove troublemakers from the school system. While on the surface this may help control some school violence, removing or putting violent students in special schools merely shifts the problem. If these students are together in separate schools, will there be enough educational, social and psychological resources to change their behavior? What about students who are suspended and expelled because of their behavior or because they have been caught carrying weapons? A legion of expelled adolescents, who do not want to be in school, roam the streets and get themselves into even deeper trouble.

No matter how many initiatives are taken within the schools, it is ludicrous to think that there can possibly be a change of attitude and behavior without first teaching students the value of human life and the principles of respect and dignity for others. Teachers, principals and school board administrators can help students learn how to resolve conflicts without having to resort to violence. They can help students discover what they excel in and serve as positive role models. However it is clear that teachers and principals cannot accomplish this on their own, nor can they resolve problems associated with drug use, family violence and the easy accessibility students have to guns.

Young people need an education—not only to prepare them for the workforce but for how to live. They need to be taught the benefits of peaceful coexistence. They need role modeling and leadership from the people they look to for guidance. This includes their parents, teachers, coaches, sports heroes, entertainment celebrities and community leaders. Finally, to succeed in changing attitudes and the culture in schools, all students must be involved in the process of change. Students are in a better position to influence their peers to support a philosophy of zero tolerance for violence and peaceful dispute resolution. Students can help make any initiative a successful reality.

Everyone, including school administrators and elected leaders, need to do these things and do them quickly, because we have already created a generation of young people who see the world as an intolerant, violent place and who have easy access to drugs and weapons. These students, who will become the adults of tomorrow, will bring to the workplace what they have learned about survival in the schools. They will form a society of young people who are callous about violence, who readily accept it and are predisposed to it.

VIOLENCE IN COLLEGES AND UNIVERSITIES

Topics to be discussed:
- A Hotbed of Violent Activity
- A Kaleidoscopic View
  - Chilly Climate for Women
  - Disruptive Behavior

- Abuses of Scientific Ethics and
  Academic Practices
- Why Universities Are Ripe for Violence
- Advancing Peaceful Coexistence

A Hotbed of Violent Activity

The problem of violence in colleges and universities is no less of a problem. While statistics and surveys are less available than for schools, the number of media reports and some published statistics quickly dispel the idea that higher educational institutions are safe places. The most prevalent types of interpersonal violence on campus are: 1) rape and sexual assault, 2) nonsexual physical assault, including fights, muggings, hazing, and dating violence and 3) hate crimes.[13]

Many female students do not report sexual harassment and date rape incidents. Many soft forms of violence such as disruptive behavior and abuse of power are not reported either. Yet these events profoundly affect student and faculty life and the dynamics of teaching and learning. An environment filled with tension, strife, hostility and danger diminishes learning and affects teaching.

Throughout time, universities have been at the forefront of new political ideas, characterized by energetic political debate leading to demonstrations and at times social unrest. It is not surprising that universities have been the catalysts for social change. One of the aims of higher education is to expand horizons and encourage critical thinking, which challenges the prevailing belief system and promotes new ideas.

Social activism by students and faculty tend to minimize other expressions of violence that plague campus life: a new wave of racism with political overtones and hate crimes plague many campuses, creating a hostile and even dangerous environment for targeted religious or ethnic groups.

Universities are often uncomfortable if not threatening places in which to study and work. They are beset with all kinds of abuse which includes: cheating and scientific plagiarism, verbal abuse, fighting, date and acquaintance rape, sexism, sexual harassment, racism, gay bashing, ethnic and racial clashes, vandalism, disruptive behavior, death threats and even murder. Students, faculty, administrators and even strangers perpetrate the violence. As in the case of other workplace settings, violent incidents are largely unreported or tend to be hushed up. Victims frequently receive little or no support and management deny or minimize the problem. In general higher education institutions seem to have little interest in keeping or publishing data about the nature and amount of violent incidents on campus.

A Kaleidoscopic View

An inside look at universities shows how troubled these organizations can be. Besides verbal abuse, intimidation, threats, racism and abuse of power that characterize many workplaces, some unique forms of abuse and violence plague many universities. Three distinct but systemically interconnected problems create a tense and hostile environment: a chilly climate for women, disruptive behavior and abuses of scientific ethics and of academic practices. These lead to a hostile environment.

News media regularly report incidents of disruptive behavior, sexual harassment, shootings and murder, involving both students and faculty members. Chronic interpersonal conflicts, excessive competition, antisocial behavior and power struggles characterize many higher education departments or entire institutions. This is more serious than personal relationships gone awry. These behaviors relate to different factions vying for power and control. Persistent conflicts create a highly stressful environment that is hostile to everyone within the institution—students, faculty and support staff alike. Moreover, several universities have experienced highly publicized cases of scientific and financial fraud concerning grants, highlighting another problem, namely professional behavior and integrity of academics in research and funding. While these abuses are not violent in and of themselves, they are part of a larger picture involving incessant conflicts, power struggles and abuses of power. This creates a hostile environment.

Each time a case of scientific or financial fraud becomes public, the credibility of the institution diminishes. Each sexual harassment case involving a faculty member toward a student or employee raises questions about the propriety and professionalism of the faculty. Every time a sexual assault, shooting or murder occurs, shock, disbelief and fear grip the university community and the community at large. These abuses play havoc with learning and teaching. With each case, the perception of the university as a symbol of respectability, civility, harmony, excellence and achievement crumbles.

Chilly Climate for Women

Colleges and universities describe themselves as fostering and supporting liberal thinking and new ideas. Yet at times they have a hard time practicing what they preach, particularly when it comes to women and minorities. Contrary to being an open society, colleges and universities have a history of being ultraconservative, elitist and racist. In addition, certain faculties such as Engineering have a long history of resentment toward women.

Men and women have different perceptions of the place of women in university life. Men claim that more women are now in faculty positions than ever before. Women acknowledge the gains in student enrolment and their progress into academic positions. However, men far outnumber women on faculty, in powerful, senior administrative positions and as CEOs. Despite the fact that more women now study and teach in universities, many female faculty members perceive the environment as thawing, but being far from welcoming. Female students also experience university life differently from male students. Potential for violence makes many women fearful. Three forms of violence threaten female students: date rape, sexism and sexual harassment. Sometimes women are victims of murder. One such incident occurred within a 48-hour period in the summer of 1990 in Gainsville, Florida. Four of the five college and university students who were victims of mutilation and murder were female. Another tragedy took place in December 1989 at a university in Montreal, Quebec, where a killer systematically roamed the halls, finally entering a classroom, searching out and shooting female Engineering students. He killed 14 young women and injured 13 more before killing himself. He had been refused admission to the Engineering program and had a grudge against the women who he believed took his place.

Another aspect of violence to which young female students are vulnerable is date rape. The findings of studies related to date rape of and by students and its connection with alcohol and drug use are disturbing. The National Institute on Alcohol Abuse and Alcoholism (NIAAA) 2002 report on college drinking estimates that, more than 70,000 students between the ages of 18 and 24 are victims of alcohol-related sexual assault or date rape each year. The same report estimates that more than 600,000 students are assaulted by drinking students on a yearly basis.[14] Study after study shows that the risk of date rape and assaults in general, increases with alcohol consumption and drug use.[15] Given the affinity of college students for drinking and experimenting with drugs and the general atmosphere that encourages alcohol consumption at student social activities, the correlation between alcohol/drugs and date rape and violent behavior in general is not surprising.

Female students do not only have to worry about the behavior of their dates. Sexual hostility sometimes enters the classroom. They may be exposed to sexist comments and the circulation of pornographic materials. Despite an effort to prevent sexual harassment by way of education, counseling and monitoring mechanisms, sexual harassment remains a pervasive and distressing factor on campus. As distasteful as harassment by male classmates is, it is worse when perpetrated by male faculty members making explicit or subtle demands for sexual favors in exchange for a passing mark or higher grades.

Female faculty members often work in a chilly climate. Although they are increasingly present, males hold most of the coveted tenured faculty positions and occupy most of the senior positions—departmental chairs, deanships, vice presidential and presidential appointments. The situation is compounded when women are part of a visible minority. Women may have to contend with devaluation of their work, exclusion, isolation and a double standard in work expectations. It is frequently a struggle for them to fit in and adapt to a male-oriented environment.

Without academic standing, female support staff are the least protected as they are the most undervalued in the institution. They may face harassment, unfair work demands and sexual harassment. This usually involves the threat of losing their job or the promise of a better position or improved working conditions.

Many female administrators, finding that their presence in senior administrative positions is resented, or facing hostility when they attempt to move into them, try to fit into the patriarchal world. They do not want to show that they are in any way different from their male colleagues.

Even with policies against sexual harassment, equity policies and support to help people deal with injustices, most women choose to quietly endure the abuse. Women—students, support staff, faculty and administrators—worry that coming forward and complaining about sexism, sexual harassment or a hostile environment, might result in a new wave of resentment against them. Frightened, embarrassed or concerned that they will be blamed, ostracized or ridiculed, women are reluctant to denounce the improper conduct of male professors, colleagues or employers. They worry that no one will believe them. They are concerned about the possibility of reprisals. More particularly they worry about the impact of their complaint on their grades, their career or their job security. Besides, they realize that the complaint process is a long, arduous one which rarely produces change in the short erm. Frequently by the time the hearing or a complaint is scheduled a student has long since left school.

Sexism, date rape, discrimination, sexual harassment and murder form part of a continuum of violence against women in universities, and are a reminder about the darker side of male dominance in academia.

Disruptive Behavior

Antisocial behavior is a serious problem. Increasingly, the behavior of some students and faculty is unacceptable and out of control. At best, the behavior is characterized as extremely bad manners and a general lack of civility. Sometimes disruptive individuals threaten or become physically violent. Their disruptive behavior interferes with academic, administrative and social activities. It impedes the teaching and learning dynamic in the lecture room. It also threatens the physical safety and psychological well-being of students, faculty and staff.

Disruptive behavior on campus has become defined as a wide range of antisocial attitudes, behaviors or activities that are generally persistent in their nature. The behavior includes: belligerent, manipulative or unruly conduct, harassment, threats, assaults, incessant arguments and monopolization of class or meeting time. It uses the time, energy and attention of teaching, support and administrative staff. Passive disruptive behaviors include lack of personal hygiene and unkempt appearance, offensive body odor as well as students repeatedly falling asleep in class where oral participation is an academic requirement.[16]

While any member of the university community can manifest disruptive behavior, students are the primary source of this misconduct. These students often have difficulty coping with stress, experience emotional problems or may have an untreated psychiatric illness such as schizophrenia or manic depression. The behavior can also be a symptom of alcohol or substance abuse or, it may be the result of learned behavior from dysfunctional families or from elementary or high school.

Jerry, a 38-year-old Sociology professor, had been shadowed and harassed for three years by a 20-year-old female student who formed an erotic attachment to him. Nancy would pester him daily, wait for him after class or seek him out in his office. She would find excuses to call him at home at night and over the years managed to "meet him by chance" in the parking lot or at community meetings. At first he was flattered by her attention. When Jerry later tried to discourage her behav-

ior, Nancy's history of suicide attempts made him reluctant to get tough with her for fear of provoking a crisis. He remained silent and endured the constant harassment because of his fear and embarrassment over his inability to handle the situation. The competitive culture in his department made it hard to admit to any kind of difficulty.

Disruptive behavior makes life difficult for everyone. In the classroom it interferes with and undermines the teaching and learning process. Disruptive student behavior directed at a faculty member results in the professor's preoccupation with finding ways to control the behavior and with safety and security measures for himself, other students and sometimes even family members.

Mike, a 24 year-old male student, was angry about his course grade. During a meeting in the office of his 31-year-old Biology lecturer, he tried to convince her to change his grade. Picking up a picture of Theresa's four-year-old son, he suggested she had better "watch out for him in day care, because you never know what could happen to a child when you are not around." Fearing a reprisal if she reported the incident and worrying that no one would believe her, she took what seemed to her to be the only logical approach. At the end of term, she gave Mike a passing grade although she knew he did not deserve it.

In the past, a disruptive faculty member was often considered to be eccentric rather than disruptive. The disruptive faculty member is often egocentric and disrespectful, verbally abusive and overly demanding of students or staff. In department meetings he may be argumentative, uncooperative or obstructive and often display a lack of collegiality. This behavior increases the opportunities for infighting and the preoccupation with conflicts diverts people's energy and attention from their work.

An Engineering Department was under constant tension because of the behavior of a faculty member. Over months, Gordon's cantankerous, eccentric and argumentative behavior escalated. His disruptions at meetings made discussion and decisions on most issues impossible. He was angry about perceived scientific plagiarism, favoritism and obstacles to his gaining tenure. As he took his complaints further up the university hierarchy, his charges became increasingly grave. Not receiving any satisfactory response, Gordon's vague and incessant grievances increased. His abrasive personality, anger and threats worsened. Since he was so difficult to deal with, people simply avoided him. They feared that Gordon would eventually lose control and harm himself or his colleagues.

Disruptive behavior has another twist. Severe conflicts and intense, long-standing lack of civility and collegiality among the faculty can be severely dysfunctional. Competition or intolerance of each other's cultural and ethnic differences or sexual orientations, favoritism and petty politics can lead academics to snipe constantly at each other and worse, make them incapable of any kind of collaboration. This total lack of collegiality disrupts teaching, research and the functioning of a department.

The Dean investigated the English department when the secretaries complained of harassment, intimidation and threatening behavior by a small group of faculty members. They reported an exploitive and abusive climate, continual infighting and lack of leadership. This had been going on for years. During the investigation, a group of graduate students came forward to complain about a professor who was terrorizing faculty, staff and students. He subdued people by coercion, harassment and threats to their careers and lives. In order to survive, many faculty members adopted similar conduct. Others remained silent and for their own protection removed themselves as much as possible from contacts with colleagues and even students. Over the years a poisoned environment had developed, affecting the quality of teaching and the running of the department. The culture was hostile and the department had become dysfunctional. An unusually high level of unprofessional ethics and conduct, favoritism and racism characterized the department. A climate of fear, distrust and suspicion had spread with increasing incidents of bullying and harassing behavior, lying, manipu-

lation of students, lack of collegiality and incessant internal political conflicts. Thefts and loss of computer equipment, software, documents and correspondence plagued the department. So frightened were the students, secretarial staff and junior faculty, they refused to speak to officials unless guaranteed absolute secrecy and protection. Eventually the professor was suspended pending further investigation. He left the country.

Far from being a mere nuisance, disruptive behavior is hostile, volatile and sometimes dangerous. It can lead to other forms of violence, as pointed out on the *Workplace Violence Continuum* in Chapter 2. It can also be a traumatic experience, particularly when the intended victims perceive the harassment or menacing behavior as life-threatening. Disruptive behavior damages the university climate. Students are obliged to study in an atmosphere fraught with tension, disturbance and conflict. Everyone exposed to continual disruptive behavior suffers high levels of stress since they become worn down by the persistent behavior.

Since most of the disruptive behavior is caused by students one must ask, "what makes students disruptive?" One important factor is that today's students have little respect for authority. They are graduates of the previously discussed elementary and high school cultures. They bring into higher education institutions the behaviors and survival skills already learned.

Another factor relates to economic stress. Tremendous pressure is put on students to do well in the current difficult job market. When students become obsessed by the need to obtain high grades to get into graduate school or to obtain a decent job, they sometimes will go to extraordinary lengths to assure themselves those grades. Stress increases emotional and relationship problems and causes behavioral changes. With fewer resources in the community, it is difficult for students to access treatment.

Colleges and universities do not generally do well in controlling disruptive behavior. They usually tolerate this kind of behavior until it reaches a crisis point and escalates out of control. At that point, stopping it requires severe or drastic intervention. There are many reasons why disruptive behavior is difficult to manage in a university setting and why it is not controlled right from the beginning. These include the following:

- A notion that disruptive behavior is simply eccentric.
- Cross-cultural differences and communication gaps.
- Lack of information and training for faculty and administration.
- Institutional structures and processes that make a coordinated response difficult.
- Increased tolerance and acceptance of the behavior and a reluctance to take action because of fear.

Disruptive behavior is sometimes confused with eccentricity. To some extent the display of disruptive behavior is often misread and mistakenly treated as though it were harmless. In a way, eccentrics are perceived as special people. A professor or student, who is unkempt, appears rude and exhibits strange behavior or poor social skills may also be brilliant and next year's award winner.

The sensitive issue of cross-cultural differences is another problem in today's multicultural student bodies in large urban universities across North America. Different cultural communities use gestures, tones of voice and levels of emotion, which can be viewed as aggressive, argumentative and disruptive, when they are simply different. Different cultures have diverse views about authority, conduct and relationships, which can lead to tension and conflict. For example, students who have experienced repression may understandably mistrust people in positions of authority. For them it may be normal to question a decision several times because they have learned to distrust information. Yet to a North American staff member working for example in registration, the student's queries about fees on three or four successive days may be more than annoying—the student may be perceived as being disruptive.

On the other hand, academic administrators often lack information, or skills and training to deal with problems of deviant or perceived disruptive behavior. They may not recognize their authority and responsibility to intervene. They may refuse to accept responsibility or be reluctant to exercise it because they are uncertain whether the community at large will support their actions. They frequently procrastinate or delegate action or decision-making to others to resolve problems that they should resolve themselves. The ombudsperson, sexual harassment officer, code of conduct officer or other professional support staff are often delegated the responsibility of handling the problem without backup or support. This makes acting in cases of disruptive behavior almost impossible. Inadequate information-sharing, the absence of a management information system, or poor communication further hamper attempts to handle disruptive behavior in a coordinated way. Fragmented and inconsistent organizational responses make handling disruptive behavior difficult. As with all forms of violence, managing disruptive behavior requires clear policies and procedures and a rapid and well orchestrated organizational response.

The administration's unwillingness to recognize people's behavior as disruptive and to deal with it promptly allows the behavior to continue. It often gets worse, causing an increase in tension, fear and conflict. When faculty or academic administrators are victims, they frequently hesitate to report the problem, since they believe they should be able to resolve it themselves. Embarrassed by their inability to handle the behavior and feeling incompetent, they remain silent. They believe their colleagues will blame them for not having taken corrective action earlier or for having allowed a situation to get out of control. Or, they worry about being chastised or ridiculed by their colleagues or superiors for their fears. Their solution is simply to tolerate the behavior or to expel the student. When the disruptive person is a faculty member, colleagues, staff and students often remain silent. They may excuse the behavior or they may tolerate it because they feel they have too much to lose by complaining or reporting the academic. They may also feel that nothing will change since others who have complained have achieved nothing. Controlling a disruptive faculty member is difficult in a milieu where academics enjoy power, protection and preferred status.

The university community often fails to perceive disruptive behavior as an actual form of violence as it is laid out on the *Workplace Violence Continuum*, accepting instead the behavior as eccentric. This is the biggest problem in controlling the behavior. Only when the university establishes an effective code of conduct that applies to all members of the community and is committed to enforcing it, will the university or college be able to manage disruptive behavior. Without the will to address the issue and in the absence of adequate resources, disruptive behavior will continue to be problematic and pose a threat to the community.

Abuses of Scientific Ethics and Academic Practices

A popular image of academics portrayed in the cinema and described in literature is of slightly eccentric scholars or scientists who are respected by both students and colleagues and known for absolute dedication to teaching and for their scholarly integrity.

Unfortunately this image runs contrary to several high profile cases involving questionable professional conduct. This includes conflicts of interest, academic and scientific fraud, abuses around authorship of intellectual property, shared authorship, financial malpractice, plagiarism, divided loyalties and misappropriation of work done. Something has gone awry in universities, which are supposed to be dedicated to the pursuit of truth and the advancement and dissemination of knowledge, and where governance and practice are expected to be conducted according to the highest ethical standards.

Abuses of scientific ethics and academic practices are more a form of misconduct than they are violent. However, the behaviors and actions can create an atmosphere of "anything goes." This sometimes leads to other abuses and can contribute to a hostile, poisoned environment. When academics fight over the ownership of their research or credits for a publication, it may not take much for the dispute to get out of hand. Infighting, bullying, intimidation and escalating conflicts can be by-products of intellectual property disputes.

Not all disciplines or universities are tainted. Most in fact are above reproach and most academics and researchers are honest, highly principled and reputable people who conduct themselves admirably. Yet enough abuses exist to draw attention to some undesirable academic behavior and the way the academic world conducts and governs itself.

Questionable behavior around scientific integrity, academic fraud, misappropriation of work and fraudulent practices with research money are abuses of the system, but no one would consider this conduct and practice violent. However, in one case, allegations of such abuses set the stage for a more extreme form of violence. Amid a background of accusations of theft of intellectual property and misappropriation of funds, a disgruntled and disruptive university professor did the unthinkable. He lost complete control and murdered four of his colleagues.

A 51-year-old associate university professor and researcher, dressed in a business suit, took the escalator to the ninth floor Engineering Department. Once there, he took out two semi-automatic pistols which he had concealed on his person and shot and wounded a secretary. He shot at close range and fatally wounded four of his faculty colleagues. He then locked himself in a room with two hostages. They later overpowered him and he was finally arrested.

These shootings were not random happenings. They were the culmination of years of disruptive behavior, allegations, conflicts and complaints about academic and financial fraud and tenure. Unsatisfied with and frustrated by the way his own faculty administration was handling his complaints, he drew more and more people into his disputes. The list of people and departments who tried unsuccessfully to contain his anger and resolve his problems grew. Several colleagues, the chair and dean of his department, senior administrators, human resources, security, health services, ombudsperson and even his own union were among the people who tried to help. Angry about the way his complaints were being handled, he became increasingly agitated, intimidating and demanding. Many people at the university felt threatened by him; many feared him. No one seemed able to deal with him effectively. In his quest for "justice," he went on a shooting rampage.

The court found the professor guilty of committing four murders. He alone is responsible for his actions, although years later he continues to try to lay the blame on others. He charges that the corrupt behavior of the university pushed him to commit murder.

This case and others involving murders and suicides, prompted by disputes over grades and intellectual property, highlight several problems confronting colleges and universities. This unethical behavior may have far-reaching repercussions and needs to be understood.

A university is a highly competitive and stressful environment. The culture is permeated by a drive to publish. There is constant pressure to produce and publish new scientific and scholarly research. This is essential for peer recognition, tenure and scholarly honors and continued grants and research contracts.

Research and academic fraud take place easily in a decentralized environment with loose social controls and a laissez-faire leadership style. The tradition of autonomy and non-interference in the researcher's work is based on the principle of academic freedom. This promotes an environment with little supervision and an honor system for conduct and ethics in research and finances.

Universities today place a high value on the ability of the academic community to bring in money. This puts pressure on academics to obtain government, industrial or private research grants which are necessary for the expansion of facilities, such as labs or to obtain the latest computer technology. It also serves to attract the best researchers and top graduate students worldwide. All of this is vital to the university because it increases in stature, which in turn attracts more paying and highly qualified students. It can also result in endowments and other financial awards.

Thus the policy of non-interference in academic matters, a production-driven research culture, loose financial controls and the need for personal recognition, control and power, all may set the stage for abuses in academic and scientific integrity. Sometimes the environment becomes untenable and hostile for students, faculty and administration, leading to extreme forms of violence.

Why Universities Are Ripe for Violence

What makes universities prone to different forms of violence such as disruptive behavior, violence against women, abuse of power and financial and scientific fraud? The reasons are complicated, because the university is a complex organization and the world of academia is steeped in tradition and rules. Universities are unique as work organizations because each faculty and department has its own administration and is largely self-governed and self-regulated. Comprehensive consultation in decision-making and extensive peer participation in leadership selection is based on advanced democratic principles that do not exist in traditional workplaces. The university promotes fairness and due process in its governance and policies. At the same time, the structure ensures faculty control, power and independence. When things work well, the model is admirable. However, these same features, in a culture strongly rooted in traditional practices, are the basis for many of its problems in management and social controls.

The world of academia is a special milieu created by academics for themselves. Academics are considered the builders of future society and are viewed as the creative force in our scientific, philosophical and political worlds. Since intelligence is of the utmost importance in this environment, abusive behavior can be, and often is, excused as eccentric.

The university culture has its roots in patriarchy with historical attitudes of resentment of women. The violence, abuse and harassment women experience on campus can be explained in this context.

Higher education institutions are elitist organizations. Change occurs through a struggle. Traditional practices are deeply entrenched and considered sacred. Resentment and hostility occur between one constituency, which wants to maintain traditional practices and acquired rights and others who want equal status. The "haves" are mainly tenured white male faculty members and administrators. The "have nots" are the untenured female or male faculty and students (undergraduate, graduate or postgraduate).

Privileges, rights and protected status are envied. The situation is ripe for hostility, power struggles and conflict and for an angry person to become ever more disgruntled, enraged and prone to escalating violence.

The notion of academic freedom, that is, the freedom to teach, conduct research or publish without interference, is a cherished, fundamental academic right. Yet sometimes academic freedom is used as an excuse for all kinds of unacceptable behavior and activities.

Eccentric behavior, abusive conduct or outlandish comments are sometimes accepted and justified under the guise of academic freedom. Although the conduct may have little connection to academic issues, the behavior is tolerated. A cycle of violence may begin when professors assume the right to mistreat students, who in turn react and become abusive themselves. Sometimes the environment inadvertently condones such practices as drunkenness, hazing in initiation rituals or sexism. All these behaviors are excused in the context of "boys will be boys" and as simple fun.

Each department or faculty is set up to be independent with control over its own administration and budgets. This creates a highly decentralized organization that is difficult to administer and to control and lends itself to financial abuses. The university administration is slow to deal with problem situations regarding academics because they wish to respect individual liberties, because of professional or labor agreements or guidelines and mostly because of an utter dread of raising the ire of their colleagues.

Universities are unique models in management, because their professional, traditional and labor agreements (the latter particularly in Canadian universities), strictly regulate them. There are strict guidelines for everything from job descriptions to the hiring process. The traditions and regulations also describe how to deal with problems relating to professors' behavior or performance. These include an elaborate consultation process in decision-making and an intricate, arduous system for dealing with complaints and grievances. This results in a multi-layered bureaucracy that is slow, cumbersome and difficult to administer.

Although this protection can be advantageous for the academic, it is sometimes a nightmare for the administrator who wants to take immediate action to curtail abusive behaviors. Even support personnel, protected under labor agreements, do not usually have the same rights and privileges as academics. In many universities a code of conduct guides student behavior, giving them similar rights to due process but with much less protection. In cases of harassment or coercion, students feel that complaining about faculty members is useless because of their "protected status." Secretaries have little recourse against an abusive professor because few people are attentive to their complaints. The university community views them as faculty support, with little status. Even faculty members, particularly women, who have complaints against one of their own colleagues, find it hard to file a complaint. The sanctioning or firing of a tenured professor, even one who exhibits dangerous or extreme behavior or malpractice, is a very serious, complicated and difficult endeavor. This contributes to the difficulty in managing the organization. Administrators have to rely more on their ability to lead by influence than on the power of their positions. Not always fully understanding the parameters of the powers they have, academic administrators sometimes either abuse their power or do not accept the responsibility that goes with it. Since strong traditions define so many situations and conditions, often the hands of the Dean or Vice President are tied. Academics do not have a supervisor to whom they report as in other organizations. Although each department has a chair, he often has no real authority over his faculty members. This lack of on-site supervision makes it hard for the university to take action against them.

The selection process for administrators represents another obstacle to decisive and quick action against abusive behavior and practices. Administrators generally come from the faculty: they are often selected for these positions because of their reputation, their ability to protect the rights and views of their colleagues or for their public relations skills. They are not necessarily good administrators. Most academic administrators return to the teaching ranks after completion of a term in administration. Consequently they must be careful to retain the support and approval of their peers while in administrative functions. Moreover, since so much administrative decision-making relies on the goodwill and collaboration of the faculty it is tough to take a firm stand or make an unpopular decision.

Administrators have little or no training for administrative roles and responsibilities. They frequently have no experience in handling labor relations, interpersonal conflicts, behavioral problems or other administrative tasks. Many administrators flounder when it comes to the all-important task of enforcing discipline and controlling abusive behavior and are reluctant to risk exercising their authority for fear of offending their colleagues. They do not know what actions to take.

The continual rotation of administrators does not allow for continuity in management philosophy, style or objectives. This lack of permanence makes it difficult to maintain authority, to develop new rules and procedures or to undertake disciplinary actions.

Barriers to the control of violence in universities are inherent in their organizational structure. These include: protected faculty positions, old boys' network, complex governance, trend toward individualism and weak management structures and practices. How can violence against women, scientific fraud and abusive and disruptive behaviors be managed effectively when so many restrictions are placed on administrators, including those by unions who protect their violent members? How can the system effectively control the anger of disgruntled students and faculty members, when so many bureaucratic levels have to be consulted regarding recommendations or actions? How can a university community prevent homicides when the administrators are powerless to control violent behavior? The principles of academic freedom which universities hold sacred are ironically, an impediment in controlling violent behavior. This very freedom allows unchecked uncivil behavior, discrimination, racism and harassing or threatening conduct. Academic excellence and the very principles the university promotes suffer.

Unattended to, these behaviors lead to extreme forms of violence. When universities allow angry, hostile and frustrated individuals to become even angrier, they risk having to contend with more extreme forms of violence, including assault and murder. Their failure to respond appropriately touches four distinct areas. Failure to:

- Respond in a timely manner to the complaints of disgruntled students, faculty and staff.
- Detect warning signs of danger and take action.
- Manage conflicts or disruptive behaviors before they escalate.
- Control weapons and the flow of alcohol and drugs on campus.

Weak leadership, complex decentralized decision-making and inadequate response mechanisms allow professors and students to become disgruntled, create havoc and occasionally to "go over the edge" and commit more extreme forms of violence, including murder.

Advancing Peaceful Coexistence

Colleges and universities share similarities with other work settings which experience problems with abusive, intolerant and violent behavior from their employees. Yet central to the issue of violence in these institutions is the purpose of education. Is the educational mission to train people for the job market? Or does the vision include education for ethical, physical and moral leadership? If so, this means a shift in the way higher educational institutions are administered.

Senior administrators need to challenge the status quo and promote a culture committed to respect for civility and human achievement. Leadership must show by words and actions the values of justice, equity, human rights, integrity and respect and dignity for *all* members of its community. The university must treat everyone equally. Cultural diversity must be viewed as a celebration of human richness. Striving for excellence in all endeavors should be the predominant goal.

Peaceful coexistence on campus will be achieved through justice, integrity and a code of conduct that apply equally to all community members, evolving into a partnership in which there is a shared vision and common values. When the university culture promotes civility, respect, collaboration and academic integrity, its community will more strongly identify and support it. The university will be transformed into a organization with a common vision. Its goals will be achieved through peaceful, collaborative efforts.

Universities of today require courageous administrative leaders who are highly ethical and charismatic change agents. The challenge for the leaders is to inspire the community to embrace exemplary conduct. Since the university community is made up of people with diverse political and social beliefs, and ethnic, religious and cultural backgrounds, the leadership has to be skilled in conflict resolution and consensus-building. Moreover, It has to act as a role model in peaceful coexistence.

A greater accountability for the actions and behavior of all university community members and a shared responsibility for the institution's well-being will facilitate decision-making and decrease abusive behavior. Improved self-regulation can prevent and control many existing systemic abuses. The university can promote a culture that does not tolerate abusive conduct of any kind, when it is understood that this new culture is in everyone's best interest.

A renewed organizational culture can blend the best in traditional practices with enlightened self-government. An environment, which is open and hospitable to all, will advance the ideals upon which universities were founded: justice, ethics, and social and political responsibility thus creating a more humane and peaceful world. The entire university community—leadership, faculty, students and support staff—face this challenge to renew their commitment to these principles.

TRANSFORMING THE EDUCATION SYSTEM

Campuses from elementary schools to universities operate within the context of the larger society. The types of interpersonal conflict, violence and crime prevalent in our educational system parallel life off campus, in students' families and in their communities. Along with math, literature, football games, dances, fraternities and sororities, students routinely experience sexual and physical assault, theft, harassment and xenophobia.

Children and young adults learn from observation. What they see today are competitive and overwhelmed adults who are unable to control their anger or maintain violence-free personal relationships. Many children face intolerance and rejection. Everywhere young people go, they receive messages that normalize violent behavior. Violence on television, in movies and in music bombards youth. Every day young people see how poorly adults resolve conflicts. They learn though this exposure that violence is normal, acceptable behavior: for parents, community leaders and governments. They receive a strong and clear message from the adult world that the use of violence as a coercive force to control others is all right. Exposure to violence at an early age desensitizes children to acts of brutality. It makes them so callous that it deadens their own pain or prevents them from seeing the pain abusive actions cause others.

Inattention toward school violence shows that bullies can get away with harming people and that victims should not expect protection from the adult world. The tendency to use counseling alone to treat offenders, without recourse to constructive discipline, fails to teach them that hurtful actions have consequences. Inability to teach students how to settle disputes in peaceful ways leaves children ill-equipped to live in what they perceive to be a hostile, conflict-ridden world. Unless they are taught how to conduct themselves, more and more youth will learn to resolve problems through violent means.

When violence in schools and on campus is dealt with in a planned, respectful and collaborative way, it will decrease. Although creative initiatives are in place in many cities to deal with the problem, the approaches are still not working well on a large scale. More global strategies are needed to deal with social conditions that create a climate ripe for abuse. Children should be educated in conflict resolution, collaboration and respect for their peers. This problem must be tackled proactively and speedily because the wave of violence sweeping elementary and high schools, colleges and universities represents a social trend. A commitment to action must be taken at the highest political levels because money is required to develop these initiatives. In reality, these are not big budget items.

When faced with an immediate problem of violence, a school can benefit from advanced planning and swift actions can cool down a hot situation. This includes the following actions:

- Enforce the ban of drugs and weapons on campus. Promote responsible use of alcohol.
- Take immediate action on verbal or behavioral cues of hostility, aggression, frustration or despair, especially expressions of revenge, death threats or suicide.
- Respond quickly and in a coordinated way to grievances and complaints. Resolve problems!
- Develop expertise in the school to help others identify and respond to troubled individuals.
- Engage students (leaders, average performers and troublemakers), teachers, parents and community members in a collaborative effort to create a violence-free school environment.

School violence is a health and safety issue that results from individual, community and political disregard for human needs and human rights. Controlling violence on campus is not the sole problem of administrators, teachers, parents or students. It is a problem for every one of those groups and for society as a whole.

More "tough love" measures should be adopted to rid campuses of violence. We need to say, "No! This behavior is not acceptable here." At the same time we need to continue working to make our educational system a positive reinforcing environment for young people. This means making the rules and consequences known for abusive, disruptive behavior and violence of any kind, no matter who the perpetrator is. It means setting limits and teaching young people to have pride in themselves and in their schools and to take responsibility for their actions. It means teaching, by action and words, the value of peacemaking over war-making. It means setting standards of conduct that everyone is required to follow and promoting equal treatment and respect for students, teachers, support staff and educational administrators.

The violence sweeping our educational system is flashing a dangerous warning signal. How our youth deal with each other and with adults has an impact on the kind of society we will be in the future. Unless we act now to stop the decay of our educational systems and say no to violence, we are in for big trouble. Young people who have learned that they can get what they want through intimidation and threats or who have learned that they need to be fearful and on guard for attacks, are taking into their homes, into their communities and into our workplaces the same lessons they learned in school—trust no one, do what you have to do to survive and arm yourself with any kind of weapon to protect yourself. Breeding a lawless, abusive and violent youth culture will have a severe effect on our future workplaces.

- 7 -
Caregivers' Dread: Violence in Health Care

They nurse us when we are sick, attend to us when we are too ill to care for ourselves and comfort us in times of crisis and distress. These health care professionals—registered nurses, nursing assistants, orderlies and home care workers dedicate their lives to healing the sick. Their jobs are tough and undervalued. Yet their contribution is vital. Without them our hospitals and health care facilities could not operate.

This group of professionals, most of whom are women, work in hospitals, emergency departments, nursing homes, custodial care facilities, psychiatric institutions, health clinics and home care programs. Together with doctors, medical technicians, therapists and other health care professionals, at one time or another they provide care for every one of us.

Health care workers do not enter their chosen field for the money. Many other jobs pay much more and demand far less. They do it because they want to help people. For the most part they are kind, concerned, gentle and compassionate human beings. To learn that health care workers are at high risk for violence in the line of duty is disturbing.

The violence is committed in large part by the very people they nurse and try to help. Confused, aggressive and paranoid victims of Alzheimer's disease may lash out and strike them. Patients in the throws of delirium from infection may punch and kick them. Delusional or out-of-control psychiatric patients may yank their hair, bite, scratch, or try to strangle them. Alcoholics or drug addicts may swear and shout insults and even pull knives or guns on them. Danger and abuse lurk in every ward and in every bed. The patient, one moment a quiet, meek individual, may suddenly turn into an aggressor.

Studies and surveys show that violence in the health care sector is a global phenomenon.[1] The literature has repeatedly identified nurses, psychiatrists, physicians, psychiatrists, patient care attendants, therapists, technicians and social workers as being particularly at risk. In the United States, the Bureau of Labor Statistics reports that for the year 2000, 48 percent of all non-fatal injuries from occupational assaults and violent acts occurred in hospitals, nursing and personal-care facilities and residential-care services.[2] Nurses, aides, orderlies and attendants suffered the most non-fatal assaults resulting in injury. In fact the injury incidence rates (measured per 10,000 full-time workers) placed nursing and personal care facility workers at 25, social workers (another high risk group) at 15, and health service workers overall at 9.3. This compared to an overall private sector injury rate of 2.[3]

Nurses in the United States are second only to police officers in being physically assaulted on the job. According to a Bureau of Justice Statistics special report, between 1993 and 1999, 429,100 nurses annually were victims of violent crimes in the workplace. That is an average of 21.9 attacks for every 1,000 nurses. In comparison, physicians experienced 71,300 attacks, or 16.2 for every 1,000 doctors.[4] In the United Kingdom, compared to the average risk for assaults and threats across all occupational groups, health care workers have a three to four times higher risk for these forms of violence.[5] In the developing and transition countries, more than half of the health sector personnel surveyed had experienced at least one incident of physical or psychological violence in the year previous to the study.[6]

These reports are part of a growing body of literature in both industrialized and developing countries describing the problem of violence in health care: nurses, doctors, social workers, ambulance drivers and other health care workers are at high risk for violence.[7] The violence includes assault, threats with a weapon, bullying and verbal abuse.

ABUSE OF CAREGIVERS—AN OLD ISSUE

This is not a new problem. Long before any significant data was available, professional journals featured articles about patient assault. Researchers investigating this issue in the 1970's were then publishing their findings in psychiatric and nursing journals. Most of this research took place in psychiatric institutions, nurses being the subject of most of the inquiries. Investigations related to patient assault were and are still mainly patient-focused. Researchers have been trying to understand why patients, particularly those in psychiatric settings and emergency rooms, become violent and how staff can better treat and manage their violent behavior.[8]

For years, psychiatric inpatient units and mental health clinics have been recognized as high risk settings for assaults on staff. In the 1990's, professional and union surveys in United States, Canada and Britain drew attention to these as well as other areas. Emergency departments, geriatric services, nursing homes, home care programs, critical care, medical and surgical units, and maternity wards have all been identified as trouble spots.

Given the history of the problem, the number of high-risk areas cited, and the number of injuries reported in recent years, one would have to conclude that safe workplaces are practically non-existent in the health care sector.

Partly because of the work of the U.S. Occupational Safety and Health Administration (OSHA) in the late 1990's and its counterpart in the state of California (Cal/OSHA), violence in health care institutions received unprecedented attention. However, as is the case with other occupational groups, the violence is downplayed by health administrators and health care workers. Institutional resistance to reporting still exists, leading to a problem of serious under-reporting of incidents. Since data collection methods vary across institutions and countries, one can speculate that the problem is much larger than previously thought.

Long before government surveys and statistics were available, unions conducted surveys of their membership. Because of widespread reported abuses, unions across North America made violence toward staff a priority health and safety issue. Some began educating their members about patient assault long before government health and safety agencies recognized the problem. For example, the Service Employees International Union and the Canadian Union of Public Employees are two unions that produced and distributed information kits in the early 1990's to alert their members to the problem of on-the-job violence and how to deal with it.[9]

If listening to health care workers talk about their working conditions is any indication, one would agree with unions that what is being reported is only the tip of the iceberg. For a variety of reasons that will be discussed later, violent incidents are generally reported by people whose physical or psychological injuries leave them too incapacitated to work.

ABUSE COMES WITH THE TERRITORY

The abuse, highlighted in the following examples, is dreadful. However, since abuse is considered "part of the job," not nearly enough attention is paid to caregivers' complaints.

A 73-year-old male in a residential care facility attacked a nursing assistant while she was feeding him lunch. He grabbed her breast, pinching and jabbing it with his fingers. She sustained a large bruise on her breast.

An elderly resident in a private nursing home, repeatedly hit a senior nurse on the head with his cane. The man had been the nurse's favorite patient for years and he would allow no one but her to attend to his needs. The incident left the nurse with a severe concussion and an acute stress reaction. She was off work for four months.

A 32-year-old male patient attacked a psychiatric nurse from behind and attempted to strangle her. As she slipped into unconsciousness, two orderlies managed to free her, but not before they too were kicked, bitten, punched and scratched.

A 62-year-old white male nursing home resident repeatedly uttered racial slurs and harassed a black nursing attendant. One day the resident smeared feces in the attendant's face, up her nostrils and into her mouth.

For years a 42-year-old male accident victim who was confined to a wheelchair terrorized the entire nursing staff at a chronic care hospital. Over a nine-month period he assaulted three staff members and repeatedly threatened to kill nine others.

A 28-year-old drug addict stabbed an emergency room doctor as he began to examine him.

A 37 year-old male psychiatric patient, suffering from depression and violent tendencies, severely injured an occupational therapist during a group activity session. The patient went into a sudden fit of rage, picked up a table and threw it at her. She suffered a cracked pelvis, minor concussion and contusions.

A female Alzheimer patient in an acute care hospital kicked a pregnant nurse in the stomach. She went into premature labor and lost the baby.

These anecdotes typify the violence that health care professionals have to contend with on a daily basis. When health care workers have an opportunity to talk about on-the-job abuse, the stories flow. Nurses, attendants and other health care workers endure constant verbal and physical attacks. They have their glasses ripped off and broken or smashed in their faces. They are beaten with fists and elbows or thrown across rooms. They are routinely yelled and sworn at, scratched, slapped, kicked, punched, bitten, spat at, pushed, struck with objects, and racially or sexually harassed or molested. They are knifed or shot. Sometimes a health care worker is even murdered. These attacks are made on people whose desire is to make life more comfortable for their patients.

DEPERSONALIZATION OF PATIENT ASSAULTS

Many health care professionals tolerate violence on the job even though some of them are subjected to terrible abuses. Often administrators ignore the problem, even when they are aware of it. Understanding the health care perspective regarding abusive patients and the culture of the helping relationship explains why this happens.

The literature of the 1980's provides an insight into institutional response to patient assault in psychiatric institutions. Rather than identifying the problem as violence perpetrated by patients on individual staff members, it was depersonalized and presented as violence directed at the institution. The focus was on what caused a patient to be violent. The impact of these incidents on the personal and professional lives of staff members was overlooked.[10]

Depersonalization of workplace violence is not unique to the health care field. As has been pointed out in previous chapters, this is a common reaction. Since patient abuse of caregivers was, and often still is, viewed as striking out against the institution, the assumption is that no one gets hurt. This allows the organization to tolerate and even ignore such assaults. In this context it is little wonder that the assaulted caregiver tends to minimize the significance of a patient attack.

The problem has been further obscured by the lack of a clear definition of violence even within the same institution, inconsistency in reporting, and unreliability of data collection methods. Statistics about the nature and scope of the problem are confusing and contradictory because of a lack of a standardized definition of what constitutes violence in health care. While some studies limit a violent act to physical injury, others include incidents of verbal abuse, harassment and bullying.

INTERNAL VIOLENCE ANOTHER DIMENSION

Although not unique to health care, internal violence, that is, violence by a colleague, is particularly striking in this industry.

Perhaps this is because the health care sector has the most documented evidence. Whether people report being mistreated, bullied, badgered, harassed, teased or excluded by colleagues or other members of the multidisciplinary team, national and international reports show that this problem is as huge as it is widespread. Nurses in particular report a high level of verbal abuse associated with the behavior of physicians, administrators and colleagues.[11] They are not alone. High stress levels and conflict between co-workers and across disciplines are common. This creates tension, leading to the hostile environment described on the *Workplace Violence Continuum* in Chapter 2.

"PART OF THE JOB"

In many institutions, employees' assertions about unsafe working conditions and protests about violence—either by patients or by colleagues are met with stony silence. Violence in health care has always been considered as "part of the job" and workers are expected to cope with it. Complainers tend to be viewed as troublemakers and receive little sympathy. Administrators who are confronted with government cutbacks, large deficits and patient overload tend to view the problem of patient assault and internal violence as comparatively insignificant.

Several years ago I attended a meeting with a group of hospital psychiatric staff, including nurses, orderlies, occupational therapists, and psychiatrists. When invited to talk about their experiences, they were eager to share their stories. What they had to say was no different from that expressed repeatedly by health care workers today.

"Do you know what it's like to take care of someone who is abusive? There are so many incidents around here, it feels like a war zone, not a hospital."

"I thought I was treating the sick. Patients are so abusive. What did I do to deserve this?"

"My attitude has changed. I realize there is no protection. Anyone can die at work, including me."

"Sometimes I've called in sick. Most of the time I cope by hoping my shift will end without me getting hurt. When you're worried about safety, it's hard to do your work. There's no way I can smile and be nice to people who hurt me."

"Until now I've kept silent about the violence. Thank you for letting me talk about it. Thank you for letting me know I'm not the only one to feel angry, hurt and violated. Thank you for letting me know I am not crazy."

"I'm tired of getting yelled at, humiliated and bullied. I'm an operating room nurse. I don't need this, certainly not from my team members!"

WHY HEALTH CARE WORKERS GET ABUSED

Why is so much abuse by patients and their families heaped on health care workers? The reasons are many. An analysis of the way hospitals and other health care facilities operate points out the extent to which the environment and organizational procedures incite frustration and hostility. Even people who are not violent by nature can become frustrated and easily angered by an experience with the health care system.

The physical design of health care institutions is one reason people become irritated. The structure of the buildings, paint colors, furniture and overall ambience, combined with overcrowding and a lack of privacy, create a highly charged environment. Many health care facilities are cold, impersonal and user-unfriendly places. This makes people feel uncomfortable and tense, adding to an already dehumanizing experience.

The way institutions operate is another factor. Simply put, the health care system may incite patients to become agitated and violent. Anyone who has had to go to a hospital emergency department knows how the experience provokes feelings of frustration, impatience, hostility and anger. This occurs at a time when people in pain feel vulnerable and distressed. A lack of privacy, endless delays for examinations, tests and results and repeated questioning by different people increase tension. Distraught and angry patients and relatives have no one to complain to or to advocate on their behalf. They therefore vent their anger on staff.

The problem of understaffing has been cited repeatedly, particularly by unions, as a leading factor contributing to patient assaults on staff. With insufficient staff, patients are unable to get the attention they need. People who are in pain, discomfort or needing attention, may lash out in frustration at their caregiver. Inactivity, boredom, lack of attention and delays also give patients more time to fret and worry, leading them to become aggressive and abusive.

Preoccupied by soaring health care costs and overextended budgets, governments and administrators look for ways to slash costs and bring budgets in line. The consequence has been major staff cutbacks resulting in increased workloads. Overworked employees try their best to do their jobs, but gradually they become highly stressed and overwhelmed. With increasing staff-patient ratios, nursing staff take longer to respond to patient requests for help and spend less time talking to or comforting their patients. All this leads to dehumanization in patient care, provoking impatience and resentment between patients and caregivers.

Admission of patients with greater needs than the institution can handle is another contributing factor to staff abuse. Potentially violent patients are literally dumped in a hospital ward, nursing home or other setting because there is no other place to put them. Without adequate physical resources, well-designed environments or enough trained people to handle these patients, employees become easy targets. The situation is aggravated when patients who have a history of violent behavior are not identified. Insufficient attention is paid to the triggers that provoke angry outbursts. Often there is no consistent approach among staff for handling patients when they do act out.

Another problem relates to medication. While the legal right to refuse medication may be seen as a victory for patient rights, it is not necessarily beneficial to staff. First, uncontrolled behavior due to insufficient medication contributes to violence. Second, the patient's refusal is often expressed in a power struggle with staff, which frequently ends in a physical struggle. The problem is further compounded when the patient's physician will not increase the dosage because he or she does not witness the full extent of the patient's aggressive behavior. Hearing about a complaint or reading in the chart that the patient screamed, kicked and scratched a nurse or attendant have much less of an impact on the doctor, than if he had witnessed the incident or was a direct target of the abuse.

Of all the factors given above for the preponderance of patient assaults on staff, one other factor stands out in the literature. Staff are blamed: for their inexperience, poor attitude and social skills, conflicts and power struggles, low morale, and fear of patients. Administrators, researchers and even staff themselves suggest that caregivers' poor behavior and attitudes are principal reasons why patients are violent toward them. Much of the past literature target- ed caregivers and nurses in particular. Time and again it has been suggested that nurses unconsciously provoke violence through per- sonality traits that irritate patients or because they are immature, have insufficient training, and are inexperienced.[12]

This theme of blaming the victim because of some personality defect or inadequacy is not only erroneous, but it also adds to health care workers' injuries. While we can all share a story about our own bad experience with a rude hospital clerk, an insensitive nurse or a callous doctor, these negative attitudes do not fully explain the propensity for violence against caregivers.

Testimonies from victimized caregivers and research results show that they are experienced professionals. Many have advanced training and years of experience. Nurses with masters' degrees, doc- tors, psychotherapists, and psychiatrists have all reported being assaulted by patients. Well-liked, attentive, compassionate and sen- ior health care workers are also abused. Mounting evidence sug- gests that most caregivers and health care professionals, including psychiatrists and physicians, can expect to suffer at least one major incident of violence during their careers This refutes the idea that inexperience, immaturity, and unpleasant personality traits are the main factors which incite patients to violence.

The issue of insufficient training in this area, however, is problematic. Health care workers receive little training on how to deal with violent patients, and how to prevent minor conflicts form escalating into violence. Somehow caregivers are expected to know instinctively how to recognize and predict violent tendencies and how to defuse hostility and handle outbursts in non-aggressive, non-confrontational ways.

The combination of high stress levels, fatigue, conflicts, staff shortages and inequalities in performance produce a volatile environment. Highly hierarchical organizations, turf issues, slow responses to problems, miscommunication, weak management skills and a permissive attitude toward offenders set the stage. All of the above contributes to creating a hostile work environment.

SICKNESS AS AN EXCUSE

When considering patient abuse toward staff, one has to think about society's perceptions about a person's ability to cope when sick, and the nature of the patient-caregiver relationship. Aside from the organizational problems discussed above, these two issues are among the leading factors for violence in the health care system. Our society views a sick person, especially one with reduced mental capacity, as not responsible for his actions. This perception stems from our feelings about illness. We tend to believe that a sick person has less control over his body, emotions or behavior. We feel sorry for people who are ill, in pain, and in discomfort. We regard sickness as a physical weakness and beyond our control.

The medical community strongly upholds the view that patients should not be responsible for their behavior. They believe that a patient suffering from dementia, for example, should not be blamed for hitting a staff member because that person is not aware of what he is doing. They empathize with a terminally ill person who takes out his anger on the staff. They make excuses for the obnoxious, threatening and violent behavior of an accident victim, because that person has to face being confined to a wheelchair for the rest of his life.

Sickness, diminished capacity and imminent death have led the medical community to accept patients' abusive behavior. Because they feel sorry for the sick person, they justify the patient's behavior, even when it causes the caregiver injury and pain. How can a health care practitioner accept their anger with a patient, or think about lodging a complaint, when the patient is the weaker and more vulnerable party?

When caregivers do stand up to their abusers and say "no more," administrators, and often the police, judges and workers' compensation agencies conspire to protect the patient. Senior management tell health care workers, "you knew what kind of environment this was when you were hired, it's up to you to cope." The police are reluctant to lay charges against the offender because they view the assault as a medical problem. In cases where charges are laid, the judge generally accepts the defense that the person is ill and therefore not responsible for his actions. Workers' compensation agencies can question and refuse to accept the legitimacy of stress-related claims resulting from an attack, especially over the length of recovery time. This results in caregivers being unsupported and even labeled as troublemakers. Moreover, patients get away with assault. The patient population quickly learns it is all right to abuse their caregivers.

BLAME THE CAREGIVER

Despite their illnesses or reduced intellectual or physical functioning, most psychiatric patients and people with reduced intellectual functioning can control themselves and know the difference between right and wrong. The use of sickness as a justification for patients' violent behavior fosters an abusive climate. When administrators excuse patients' bad conduct, they give them permission to continue the behavior. Inaction also sends a powerful message to other patients who see that it is permissible to behave this way.

A permissive attitude concerning patient assault on staff causes resentment and anger to build, as caregivers feel unsupported and unappreciated by management. A tolerance for violence splits staff between those who want to excuse the patient and those who want to hold him accountable for his conduct. The escalation of conflicts among staff members heightens stress and tension on the ward and among the patients. A charged climate intensifies, when victimized employees feel unsupported by their team members. When patients sense tension and conflict, they become even more insecure and anxious. They then act out their frustrations and anger, heaping further abuse on their caregivers.

Besides having to cope with their injuries, victimized caregivers have to contend with their feelings about the abusive patient, their own inadequacies, and the worry that they consciously or unconsciously provoked the incident. Doubts about their professional competence, self-worth and their suitability to work in this particular setting lead victims to question their actions and to blame themselves for the assault. "I must have done something wrong" or "I must have done something to provoke the behavior" is a frequent lament of the victimized health care worker. This self-blame is reinforced by team members. Since health care workers dedicate themselves to serving the sick and cannot understand how patients could be abusive to people who care for them, they believe their victimized colleague must have done something to cause the patient to become abusive. This "blame the victim" attitude works for team members, until they too become targets.

The tendency to shift responsibility for the abuse from the patient-offender onto the caregiver-victim is wrong. The same holds true when the offender is a co-worker. Abusive people—patients or co-workers—need to be held accountable for their actions. Patients and staff alike need to be reminded that abusive behavior of any kind is inappropriate and unacceptable. At the same time, the organization has to analyze the events leading up to the incident and address the "triggers." Many provocations in institutions are operational. Clear action to make people responsible for their behavior and address organizational problems will place the onus where it belongs: on the offender and the health care system.

HELPING CULTURE FOSTERS VIOLENCE

The health care culture provides clues about why patients are allowed to get away with assault and why the responsibility for incidents shifts from the offender to the victim. A hospital is a closely-knit community with a strong shared mission, well-established rules of conduct and norms of behavior for staff, and a well-defined chain of command.

In comparison to nurses, medical doctors, psychiatrists and chiefs of staff all represent a higher authority for patients. Their relationship with patients is more detached. Patients are more respectful of them and in some instances fear them. Since their roles distance and protect them from patients' acting-out behavior, they do not realize that patients act differently with them than with other staff. Since they have no difficulty controlling the patient, they believe the patient is easy to manage. When a patient does act out against a member of the nursing staff, senior doctors and administrators rationalize that the incident happened because of the nurse. He was unable to control the patient, lacked the skill or ability to handle the situation, or must have done something to provoke the patient into becoming angry and aggressive.

This rationalization is typical and can be easily understood through the following example.

Nurses at a psychiatric hospital repeatedly endured verbal and minor physical attacks by patients. The male psychiatrist in charge of their ward did not listen to them or respond to their complaints. Carolyn, a 28-year-old nurse, wanted to charge one of the patients with assault after he had hit her. The psychiatrist, who had trouble understanding Carolyn's fears and anger, convinced her she was overreacting and that any such action would be detrimental to the patient's progress.

There were several reasons for the psychiatrist's insensitivity toward the nurses and his lack of concern about his patients' abusive conduct. Not surprisingly the patients behaved differently with him, because of his status and authority. Since they were submissive towards him, he believed their aggressive behavior was an expression of hostility and anger related either to patients' problems or to the way the nurses were interacting with them. He viewed patients' screaming, use of obscenities, verbal threats, and harassment of staff, as normal acting-out behavior of disturbed people. The psychiatrist also believed that venting anger was cathartic for sick patients. Since he spent little time on the ward, he was rarely exposed to the patients' aggressive behavior. He could not support Carolyn's desire to charge the patient with assault, because he did not perceive the patient's behavior as violent. He believed the patient needed help in order to understand the emotions that caused him to lose control, rather than be sanctioned for his actual behavior.

This example highlights why health care workers generally tolerate abuse and why they minimize and excuse patients' behavior. Doctors, nurses, orderlies and therapists believe their role is to take care of sick people and make them well. Since they view anger and hostility as a normal expression of feelings associated with illness, they accept that "abusive patient behavior is normal, comes with the territory, and is part of the job."

AVOID MAKING WAVES

Caregivers hesitate to report incidents. They feel tremendous pressure from management, treating physicians and colleagues to tolerate and keep quiet about the abuse. Everyone gives them messages, either directly or indirectly that "they are professionals and should be able to cope." The *helping culture* frowns on any display of vulnerability, especially toward patients. Since caregivers believe they should be strong and in control, they never want to appear weak or fragile. Those who are abused feel guilty, incompetent and inadequate, because they believe that in some way they may have provoked the incident, even when in their harts they know they did not. They therefore keep quiet about much of the abuse they endure.

Caregivers have good reasons to remain silent. Filling out workers' compensation claims and incident reports are time consuming and often a wasted effort. Experience has taught many of them that not much change comes about from the filing of reports. They have also learned that reporting the incident can increase their problems. Their behavior might be scrutinized or they might be reprimanded for their errors or perceived poor judgment. The incident goes into their file with the unspoken threat: "You are a problem!" They might have to contend with hostility from team members and management for disturbing the status quo. In other words, employee-victims are isolated, blamed and even viewed as troublemakers.

Knowing that they may receive little sympathy from their colleagues and employers and, experiencing embarrassment, guilt and shock, health care workers often endure abuse and even become callous about it. They cope by stifling their natural fears and reactions, until they become so overwhelmed, they are about to "blow up." Over time, victims can become aggressors. They may lash out at patients, colleagues and management. When fear or stress becomes too much, they may call in sick. However their guilt about their absence and therefore, letting their colleagues down increases their distress. Not knowing that they are responding normally to a highly stressful situation, abused health care workers think their fear and other reactions are signs of weakness and professional incompetence.

Negative messages and lack of support from colleagues and supervisors heighten their feelings of inadequacy. Depression and apathy set in. Because they see things differently from others and no longer feel they fit in, abused workers tend to withdraw physically and emotionally from the team. They feel trapped in a career they love, but in a job they hate.

CAREGIVERS AS VICTIMS

In recent years, nursing journals have been focusing on the reactions of nurses and other health care workers to both patient and collegial abuse. It is now generally accepted that patient attacks on their caregivers result in what has become recognized as normal victim reactions, namely: anger, anxiety, helplessness, flashbacks, depression, shock, disbelief, apathy, self-blame, loss of control, increased irritability and resentment. The same reactions apply when the offender is a colleague.

Not surprisingly, nurses and other health care staff who suffer continual abuse from a patient or colleague feel unappreciated, mistreated and exploited. They develop fears: of being alone, of having to deal with the patient or colleague again, and of suffering further abuse from the patient or from others. At the same time they feel sorry for the patient who assaulted them. Or, they become angry, frustrated and hurt by their team member's behavior.

They become preoccupied and concerned about their safety. They worry about their vulnerability to violence. They suffer debilitating fatigue and become discouraged. They become frightened or overwhelmed. Their perception of the world as a just place is shaken. Beside psychological effects and loss of income when they are unable to work, health care workers suffer physical reactions common to all victims of violence. These include increased stress, loss of appetite, headaches, disturbed sleep, nightmares, gastrointestinal problems and stress-related illness. Trying to cope by using alcohol, illegal or prescription drugs, or over-the-counter medication is normal for stressed-out caregivers—and very dangerous for people in their positions. Sometimes they burn out. At other times they become even more disturbed, when the incident triggers memories of past traumas, or causes unresolved personal conflicts to surface and overwhelm them.

Abused caregivers always struggle with doubts about their professional competence and with feelings of powerlessness, helplessness, vulnerability and anger. They often become isolated from family and friends and withdraw from their normal activities. Because of their fears, they force themselves to go to work. As their anger builds up they may become more argumentative, aggressive and difficult to be with. As a result of the experience and their reactions, they often have trouble doing their work.

The damage caused by an attack on a caregiver or by a hostile environment created by colleagues, has been grossly underestimated. In addition to any physical injuries, victimized employees suffer acute stress reactions. When the caregiver is placated, ignored or blamed, receives little or no support, and continues to be exposed to high levels of stress, the stress reaction gets worse. Sometimes the caregiver suffers from a post-traumatic stress reaction from the incident and from associated secondary injuries.

HIGH COST OF ASSAULTS

Assaults on health care staff take their toll, regardless of whether a patient is the offender or it is a co-worker. Everyone suffers. The institution bears the financial costs associated with absenteeism and sick leave claims. The victim endures lost revenue, pain and suffering. Patient care is compromised.

When caregivers are preoccupied with their own safety, they cannot do their jobs well. Patients do not get the type of care they need and deserve. In departments where abuse is a way of life, team relationships become strained, conflicts increase, and morale declines. Employees and patients all feel the increased tension. Other patients, sensing the discord, become anxious, nervous, and act out their feelings. When the situation is not properly managed, the unit where abuse occurs becomes a hostile environment. Conflicts increase between patients and staff, among staff, and between staff and management.

Most caregivers acknowledge the extent to which such a hostile climate affects their job performance. Many request transfers to safer areas within the institution. Some quit their jobs and leave their chosen profession. Each year, health-care institutions lose experienced practitioners due to violence which causes stress, burn-out, illness and injury. The system can ill afford to lose competent nurses, doctors and other health care professionals. Nor can it afford the associated financial costs.

ENDING THE ASSAULT ON CAREGIVERS

When health care administrators do take action against patient violence directed towards their staff, they usually begin by addressing the problems in the following ways:

- Form a task force to examine the situation.
- Undertake a survey to learn the extent of the problem.
- Review institutional procedures regarding medicating or restraining patients.
- Establish an emergency response team to control patients' violent behavior.
- Improve security measures (metal detectors to screen for weapons, alarm buttons, armed security guards, use of chemical mace and electrical immobilization interventions like the Stun Gun).
- Train staff in nonviolent physical intervention techniques.
- Offer counseling to victimized employees.

These measures do address the problem but they may not resolve it. They do not go far enough to get the violence under control or to reduce the frequency or intensity of incidents. Nor does it address the issue of internal violence. What is needed is a more comprehensive approach to tackling this problem. In addition to the important actions listed above, the following strategies should also be considered:

- Form a multidisciplinary committee, with labor-management representation, whose task is to monitor and investigate incidents and rapidly provide practical recommendations for handling particular situations.
- Standardize the definition of violence to include threats, verbal abuse, physical and sexual attacks, bullying and near misses.
- Establish consistent incident reporting and data collection methods, and require employees to report all incidents of violence.

- Develop a plan to deal with aggressive patients, relatives, the public and colleagues.
- Create and promote a clear policy of zero tolerance for violence with sanctions against all offenders: patients and their families, employees, professionals and managers.
- Develop a code of conduct that applies equally to patients, visitors and staff.
- Handle complaints and resolve problems at the first sign of abuse.
- Take action and, when appropriate, support victims in the pressing of criminal charges.
- Accept workers' rights to refuse dangerous work as an opportunity for cooperative preventive action.
- Help and support employees who wish to file workers' compensation claims and arrange for financial compensation to reduce their hardships.
- Set up a confidential employee assistance program and crisis response service to provide individual and group debriefing sessions for staff and patients following incidents.
- Develop a system that flags abusive and potentially dangerous patients and ensures a unified approach to containing the behavior and calming the individual.
- Identify and resolve organizational irritants.
- Address conflicts, hostilities, bullying behavior and abuse of power issues among staff and between disciplines.
- Train staff and managers to identify early signs of distress, in communication skills, anger management, conflict resolution and problem-solving. Ensure that the same training is given at all levels of the organization.
- Clarify the organization's legal position and establish guidelines regarding the admission and care of disruptive and violent patients.
- Deal with high patient-staff ratio levels and modify shift-rotation procedures to better respond to patients' needs.
- Ensure that the physical environment is warm and user-friendly.

RESPECT FOR THE CAREGIVER

Evidence suggests that health care workers have a higher injury rate from patient assaults than construction workers have from work-related accidents. We need to respond quickly to the crisis that is decimating the ranks of caregivers and ruining the quality of patient care in our health care institutions.

Florence Nightingale worked in dreadful, primitive conditions. However, this caring human being, whose life work was the improvement of health care conditions and providing comfort and care for the sick, probably never had to contend with the knowledge that the very people she was helping could assault her. Today's Florence Nightingales, be they nurses, doctors, therapists, technicians, or personal care attendants do not deserve such terrible treatment. Being sick is not a reason to abuse a caregiver. Nor does working in a high-stress job give people license to take out their frustration on a colleague. For the sake of our health care workers and health care systems worldwide, the problem of violence in health care organizations needs more attention and better solutions.

- 8 -
Biting Hands that Care: Violence in Social Services

Social workers are people who care. They care about the disadvantaged, the wounded and the powerless. They care about improving the quality of life of other people. Since they care so much about people, they never expect to be hurt while doing their jobs.

Social workers deal with violence every day. Yet unlike the police who have the full force of the law on their side, as well as the training and means to protect themselves, social workers do their work without protection of any kind.

The profession is female dominated and therefore a high-risk occupation.[1] Social workers are employed mainly in child protection services, hospitals, psychiatric institutions, schools, and family service and social agencies, community organizations or private practice. While these venues are high-risk areas for on-the-job violence, it is their roles and mandates which make them particularly vulnerable. Social workers have the legal authority to remove abused and neglected children from their families. They have the social responsibility to protect the elderly, mentally ill and other vulnerable groups. It is also their responsibility to evaluate whether people are eligible for financial, material and community resources.

Their work is indispensable yet social workers get little encouragement for the good they do or appreciation for the dangers they face. Although they have tremendous influence and authority over people's lives, they often feel frustrated, disillusioned and demoralized. Their work is greatly misunderstood and undervalued. More often than not, they are blamed for failing to provide solutions for horrendous social problems, as if they alone could fix the malaise created by society.

Although social work requires a university degree, it is not a high-status or highly-paid profession. Social workers intervene in hostile situations and with the marginalized, deviant or poorest people in our society. They are often a desperate person's last hope. Because of their skill, dedication and caring, social workers help improve and even save lives, especially those of children at risk.

Their legal and social mandate to protect the vulnerable and the weak, place them at risk. They provide a safe haven for people in danger. They also arrange for the confinement of violent, out-of-control people. They are required to go into dangerous crack houses or cult communities to investigate complaints and they provide protective services for children who are neglected or physically, psychologically and/or sexually abused. They are obliged to deal with disturbed people for whom they must petition the court to arrange involuntary psychiatric hospital admissions. They are expected to place incapacitated elderly people in nursing homes or other custodial care facilities, sometimes against the person's will. They are required to find shelter for battered women and their children. They are obliged to deal with aggressive young offenders for whom they may recommend a closed treatment facility. They are forced to confront belligerent and vicious youth gangs when they intervene to protect younger and more vulnerable children from attacks. They do all these things to protect their clients. They do so at all hours of the day and night, mostly without police backup or protection, and with little regard for their own safety.

Social workers suffer abuse from every quarter, starting with their own clients. They face hostile angry parents who are forced to meet with them because of their legal mandate to investigate a complaint or a suspicion of child abuse or neglect. They deal with children so marked by abuse that they take out their hatred on the very person who has rescued them. They are confronted by the frustration and anger of people suffering from life-threatening illnesses, by the rage of battering men, and by the desperate fury of a needy person for whom there are no resources. Although they know that much of the anger is misdirected, facing someone who is in a rage is terrifying. They are expected to do their jobs, while ignoring their own fears and taking hostility in their stride.

Besides anger from their own clients, social workers often encounter pressure from doctors, police, judges and other professionals who believe they do not work hard enough or quickly enough. Yet social workers are often prevented from carrying out their mandates, because of unrealistic workloads and a lack of cooperation from other professionals. In hospitals and psychiatric institutions, social workers are charged with the task of placing the elderly and chronically ill in nursing homes, foster homes and alternate custodial care facilities. Although the lengthy delays in finding new facilities for these people are due to the lack of resources, it is the social worker who is made to feel responsible.

If all of this were not enough, they endure complaints from an unsympathetic public who are unaware of the complexities in their work, their heavy caseloads, long hours and their dedication. They have to endure bad press and criticism the minute something happens to a vulnerable child or adult, or because they are unable to resolve complex social problems.

Social workers assume very important roles because they act as society's conscience and work to improve the quality of people's lives. Somehow, despite the bad press, dangerous work environment, hostility and low-status jobs, most social workers love the work they do. Their satisfaction lies in knowing they can make a difference in a child's life, reunite a family or make life a little easier for an elderly person. Many young people, who want to "make a difference" make social work their career choice.

TARGETS FOR ATTACKS

The manner in which social services are delivered, inadequate funding, unwieldy caseloads and a lack of resources, set social workers up as targets even before they meet their clients.

Social workers have been mandated to assume a law and order role without having the necessary protective means, adequate resources, or clout to do their jobs. They are often placed in a no-win situation and are even scapegoats for the ills of the world. Social programs traditionally address the symptoms of larger social problems, rather than tackle the root causes. Society does not adequately deal with issues of poverty, despair, alcoholism, drug abuse and family violence. Thus every day social workers face the outcome of these social problems.

In assuming a law and order role, they are set up as targets. Their mandate to protect abused and neglected children makes social workers targets of hostility the moment they start their investigation. Parents feel that the way they bring up their children is nobody's business but their own. As soon as social workers insist on meeting parents to conduct an investigation, they are confronted with angry people. This can turn to rage when social workers recommend restricting parental access to their children and the conditions under which they will have this access.

Social workers involved with other at-risk populations are placed in equally vulnerable positions. At times they take on a role of advocate for women who are victims of conjugal violence, by finding them safe shelter and withholding information of their whereabouts from their enraged, controlling partners. They may have to take steps to arrange compulsory admissions to psychiatric institutions, alcoholism or drug treatment programs or other treatment centers for out-of-control clients. They have to confront adult children about their abusive and neglectful behavior toward their elderly parents. All these actions provoke strong reactions, such as hostility, suspicion, mistrust and anger. Unfortunately the person on the receiving end of these emotions is the social worker.

Their vulnerability increases with the messenger role they assume. Social workers often deliver messages clients do not want to hear. They tell parents that their children will be placed in a foster home. They tell young delinquents that they must go into a group home or residential treatment facility. They tell paranoid psychiatric patients that they must be re-hospitalized. They tell people in desperate need that there are no resources available to them. Feeling trapped and having no one else on whom to vent their anger, clients hurl abuse on their social worker. As the bearer of bad news, the social worker is in the direct line of fire.

If intervening in matters of family violence were not enough to set them up as targets, their role as gatekeepers for services or resources places them at risk. Continual government cutbacks to social programs leave low-income people without the bare necessities of life. Social workers have the power to recommend or limit people's access to community and government resources that provide money, food, shelter and health-related services. Their intervention can at times open or close doors for people in need. At other times despite their good intentions and desire to advocate for their clients, they have little power to influence an overburdened system.

As people's frustration against perceived or actual injustices builds, and the availability of help to meet their basic needs shrinks, their desperation increases. Clients push to get their social workers to "see" their point of view. This combination of poverty and insufficient resources makes the situation ripe for an explosive reaction.

Sometimes social workers' attempts to fairly assess a situation, cause humiliation or anger in the client and inadvertently set off violent reactions. Social workers may have to ask intrusive questions or comment on clients' priorities to ensure they are really in need. The lack of adequate resources means that people have to be very closely screened. When social workers are obliged to question someone's need or withhold help, a backlash of frustration, desperation, disappointment and anger can easily be redirected towards them.

Their clients' emotions heighten when people in positions of authority, such as the police, doctors and judges assure them that the social worker can provide financial and material resources or counseling services to remedy their problems. When social workers are unable to do these things, they are left to deal with angry and disappointed people whose hopes and last chances for help have been dashed.

These professionals, who want only to make the world a better place, and whose aim it is to help people feel better about themselves, are set up for failure, disappointment and violence. They feel terrible about the calamities befalling their clients. They believe they can never do enough to make up for the abuse and bad breaks so many of them suffer. Enormous caseloads and a lack of resources force them to make judgment calls every day about who gets help and who does not. They hope that they have made the right decisions. They worry that by turning people away or not being able to provide them the time, support or material help they need, they may be perpetuating family violence, drug and alcohol abuse, crime and suicide.

The responsibilities of social workers are enormous. Though they derive satisfaction in helping someone out of a terrible situation, they know they will face more of the same. Moreover, tomorrow and the next day and the day after that, they will be placed directly in the line of fire. Still, social workers remain loyal to their mission to improve the quality of life of people in need.

DANGER LURKS EVERYWHERE

Few people are aware of what life is really like for social workers. The work is highly stressful. The stress comes from many sources. It comes from the lack of available resources and the perpetuation of poverty and family violence. It comes from the constant exposure to terrible acts of violence, such as those committed by parents against their own children. It comes from the onerous task of assessing and providing protection services for more vulnerable groups than the system can handle. It comes from the knowledge that one false move or one bad judgment call can place a vulnerable child in even greater danger and may even result in his or her death. It comes from knowing that, to help children, they must forget the dangers to themselves and in some cases to their own families.

Give social workers an opportunity to discuss the dangers in their jobs and they are at first remarkably quiet. Of all the professional groups, social work literature pays the least attention to the problem of on-the-job violence. Considering the literature is written by social workers themselves, it is clear they hesitate to address the problem of client abuse.

When social workers do acknowledge the problem, they do not talk about themselves first. They speak about the horrendous abuse to which many senior citizens, women and children are subjected. They worry about the 64-year-old woman who lives alone in pitiful conditions without food or furniture because her 32-year-old son steals her old age security check to feed his drug habit. They deliberate over the plight of the 28-year-old woman who has been repeatedly beaten by her husband. Or they agonize over the two-year-old girl who was twice sodomized by her abusive father, the four-year-old boy who had cigarette burns and scars all over his body, or the twelve-year-old girl who for two years has been sexually molested by her stepfather.

What ensues is their overwhelming fear. Their fear is not for themselves. Their never-ending nightmare is that someone for whom they are responsible will die. Their sense of responsibility toward their clients, both children and adults, is formidable. Moreover, they are burdened by the fact that should a death occur, particularly in the case of a child, they would be blamed. They know they would be held accountable for failing to protect the child, even though in their best judgment and experience this was not anticipated. They are aware that with limited human resources, cases must be prioritized and some difficult situations simply must wait. Sometimes these difficult situations explode when time runs out.

When they are attacked, getting angry with the offenders is hard because they know that the anger and hostility are not necessarily directed against them personally, but against the agency, the laws which they must implement, or because of the abuser's build-up of frustration or anger at "the system." Moreover, they know that under the facade of aggression and the tough exterior, the people they are dealing with are hurting inside and need their help.

When they are encouraged to look at the dangers they face in their work and the risks to their own lives, the stories spill out. At first they tell horrifying tales about abuse and violence in their caseloads. Then they talk about the abuse directed at them.

They sat in a semicircle and waited. Sixty social workers employed in the child protection field were crammed into a room. When they were first invited to share an experience of on-the-job violence, a long silence followed. Then, with a little encouragement, each one began to talk. One brave man, fighting back tears and then openly crying, told the group of the circumstances in which a child in his caseload had almost died, and how he had suffered, because that child had been the same age as his own son. Others told of being screamed at, sworn at, pushed, kicked, punched, threatened and having the lives of their families threatened as well.

Soon other heart-wrenching tales began to flow. Many told of episodes they had never before talked about and some revealed incidents they had tried to forget. A twenty-five-year-old woman talked about how frightening it was to go alone into a drug dealer's home to remove a three-year-old child. The father threatened to kill her and pushed her out of the house. It was only when she returned with the police that she was able to remove the child. Others told stories of slashed tires, being pushed down flights of stairs and receiving harassing telephone calls in the middle of the night for months on end. Male and female social workers related harrowing accounts of being threatened with knives, guns and even, in one case, an axe. Several women in their twenties told of being sexually harassed. One experienced worker sobbed as she told of being sexually molested at knife-point by a client, fifteen years earlier.

Again and again they revealed how angry parents had threatened their lives when they went in to protect a child and how upset they had been that no one had taken the incidents seriously or given them protection. During the telling of these stories, only the voice of the storyteller was heard in the room.

At the end of it all, they talked about their feelings. They were relieved that they were finally able to talk about the incidents and that they were listened to. They expressed shock and disbelief that so many of them had been attacked, when most of them thought their own experience had been unique. As the realization of their collective experiences sunk in, so did the dread and fear. They realized that the nature of their work put them at risk. Finally, they became angry because the agency administration did not understand how hard a time they were having. They were frustrated that the police, government, public and media all seemed oblivious to the dangers in their work and their need for protection.

The stories of these workers are not unique. When given the chance, social workers will speak out about the violence to which they are continually exposed. The more they talk about their experiences, the more it is apparent that these professionals are at times in grave danger.

Moreover, the stress that comes from being constantly exposed to violent situations takes its toll on social workers. Each case seems worse than the previous one. Knowing that budget constraints prevent them from totally resolving the problem, they can only apply band-aids and hope they will stick. They do their jobs, hoping they did the right thing and that nothing worse will happen to their clients, particularly the children for whom they are responsible.

Although it is clear that the violence to which they are exposed is an occupational hazard, most social workers see the violence primarily as a personal failure. They believe that if they were skilled enough, they would be able to prevent the attacks. A source of stress and helplessness comes from the constant accounts of violence by their clients. Since social workers have to contend with so much abuse in their jobs, they begin to see the violence as normal.

SILENCE AND UNDERREPORTING

As is the case in so many other occupational groups, incidents are underreported, perpetuating the myth that social workers work in "safe environments," where nothing bad happens to them.

Sufficient data is available to tell us that this is not true. Work-related violence in social agencies is as much of a problem as it is in health care settings. The Canadian Union of Public Employees surveyed 9,000 Ontario social service workers employed in developmental services, workers' compensation and child welfare in 1999. Almost three quarters (71%) reported having been subjected to a combination of physical assaults, verbal abuse or threats at work.[2] These findings support an earlier CUPE report of Children's Aid social workers surveyed in Toronto. In 1990 it found that 52% had been subjected to an aggressive act at work. About 20% were victims of more than three aggressive acts.[3] In the United States, mental health workers experience simple and aggravated assaults at rates higher than all other occupational groups except law enforcement.[4]

These findings are not unique to Canada and the United States. Violence toward social service workers was identified as a major problem in Great Britain in the 1980's.[5] The ILO includes social workers in a global trend for work-related violence, placing them among the high-risk occupations.[6] This recognition led the U.S. Occupational safety and Health Administration (OSHA) to produce guidelines to prevent violence in the health care and social service industries.[7]

Despite the fact that violence is pervasive in the profession, social workers generally endure abusive situations and do not report incidents. There are several reasons for this. They worry that they will be blamed for the incidents because they have been taught that a skilled counselor can defuse a client's anger and that they should be able to turn unwilling, hostile people into clients who welcome their help. People working in child protection services also believe that it is unreasonable to expect abusive and dangerous parents, who take out their anger on their own children, to act differently toward them. Since they are professionals who have extensive training in helping people, social workers feel that they should be able to cope with whatever abuse comes their way.

A lack of agency support makes them reluctant to report incidents. They have learned from experience that they can expect little understanding or help from management and that complaining about the abuse may even leave them open to criticism and reprisals. They believe that any complaint or expression of fear would be viewed as a sign of weakness, inadequacy or incompetence. They fear that a report of a violent incident could be used against them in a performance appraisal, or even as reason for dismissal.

Since they have insufficient time to handle their workload as it is, they view filing incident reports as time-consuming, arduous tasks that produce few positive results and most probably will cause them a great deal of trouble. Even if they were to lodge a complaint, they doubt that protection will be available. Death threats, obscene telephone calls and harassment are likely to be minimized as insignificant nuisances, rather than as serious events.

Social workers also worry that reporting an incident will adversely affect the relationship with their client. They believe that an already fragile relationship would deteriorate further, causing them to "lose" the client. Moreover, they are reluctant to take legal action for fear that the person whom they are trying to reach and help may face prosecution.

Overall in the helping culture of child protection and other social services, client violence is accepted as "part of the job." Dealing with injustices and abuse is the mission of these professionals and of the agencies they work for. Feeling badly as they do about their clients, particularly the children, they often minimize the risks to their own security. So do the agencies. Violence comes with the territory.

CARING CULTURE HEIGHTENS VULNERABILITY

Social work is based on the principle that caring, guidance, patience, understanding and nurturing, enable people in pain to feel better about themselves. When people heal, they better can cope with life's stresses and are less likely to hurt others. It is therefore inconceivable to social workers, as it is to all helping professionals, that the people they want to help would harm them. When attacked they conclude the incident happened because they did not try hard enough to understand their clients or because they did something to provoke the incident.

While many female social workers are victims of client assault, it is not only the female or the young, inexperienced or middle class workers who suffer abuse. Mature, seasoned professionals and visible minorities are also targets. Men, in particular, have a harder time seeing the cues or acknowledging their fear or vulnerability, because they have been socialized to accept aggressive or violent behavior and to be strong in the face of it.

Regardless of their gender and levels of experience, social workers believe that threats, angry outbursts and other forms of abuse are a normal part of their jobs. Management reinforce this position. Everyone accepts that clients with emotional difficulties or in crisis may take their anger out on them.

Social workers understand how abusive parents feel about their presence. They understand their home visit and investigation will be seen as an invasion of privacy and space and that these actions are in themselves provocative. They know they are dealing with desperate people who feel powerless and trapped and who probably have been victims of child abuse and neglect themselves. Believing that it is natural for a parent whose children are being taken away to be angry with the person making the decision, they feel pressured to take the anger or violence directed at them in their stride. They rationalize the situation: if they can divert the anger, perhaps they can divert it from a vulnerable family member, particularly the children.

In some ways their training contributes to their vulnerability. They learn in school that a skilled clinician can help people change or improve their situations. This places tremendous strain on young social workers who believe they should be able to help people change their conduct and make the world a better place. If the client does not make progress, is angry with them or if they cannot "reach" the client, they feel it is their fault. They must be empathetic, patient, caring, and skilled enough to break down the barriers and help clients overcome their difficulties.

Social work training also predisposes them to tolerate abusive behavior from clients, because they are taught that an expression of anger is cathartic and therefore good. Unfortunately, they get little training on how to defuse the anger or how to set limits on abusive behavior. Training in how to handle such psychologically demanding work is improving but still, they are ill-equipped to handle today's violent-prone population.

THE DILEMMA—CLIENT RELATIONSHIP

Social workers often find themselves in a conflict regarding their roles. Their mandate may require them to be authority figures, which is a direct contradiction to the essence of their helping role. This dual control/support role can be difficult for both clients and social workers. That the social worker has the authority to make major decisions that affect someone else's life, may be viewed as a provocation, warranting an aggressive response. People do not easily accept someone else making decisions for them or interfering in their lives.

In some situations the caring role can also be problematic. For example, while social workers try to establish a trusting, understanding relationship, clients may not always view this attempt to help them positively. People who are not used to interference in their lives, or being encouraged to talk about their problems or revealing their feelings may find this threatening. Faced with a loss of control over their lives, clients may respond in anger.

Working in child protection services presents a particularly difficult dilemma for social workers. In order for parents to regain custody of their children, they must be helped to overcome the sources of the hurt, despair and anger that caused them to be abusive in the first place. Yet understanding that any kind of intimacy can provoke a hostile and abusive reaction, the worker may hesitate to address personal issues. Without therapy and education, lifestyle and behavior changes are rarely achieved. The professionals are in a Catch 22 situation. They want to help their clients, yet they know the help may provoke aggressive or abusive reactions directed towards them.

Without adequate resources, bound by time restrictions, and with limited means, the focus can easily shift away from society's failure to provide adequate resources for its citizens, to the shortcomings of the people needing the services. Redefining the problem as personal, when it may in fact be a social one, can be damaging for the client and harmful to the relationship. As the client's frustration with the system builds and alienation increases, the anger is redirected toward the worker.

Social workers adopt survival strategies to protect themselves psychologically from the barrage of abuse and the constant pressure of dealing with so many terrible situations. This can cause them to unintentionally distance themselves from their clients' feelings. They may appear authoritarian and uncaring when they are really feeling frightened, overwhelmed or burned out.

AGENCY INCITES ANGER

An agency's treatment of its own staff, its operations, the ambiance of the setting, and how it treats its clients, contribute further to employees' vulnerability. Inadvertently the social service agency reinforces workers' feelings of inadequacy. This is due to close supervision and scrutiny of their work, years after they have received their formal education. This may be necessary, given the mandate of social agencies to protect children and vulnerable adults. The agency may need a check and balance system to protect itself against legal action, or against public cries of ineptitude directed towards the agency should something go wrong. However, this does little to encourage independence, feelings of competence and self-worth. Given this backdrop, how can social workers deal effectively with aggressive, hostile and violent clients?

Many clients are furious even before they walk into the agency because they are there involuntarily. The ambiance does little to put them at ease. Many social agencies are located in badly lit, poorly decorated, dreary-looking buildings. Little attention is paid to clients' comfort, which heightens their frustration, nervousness and anger. It is not a welcoming atmosphere.

Inattention to customer service magnifies the client's already low self-esteem and uneasiness. The mere idea of going for help or being forced to go for help is stressful and creates hostility. Clients may perceive stressed professionals as uncaring or disrespectful, when they do not return telephone calls quickly or arrive late for an appointment because of another crisis. Often the receptionist is too busy to greet clients properly, adding to client frustration and anger. This sets the receptionist and social workers up for angry outbursts.

When a client calls in crisis and is told the social worker is unavailable, frustration builds. Since the secretary or receptionist is the only contact the client has with the agency, he may become the target of the client's frustration and anger.

Budget constraints place tremendous pressure on workers to do more with less. Frenzied counselors, already overburdened with extremely high caseloads, do not have the time to pay attention to every client's needs and demands. People quickly learn that the best way to obtain help is to become noticed. They learn that acting-out behavior, threats, abuse and other forms of violence and suicidal threats or gestures will garner immediate attention. Overloaded staff react when people have been forced by an overburdened system to become aggressive or abusive.

INATTENTION TO VIOLENCE

Many social workers believe their direct supervisors and managers do not understand what they are going through or seem uninterested in resolving the problems that lead clients to become abusive. They have learned from experience that only dramatic incidents receive attention and so, action is often too late or inadequate.

The reluctance of supervisors and managers to become involved or take action is understandable. They are not in the line of fire. They may be too far removed from direct service to understand what the staff have to contend with. Although most supervisors or managers are former front-line workers, they probably never acknowledged the risk of violence in their own work. As agency managers or directors, their preoccupations are different from the workers. Their seeming indifference to the violence suggests that either they have forgotten what it is like on the front-line, or that their priorities and objectives are different.

Management's inattention to the plight of their workers may be the result of increasing social demands and budget constraints rather than a lack of concern for their employees. They do not want to deal with another overwhelming problem. Attention to the problem of client violence toward staff places further demands on management's already limited time and resources. It is easier not to address the problem at all. It may take a major incident before management is forced to accept the reality—that violence against social workers is a major problem in their own agency and will not disappear.

As in other industries, social service administrators seem concerned that violence will be perceived as a reflection of their poor management skills. They therefore tend to react slowly to this problem. Not only does their slow response discourage employee-victims from revealing the true extent of the problem, it creates tension between front-line workers and management. Frustration and anger builds against management over their apparent lack of concern for worker safety and the lack of proactive initiatives to end client abuse. This creates a hostile work environment. Importantly, the lack of resolution of this problem places employees at even greater risk.

Management's inattention damages staff morale. Employees do their work and try to help their clients, yet they become cynical. When helping professionals feel demoralized, powerless and victimized, it is unlikely that they can transmit messages of hope and encouragement to clients who feel the same way.

AGENCY'S ROLE IN STOPPING VIOLENCE

Budget constraints, other pressing priorities and lack of time and energy may keep management from openly acknowledging the problem and taking action to better protect their workers. Yet inattention to the problem of client violence is expensive. Agencies are forced to spend large amounts of money on security measures to protect staff and their families when a worker's life is in danger. Employees lose valuable time and energy because they are unable to concentrate on their work.

In addition, stress-related medical leave because of work overload or overexposure to violence increases the costs and burden on an already taxed system. Burnout, depression, PTSD and stress-induced physical illnesses are normal by-products of unrelenting client violence. When workers can no longer take the pressure, they "crack." They go on sick leave or they quit. This places a greater load on an overburdened system that finds it difficult to recruit and retain its workforce.

Besides needing to control sick-leave and replacement costs, management have an obligation to stop the violence. Similar to other work settings faced with the same problem, management have a legal and moral responsibility to do its utmost to protect staff. Employees have the right to work in a safe environment. Moreover they cannot possibly help other people when they are worried about their own safety and exposed to violence. However, placing staff safety on line with client safety is a tough shift in thinking for an organization founded for the purpose of protecting its clients, especially children, from danger.

Social service agencies which are dedicated to stop violence against children and adults seemingly allow violence to be directed toward their staff. While denouncing parents' violent behavior toward their children, management tolerate abusive treatment toward their own staff. This gives confusing messages to clients. To be consistent in their orientation and properly fulfill their mandate, social service organizations, even those with a child protection mandate, have to take a strong position against violence toward their staff. This should be no different from the position they assume when a staff member is abusive toward a client. A clear message that violence will not be tolerated in the Agency must be delivered and enforced. This of course applies to the different kinds and levels of violence noted on the *Workplace Violence Continuum* in Chapter 2.

The agency must examine its own practices and behavior that impel clients to become hostile with staff. To prevent violence the goal must be to rid the organization of irritants both in its operations and in its client services.

Eliminating client violence means taking a position and adopting a get-tough attitude. Agency directors have to be ready and willing to press criminal charges against any client who delivers death threats or physically assaults staff. They should consider establishing close working relationships with law enforcement in order to help them out in high-risk violence cases.

Advising clients of a zero tolerance policy with respect to violence, setting clear limits and applying swift sanctions will immediately curb a lot of abusive client behavior and effectively reduce many risks to staff.

Perhaps more than any other organization confronted with this problem, social service organizations are knowledgeable about human behavior, the grasp of the larger social context that provokes people, and the potential skills to defuse anger. Not only do they have the ability to resolve the problem themselves, they can also demonstrate to other organizations how to control and prevent violence, deal with offenders and help and support victimized staff.

CONTROLLING VIOLENCE

Although not every incident can be prevented, the following interventions can dramatically reduce the number of incidents of client violence in social agencies.

- Set up a protocol that defines violence and outlines procedures for handling potentially high risk and actual violent situations.
- Prominently display an agency policy of zero tolerance for violence and refuse to see clients when they are violent toward staff.
- Ensure worker safety through an agency security system, a "buddy system" so that workers can visit clients in pairs, police escorts when they must go into dangerous situations, cellular phones, emergency codes for home visits and on agency premises, and security of staff working alone during evenings and quiet hours.
- Standardize the definition, content and methods used to collect data about violence. Record all major and minor incidents to develop a picture of the types of violence to which the agency is vulnerable, a profile of the perpetrators and how conflicts were resolved.
- Ensure the premises are user-friendly.

- Improve client relations. Remove irritants that cause clients to become aggressive. Treat clients with dignity and respect. Demand that clients have respect for all staff.
- Press criminal charges against clients who threaten the lives of staff and/or their families.
- Establish a permanent ad hoc committee to which staff can go for help and advice regarding potentially explosive cases, or if they have been threatened or attacked.
- Provide workers with practical case management assistance and security protection when required.
- Enlist a member of the local police department to serve on the permanent ad hoc committee
- Solicit police support when dealing with situations of extreme violence.
- Set up and staff a permanent violence prevention unit whose mandate it is to monitor, manage and prevent incidents by improving processes and practices and developing a consistent approach throughout the organization.
- Provide crisis counseling, legal advice, financial support and security protection for threatened employees and their families. Offer professional help and moral support to enable victimized staff to overcome the effects of violence. Encourage peer support to cope with violent situations.
- Sensitize and increase staff's awareness of risks. Train them to recognize warning signals and potentially high risk situations. Provide training in methods of defusing anger, handling difficult or violent situations, conflict resolution and self-protection strategies.
- Train supervisors and managers to better help staff deal with client violence in their work, and provide practical and moral support to victimized staff.

By taking action to protect the workers, establishing formal procedures to address the problem and fully supporting employees when assaults occur, management display a caring attitude to their staff and deliver a strong message to clients about the use of violence. A tough approach to violent clients produces positive results. Employees are reminded that they do not have to tolerate the abuse and, as a result, feel better about themselves. Clients are informed that, not only must they stop their abusive behavior toward their children, but abusive behavior toward anyone is unacceptable and will not be tolerated.

Taking a proactive approach to stop violence will result in workers worrying less about their own safety and security. They will then be able to continue the valuable work they are mandated to do—protect the lives of children and assist adults who need their help.

- 9 -
The Flipside:
When Staff
Become Abusers

Until now the focus of this book has been on abuse of employees. However, the analysis of workplace violence would not be complete without a brief look at the other side of this issue—staff who abuse clients or patients in their care.

This issue is not merely about a frustrated store clerk or customer service rep who may be rude or indifferent to a customer. It involves vulnerable people and caregivers who steal, terrorize, neglect and abuse them. Among the vulnerable populations are: young children in daycare, special needs children in protective environments, physically or intellectually-challenged adults in foster homes and chronically ill, elderly people in nursing homes.

While hardly a new problem, from time to time investigative journalism uncovers situations of terrible living conditions or harsh treatment such as: deplorable housing conditions for psychiatric patients; stealing, neglect and physical assault of seniors in nursing homes; and physical and sexual abuse of disabled people in long-term care facilities. Administrators have had to confront issues of neglect and/or abuse. Sometimes hidden cameras and tape recorders detect the abuse, showing caregivers abusing frail, sick and elderly people: they are screamed at, restrained, slapped, terrorized and left in wet clothes or without clothes at all.

Each case of abuse receiving public attention results in an immediate outcry of shock, anger and demand for change. Government and health officials renew their pledges to investigate complaints and to introduce legislation that will establish standards of care. Until now society has been unsuccessful at protecting its most vulnerable populations and assuring quality of service.

PATIENTS ARE VULNERABLE

It is easy to intimidate, bully and sexually or physically assault vulnerable people in protective settings. Patients or residents are weak or ill and are no match for a healthy caregiver: they cannot and do not fight back.

Furthermore, residents have little power or control over their lives and over what happens to them. They are there because they are unable to live on their own or to take care of themselves. Sometimes they enter the setting willingly, more often than not they are forced to go there, having been placed by families who cannot look after them, by social workers or by judges who have declared them to be incompetent.

If they are lucid and able to speak, they have no one to tell. With families or friends not being constantly present, the majority of people who call these institutions "home" are on their own. The settings do not encourage patients or residents to speak out about an abusive staff person. Even when patients do complain, they are often not believed and instead are labeled as "troublemakers." Furthermore, discussing bad living conditions or abusive treatment is a risk: no one can protect them from reprisals. Few of these settings have an ombudsman who can advocate on their behalf. Even fewer have a consumer committee with a mandate to receive and investigate complaints and to work with the administration to remedy unacceptable situations.

A strong code of silence protects abusive staff. Other patients who witness the abuse are afraid to speak out because they can easily become the next target. Even other staff, who could stop the abuse, are afraid: the abusive person is usually abusive towards them as well. In unionized settings, the situation is more complex—unions support abusive staff because of their obligation to defend their membership.

Several factors create conditions for abuse or neglect of vulnerable people in care: lack of enforceable standards, infrequent inspections by public health officials, budget concerns and administrators who do not understand the issue or know how to address it. Furthermore, society does not value the work of staff on the front lines of care. These positions offer minimum wage salaries and do not identify prerequisite skills.

Screening procedures may not identify previous performance issues, including a history of violence. Administrators do not consistently apply their own standards of care, monitor behavior, closely supervise staff or deal quickly and firmly with the first signs of abuse. Finally, chronic understaffing and high patient/staff ratios can result in neglect and abuse. Patients' needs suffer when caregivers have too much to do and not enough time to do it or when they have to deal with difficult behaviors without adequate training.

VIOLENT CAREGIVERS

In a long-term ward of a psychiatric hospital, a 33-year old female patient with special needs was found to be five months pregnant. An investigation revealed that a male nursing assistant had been sexually assaulting her for years.

In a private boarding home, two employees terrorized the people in their charge. In one situation, they placed a blanket over a resident's head and hit him continuously. In another, they slapped a 50-year old resident on the head and put a rag over her nose and mouth.

These two situations are not unique, nor do they represent the worst cases. A 2001 report by the Special Investigations Division of the House Government Reform Committee in the United States found widespread physical and sexual abuse, staff failing to protect people from abuse from other residents and instances of residents being punched, slapped, choked or kicked by staff members or other residents, resulting in fractured bones or lacerations. It reports that the incidence of abuse has increased every year since 1996. Over 30% of the 5,283 nursing homes in the United States were cited for almost 9,000 incidents of verbal, physical and sexual abuse over a two-year period.[1]

How does a violent person enter the system and work there? It starts when administrators do not screen new hires for a history of violence or hire people with limited skills or no interest in caring for vulnerable patients. People hired as caregivers are not necessarily drawn to these settings because they enjoy taking care of the sick or disabled. They may be attracted to the setting because they believe that the job is secure or stable. Their contempt for the people they care for eventually comes across in their attitude, behavior and actions.

Without close supervision, careful scrutiny for signs of abuse, strict enforcement of a code of conduct and close monitoring of suspected behavior, violent people will continue to abuse vulnerable people in their charge.

NEGLECT—A SYSTEMIC PROBLEM

Neglect is another form of abuse seen in protective settings. In the public system, administrators have insufficient funding to ensure adequate ratios of caregivers to patients. In the private sector, administrators try to do more with less to generate a profit. The low staff/patient ratio translates into unrealistically high workloads, heavy responsibilities and patients who need more time, care and attention than they receive. Over time, staff become worn out by a system that expects them to manage, without adequate resources, training or support. This may translate into patients or residents receiving inadequate care. Neglect, the most common form of abuse of the ill or frail, is highlighted in the following examples.

It is mealtime in an acute care hospital. Dietary attendants deliver the food trays to the patients. A 90-year old bed-ridden man has to wait until a nurse's aid comes by and opens the containers and places the cutlery in front of him. She cannot stay to help him eat because she has to hurry away to answer another patient's call. The patient does not get to eat because he cannot lift the spoon to his mouth.

In a convalescent hospital the only nurse on duty in the evening has to take care of thirty people. An 84-year old women wheel-chair bound, aphasic woman, needing help to get to the toilet, keeps ringing the bell. By the time the frustrated nurse arrives thirty minutes later the patient is in tears because she has wet herself. On another day, a nurse assists the same women to the toilet, but forty minutes later, she is still sitting there, waiting for someone to take her back to bed.

Neglect is not necessarily intentional. Insufficient staffing and budget constraints translate into unrealistic demands on staff time. As a result, they either ignore patient's calls for assistance or prioritize who should receive their attention. They become hardened and ignore people's needs (e.g. pain medication, bedpan or returning to bed), responding only to the most pressing ones.

The problem becomes compounded when a vulnerable person is rude or aggressive towards the caregiver. The caregiver who may not have the skills to deal with this behavior can retaliate by ignoring the patient altogether. Ultimately the most vulnerable people, those who are dependent, alone and too feeble to protest, suffer the most.

NEGLECT TURNS INTO ABUSE

Staff members do not usually start off being abusive. Nor do they necessarily mean to act that way. However the abuse towards people in their charge stems from a build-up of tension, irritation or emotion. Caregivers feel caught in the middle: harassed by supervisors who push them to perform their tasks faster and by patients who have major care needs. Frenzied staff react inappropriately to irritating behavior or repetitive requests.

A bell from Room 302 rang at the nursing station. This is the third time within the last half hour that the frustrated attendant was called to the room. The resident wasn't fully aware of having just recently been attended to. He's elderly and forgetful. The attendant arrives and yells at the resident for bothering her again.

The bell rings, and Jessie, the patient care attendant, decides that it's just Millie again and there's really nothing wrong. Since Jessie had attended to Millie fifteen minutes ago, she assumes that Millie has forgotten and is just being bothersome. She decides not to go in. Millie has soiled herself ... but now she will lie in it for quite some time, rather than risk ringing the bell another time and be yelled at for being annoying. Finally, Millie rings her bell again but Jessie decides the call is unimportant. Millie is developing a urinary tract infection, a common condition in the elderly and she has to urinate every few minutes. Millie lies there in pain ... until she soils herself once again. After hearing the bell a third time, the attendant arrives and is angry to see that Millie has soiled herself.

Caregivers who may not have been callous can change under pressure. They often do not have the skills to deal with anxious or "demanding residents and their families. They view questions, negative comments and suggestions as a lack of appreciation and a personal insult. They struggle to handle what they perceive to be excessive workloads. They burn out or frequently become sick. Over time, they become coldhearted or bitter and angry. Feeling exploited, they become abusive or neglectful toward their vulnerable charges.

STOPPING ABUSE OF PEOPLE IN CARE

Like the many other situations of violence previously discussed, abuse of vulnerable people occurs for three primary reasons: 1. No one stops it. 2. Offenders are not educated or sanctioned. 3. Organizational problems are not resolved.

Remedying this problem requires clear standards and stricter controls on the nursing home industry and on other facilities and institutions that house and care for vulnerable people. Moreover, budget constraints and staff/patient ratios are significant factors in the management of this problem. Other strategies that can help organizations contain the problem include:

- Hiring guidelines and screening procedures such as: verification for criminal record, reference checks.
- Standards to ensure employees have appropriate training (e.g. patient care attendants, childcare workers, etc).
- Direct and close supervision of staff involved in direct patient care.
- Supporting staff when they ask for help and rewarding people who openly admit to mistakes and want to learn from them.
- Confidential mechanism (e.g. ombudsman or a board of directors committee) that encourages consumers, families and staff to report cases of abuse without fear of reprisals.
- Continuous quality improvement programs that develop humane philosophies of care and client-focused approaches.
- A zero tolerance for violence policy protecting consumers and staff.
- Staff training including orientation programs for new employees and on-going training for all staff (e.g. conflict resolution and techniques to defuse triggers that might otherwise lead to escalating behavior).
- A consumer committee with a mandate to work with management and staff to deal with consumer complaints.

In many ways this facet of the workplace violence problem is far worse than the previously described situations because this involves frail and sick people who are unable to defend themselves. To close the circle on workplace violence, new ways have to be found to redress problems that lead to neglect and violence by staff towards people in their care. An organization cannot promote a zero tolerance policy for employees and at the same time leave their consumers unprotected.

PART THREE

RESOLUTION

- 10 -
A Sympathetic Ear: Support for the Employee-Victim

Employees experiencing work-related violence suffer reactions similar to other victims of violence. The distress and pain come from verbal abuse, intimidation or threats, bullying, sexual harassment or physical assault, and precipitate a wide range of frightening feelings and reactions. Some employees find the ordeal so disturbing and overwhelming that they experience acute traumatic stress and even PTSD. They may be unable to work or even carry on with their normal daily activities.

My experience of more than two decades of practice has shown that a sympathetic and understanding manager and a supportive and caring workplace environment can make all the difference. When people feel supported after a traumatic event, the intensity and duration of their stress reactions decrease significantly. A safe environment, understanding and caring by colleagues and management, and practical support quickens recovery and enables employees to resume their work. An effective management response has the effect of reducing employee trauma and diminishing organizational costs and losses.

To contain the fallout from an incident, managers must be in tune with their employees. They need to understand what happens to employees who experience violence or who witness it. They need to be aware of the range of potential feelings and reactions common to all victims of violence. They must also understand the degree to which a single event can negatively affect their employees' lives. The more managers understand how work-related violence affects their employees and the organization, the more effectively they can respond and help employees through the recovery process.

PORTRAIT OF EMPLOYEE-VICTIMS

Employees frequently wonder why the incident distressed them so much, particularly if it was a "small" one. They question why an incident such as an assault happened to them, or in the case of harassment or bullying, why they were being targeted. They constantly replay in their minds what they did or did not do, and how they could have handled the situation differently. Victims often become depressed or angry over the way the violence has changed their lives. They go through a grieving process, mourning the changes to their personality and the loss of the person they knew. Victims feel responsible for their inability to function as they did before. Frequently recovery is complicated because of their inability to understand their turbulent feelings and altered behavior, or because they are unable to make the connection between the abuse and those changes. They feel frightened and alone.

Most people suffer debilitating reactions from work-related violence, even from seemingly minor, inconsequential incidents. Employees who come away unscathed emotionally are rare. Even without physical injury, violence usually causes some degree of psychological injury. Sometimes employees experience such deep-rooted emotional wounds that healing takes months or even years. Other times, employees feel so much distress and pain that they try to find relief by quitting their jobs. To their surprise they often find that the fear and hurt remain.

They often fear they are becoming mentally ill because of the dramatic changes to their personality and their reduced level of functioning. They do not realize that anxiety, fear, depression, self-doubt and anger are normal reactions to trauma. Often they do not understand that what they are going through is a normal reaction to a traumatic experience.

Employees frequently pay a higher price than victims of violence generally. Like most victims, they blame themselves for what happened, believing they should have been able to stop the abuse. The distress is heightened when peers or management pressure them to forget the incident or act as if it never happened. A lack of understanding or support by management and colleagues isolates employee-victims from the people they expect would best understand their plight. Their confusion, disillusionment and anger increases if people try to discredit them or if their offenders appear to receive more sympathy than they get. Institutional resistance and refusal to deal with the problem create tension and hostility, which increases victims' frustration, disappointment and alienation. They cannot understand why they are not supported or why they are being blamed. The way in which peer reaction and an unsupportive or hostile climate affect employee-victims is highlighted in the following case.

Laura, a 35-year-old counselor working in a support center for persons living with AIDS participated in a training program to help staff deal with abusive, aggressive and physically violent clients. During the second day of training, the consultant challenged the group with respect to their pattern of excusing abusive client behavior because their clients "were living under a death sentence." For the first time, Laura began to speak. Tearfully she told the group that several months earlier, an HIV-infected client whom she had been counseling threatened to stab her with a syringe. The client, a drug-addict, was angry because she refused to give him money.

Laura had not been able to discuss this incident with her co-workers because many of them felt that HIV-infected people were special. Pressure by several co-workers, who were also HIV-positive, made her feel guilty because she herself was not infected. Some of her colleagues insinuated she did not know what life was really like for a person living with AIDS. She had also picked up the message from them that she had mishandled the situation and that she had provoked an aggressive client reaction. At a time when support from her co-workers was so important, she felt isolated and rebuked. She was grateful for the kindness and support of her supervisor. Yet the condemnation of her colleagues hurt her. Since the incident, she hated going to work because her colleagues were aloof. Moreover, she was afraid that another client would become abusive and succeed in infecting her.

Laura's revelation enabled the group to talk about their attitudes toward their clients and their tolerance in accepting abusive and threat-

ening behavior because "these people had a right to be angry." For the first time many of them came to realize how punitive and hostile they had been toward Laura. At the end of the discussion the tension in the room had dissipated. When her colleagues could acknowledge her distress and apologize for their insensitivity, Laura could tell them how much their understanding meant to her. Immediately she felt as if a weight had been lifted off her shoulders. For the first time in months she felt supported and connected to her co-workers.

Although the context may differ, victimized employees often complain about negative co-worker or supervisor attitudes and comments. Apart from the lack of support, many victims complain about subtle or overt criticism regarding the way they handled a situation or the way they behave afterwards. Often they feel ridiculed and discredited by people who refuse to acknowledge the existence of a problem or who do not try to understand what they are going through. They feel re-victimized when managers or colleagues tell them that they are too sensitive or that they are imagining things, or when they are accused of being a troublemaker.

Too often employees become scapegoats for management's inability to control the problem of work-related violence. A defensive attitude prevents corrective action and gives employees the message that violence is their problem. The message they receive is that they should have prevented the incident or they should be able to cope with the aftereffects. This adds to their feelings of isolation. Employees who experience violence feel like outsiders looking in. They also feel guilty about their fears, inability to work and to forget the incident. Organizational resistance or denial prevents them from sharing their fears and apprehension with the very people who should understand and support them. When a colleague or employer seems uninterested, unsympathetic or critical, victims' anger, frustration and despair increase.

Different perceptions and reactions to the incident increase tension between those who experience violence and those who are removed from it. The more their employer's perception of the event differs from their own, the more victims feel isolated and rejected.

This lack of sympathy or support and a judgmental environment cause a secondary injury. Work-related violence hurts more than it should because, as employee-victims continually lament: "Nobody understands or cares and everyone acts as if it was my fault."

An abusive or traumatic workplace incident can cause sleepless nights and anxious moments. Even worse is the fear of going to work and the way the violence affects the quality of people's lives. Some employees never discuss their experience with anyone at work despite their need to do so because they fear being ridiculed or viewed as incompetent. They may even worry about reprisals, particularly about being fired. Other employees suffer in silence because they believe nobody cares. In order to protect themselves, victims inadvertently add to the conspiracy of silence by trying not to draw attention to the incident or to their difficulty coping.

The longer employees suffer from these intense reactions, the more the negativism toward them increases. Management and even some co-workers become convinced that their difficulty adjusting is due to emotional problems unrelated to the incident. While this may occasionally be the case, it is not usually so. It is erroneous to shift the blame for employees' troubles from the true culprit, namely the perpetrator and the violent incident, onto the victim. To suggest that the victim is predisposed to depression, anxiety or other emotional disorders is overlooking that what the victim is experiencing, is a normal reaction to violence. The lack of understanding sets the stage for insensitive comments and hostile actions by colleagues and management, thereby increasing the likelihood of a secondary injury. Perhaps unintentionally, organizations often re-victimize their employees.

Work-related violence is difficult for employees to handle because most people define who they are by the work they do, and derive much of their self-worth from their jobs. When employees change because of violence and are no longer able to work as before, their self-esteem diminishes. When their colleagues or managers criticize or blame them for the way they handled the situation or suggest they are not suited for the job because they cannot cope with violence, they suffer a further erosion of their self-esteem. The loss of self-esteem affects their work, their personal and family relationships, and in fact, everything they do. Workplace violence is a harmful social problem, not only because it affects productivity and morale, but also because it negatively impacts on every area of the victim's life.

BLAME THE VICTIM

Society blames people in many ways for having become victims of violence. Employee-victims share this fate. Too often employees are made to feel ashamed or guilty or they blame themselves for what took place, as if the incident was their fault. Many people with whom they come in contact, subtly or overtly reinforce this blame. This "blame the victim" attitude stems from many widely held misconceptions about violence and how people should handle it. Some of these misconceptions are:

- The victim must have done something to provoke or escalate the incident.
- The victim's behavior, attitude or reaction subsequent to the incident is abnormal.
- Adults should be able to cope with misfortune or adversity, no matter what harm befalls them. ("Keep a stiff upper lip" attitude).
- Adults should be strong and in control of their emotions, no matter what.
- Employees are trained to handle unusual, highly charged crises at work.
- Violence is part of the job.
- Everyone reacts to crises or traumatic events the same way.
- People should be able to get back to work right away and be able forget the incident ("Get right back on the horse" theory).
- Violence does not cause psychological injury.

These are commonly held views about the workplace and the way we expect people to respond to trauma. These beliefs are false.

Unfortunately tremendous damage is done when well-meaning but misinformed people pass these messages on to a traumatized person.

FACTS ABOUT VIOLENCE

In order to heal from the aftermath of violence, people need to ignore the negative comments they will receive about their behavior before, during and after the incident. Many of the comments listed below relate to misinformation about how people become victimized, what happens to them in the process, and how they recover after the experience.

- A violent incident is seldom the victim's fault. Victims do not generally provoke or invite violence. Victims are not to blame.
- Reactions to violence vary because of people's different perceptions about what constitutes danger and their ability to handle stress. There is no right or wrong way to deal with trauma. Nor is there a set time limit on recovery.
- People do not "overreact" to abusive or highly stressful situations. To suggest that they do is to suggest that fear and anxiety arising from a perceived life-threat is abnormal.
- An incapacitating or long-lasting reaction does not mean that victims are "ill." It means the event has overwhelmed them and their normal coping mechanisms have failed. Their life is out of control. Their view of the world as a safe and just place has been shattered and must be reconstructed.
- Healing takes time. Wishing anxiety or depression away, or being angry because of a slow recovery, will not alter the situation. In fact, self-recrimination increases stress. On the other hand, avoiding stress helps the recovery process. Patience, time, determination, faith and the right support enable traumatized individuals to work through their healing process and recover.
- People's insensitivity to victims' feelings or their ignorance about the trauma recovery process cause unnecessary pain. Downplaying the incident, dismissing employees' reactions,

telling jokes, changing the subject, or finding distractions increase the pain. People perceive any suggestion that they just forget about the incident as an attack.

- Independent and strong people have a hard time perceiving themselves as a "victim" because the word conjures up images of weakness and loss of control. Yet for healing to take place, people have to accept their limitations. Only after they have gone through a healing process and worked through the "victim state," can they accept what happened to them and become "survivors."

- The more people perceive a situation as dangerous or life-threatening, the more dramatic will be the changes to their personality and behavior.

- While victims mourn the loss of their old self, when they recover from the pain and suffering they will feel stronger and wiser. They will develop a clearer sense of personal values and life priorities.

VARYING REACTIONS

Our perception of what constitutes danger and our tolerance for high levels of stress differ. While one person may regard an incident as trivial, another may perceive it as catastrophic: one employee may respond to an event nonchalantly, while another may be highly agitated. Whatever the nature of the incident or its severity, different employees frequently display different reactions to the same event. What follows are typical responses to traumatic events.

- Seem untroubled by the incident.
- Experience minimal distress that disappears after a couple of hours or days.
- Appear to be in control, but suffer silently, seemingly unaffected by the experience. Outwardly they deny symptoms or signs of distress.
- Experience a moderate to intense stress reaction lasting days, months and sometimes years (post-traumatic stress disorder or PTSD).

- Experience a delayed reaction weeks or months after the event.
- Experience a resurgence of emotions triggered by a seemingly unrelated traumatic event, even years later.

These are normal responses to violence.

The range of reactions may be confusing because people have different perceptions of the same incident and therefore react differently. While some employee-victims may experience immediate and intense physical reactions, such as trembling, crying or total withdrawal, others may simply bury themselves in their work. These contrasting reactions can be bewildering to managers, colleagues, family and friends who may want to help but do not know what to do.

PERSONAL REACTIONS TO TRAUMA

Regardless of whether the event is a one-time event (e.g. holdup) or reoccurring (e.g. bullying), the person will be distressed. The greater the perception of danger or threat, the more intense the stress reaction will be. Furthermore, prolonged exposure to abuse such as harassment or to a series of abuses such as multiple incidents of physical assault, increases stress levels. When abuse or violence persists over time, our psyches become worn down from overexposure. *Violence overload* can be the result of psychological battering from harassment or too frequent exposure to life-threatening events like holdups.

Violence overload is similar to job burnout. The person suffers from extreme physical and emotional exhaustion and is no longer able to cope with the stress. This results in a type of psychological shutdown and inability to function. Going to work, taking care of family responsibilities and handling even simple everyday tasks becomes too much.

Fear and shock are typical reactions to sudden life-threatening events. In Chapter 5, there is a description of the physical and emotional reactions people commonly suffer as a result of a holdup.

These same reactions apply to other types of violent episodes, particularly when the incident is a solitary event, such as a shooting, hostage-taking incident or assault.

During the event, the initial response is "fight or flight." Then our bodies react physically and emotionally to the event. Immediately after the incident, a physical reaction sets in. Crying, trembling, alternating hot and cold flushes, headaches, nausea, rubbery legs, and heart palpitations are all typical reactions to shock.

As the shock wears off, we try to make sense of what happened. Sometimes what we have experienced is too horrible for us to understand. We cope by denying it even happened. We try to convince ourselves that we imagined the incident or that it was not really that bad. This may work for a time, but eventually reality creeps in. It is then that we have to deal with the full range of our emotions.

A distressing incident or exposure to persistent abuse often leaves people with overwhelming feelings, behavior changes or physical reactions. A roller-coaster of emotions, and reactions impacts on our lives.

Dealing with the aftermath of an event can be as terrifying or stressful as the event itself. Coping with overwhelming and frightening emotions, disorientation, a loss of control, and behavior changes are disturbing, particularly when they seem to last forever. A diagnosis of PTSD is frightening. A better understanding and acceptance of these reactions as normal responses to trauma will speed up the healing process.

What follows is an inventory of common emotions and reactions to trauma. These are not presented in order of importance, frequency or severity. Some traumatized people experience a few reactions; others experience many or all of them and suffer from PTSD. I must caution the reader not to use this as a tool for self-diagnosis. Rather, I offer this list to help us all better understand the symptoms and reactions to violence and trauma. These may seem overwhelming to victims and strange to managers, co-workers, family and friends.

- **Shock**: We all want to believe nothing bad will happen to us. Rarely do we think that something dreadful could happen at

work. When it does, we are shocked to realize we are not protected from danger or harm. We suddenly feel vulnerable and
like "sitting ducks."

- **Emotional numbing**: When the shock is too great, the incident
too overwhelming or the abuse persists, emotional numbing
can set in. This defense mechanism is our mind's way of shut-
ting out highly intense pain or an overwhelming situation.
Numbing buys time by allowing the significance of what has
happened to sink in gradually. Eventually though, numbing
gives way to intense pain, which is the first part of the healing
process.

- **Disorientation**: Sudden events can leave a person feeling
dazed, in a fog, or lost. This signifies the state of crisis the person is in.

- **Denial**: When the reality or pain is too great, denial is a normal
defense mechanism. Unlike emotional numbing where we
acknowledge what happened but do not feel the pain, denial
alters the significance of the event. Denial can be a protective
shield against too painful an event (e.g., witnessing the shooting
death of a co-worker) or it can prevent us from taking action to
guard ourselves against further incidents (e.g., sexual harassment by a respected manager).

- **Flashbacks**: Intrusive thoughts or memories, or repeatedly
reliving disturbingly vivid scenes of the trauma are common
reactions to violence. These repetitive scenes are uncontrollable
and involuntary, happening during the day as flashbacks or
during sleep as nightmares. A noise, sight, smell, or comment
can trigger flashbacks. These are frightening reminders of the
incident. During a flashback, we are detached from reality and
relive the attack or imagine ourselves face-to-face with our
aggressor. Sometimes victims can even experience visual or
auditory hallucinations which seemingly come from nowhere
and are very real. Hallucinations may involve aspects of present
or past traumas, or images of random attacks.

- **Fear**: Violence brings out our worst fears, for our own safety
and that of family, colleagues and friends. When fear becomes

all-consuming, staying alone at home, going out alone, or returning to work all become impossible tasks. We may feel threatened or "paranoid," believing we will be attacked again, either by the aggressor or by someone else. The fear can be paralyzing. Sometimes people fear that reporting the incident, pressing charges or going to court will provoke reprisals or another attack.

- **Phobic reactions**: In the mind of a terrified person, public places can be dangerous. Streets, buses, subways, shopping or being in any public place can cause panic. Sometimes even home may not feel safe. Trauma can also lead to generalized fears and agoraphobia.

- **Depression**: When the incident is too overwhelming and causes too dramatic a change in lifestyle, or when recovery is too slow, sadness, despair and depression set in. When the despair is too intense, suicide may be considered as a viable way to ease the pain.

- **Anxiety**: High levels of stress, loss of control, and worry over what has happened cause anxiety. Fear of the unknown and of everything outside a well-established daily routine can increase anxiety. For a while after an incident, victims often develop an exaggerated startle response; that is, becoming easily startled by sudden noises or activity.

- **Panic Attacks**: Fear of being attacked again by the perpetrator or by anyone else can turn low-level anxiety into a panic attack. A sudden overwhelming fear can cause claustrophobic feelings and produce physical symptoms such as heart palpitations, rubbery legs and shaking. Being in a public place, in unfamiliar surroundings or with too many people can heighten anxiety. A restaurant, store, theater, bus or subway and even a work site can trigger an attack.

- **Anger**: The event as well as people's insensitive comments often lead to intense anger. We become furious with the aggressor for destroying our quality of life and shattering our belief that the world is a safe place. We become resentful when family, friends, and colleagues do not understand the way we feel or what we are going through. We are furious with our employer for not having provided a safe work environment, for ignoring our suffering, and for being unresponsive and unsupportive. Exasperation sets in for many reasons: not having anticipated the attack, not having noticed the warning signs, not having followed our intuition that warned of impending danger, or not being able to get over the incident. Anger may make us irritable and cause us to argue with everyone, especially people closest to us.

- **Frustration**: Being on an emotional roller-coaster is frustrating, because nothing is as it used to be. Frustration increases with the realization that no one seems to care, fully understands or experiences similar reactions. We cannot stop the reactions no matter how hard we try. Every little thing, no matter how trivial, is exaggerated. We feel powerless and out of control. Frustration leads to conflicts and rifts in relationships, even those that were previously good. This adds to discouragement, despair, depression and isolation.

- **Guilt**: Having been unable to prevent or stop an attack or prolonged harassment provokes feelings of guilt. We may also feel guilty because we are unable to forget the incident and for having lost control. Slow recovery and the need for time off work also add to the guilt. When co-workers seem unaffected or when victims are blamed, remorse intensifies. Guilt increases with the suggestion that we "should be over it by now."

- **Shame**: Remorse turns into shame when we compare our behavior, actions or reactions with others and find ourselves lacking. We feel powerless and humiliated because we are weak, dependent, needy and a shadow of our former selves.

Exposure to violence and trauma results in physical, behavioral changes and psychological reactions. What follows is a list of the most common effects:

- Change in eating habits.
- Insomnia.
- Change in behavior patterns.

- Increased dependency on alcohol, drugs, over-the-counter medication, prescription drugs, cigarettes, or coffee.
- Crying spells.
- Health problems.
- Confusion/disorientation.
- Lack of concentration
- Inability to make decisions.
- Memory impairment.
- Fatigue.
- Hypersensitivity.
- Reduced sexual desire.
- Loneliness.
- Helplessness/hopelessness/powerlessness.
- Disillusionment.
- Loss of control.
- Loss of self-esteem.
- Loss of independence.
- Intense feeling of professional incompetence or worthlessness.

These reactions and feelings are normal responses to a trauma, regardless of where the incident occurred. Victims of workplace violence however, must return to their workplace. They have to confront the abusive person (e.g. harassment), or face the risk of another incident (e.g. holdup). The anticipation of possible further abuse increases anxiety and makes returning to work more difficult.

VARIED RECOVERY TIME

One should not blame employees for the intensity of their reactions or for the length of their recovery time. Many factors affect the intensity of the stress reaction and a person's ability to recover from a traumatic event:

- Individual's own perception of the danger and risk to life.
- Duration of the incident, severity of the violence or threat, and the extent of physical proximity and contact with the aggressor.

- Previous exposure to violence or trauma.
- Level of personal and family stress prior to the incident.
- Support of family and friends.
- Workplace climate before and after the incident.
- Degree of stress at work.
- Relationship with management, immediate supervisor and co-workers.
- Amount of understanding, support and sympathy received after the incident from management and colleagues.
- Management's ability to accommodate injured workers during the recovery process.
- Management's attitude about the incident and reaction to the perpetrator.
- Degree of secondary injury suffered after the initial trauma (that is, incidents, comments, actions and reactions that may hurt an already fragile person).
- Speed with which help (medical, psychological counseling, financial and legal) is received after the incident and the professionals' experience and skill in dealing with trauma.

An employee's recovery from a work-related trauma is dependent on all of the above. However, by far the biggest factor impacting recovery time and an employee's ability to stay on the job relates to what goes on at work.

> Employees' recovery is directly linked to the understanding, support and help they receive from their supervisors and colleagues, and to their employer's expression and demonstration of concern.

Positive, practical action to protect employees and help them recover will significantly reduce the negative impact of a distressing or tragic event. The most important person in this endeavor is the employee's immediate supervisor.

An empathetic, sensitive supervisor, supportive and compassionate collegial relationships, and a work environment that displays compassion are essential in diminishing the negative impact of a work-related incident.

RECOVERY STAGES

Victims of violence go through three distinct stages as they recover from trauma: shock, impact, and recovery. Understanding the recovery process enables everyone to better handle employees' symptoms, attitude and behavior and the associated problems. This significantly hastens the healing process.

Shock

The shock phase begins during the actual traumatic event(s) and generally lasts from a few hours to a few weeks. During the incident itself, everything seems to happen in slow motion. While in shock, people normally go through two important responses: immobilization and denial. During immobilization, affected individuals are unable to function. They are confused, disorganized and have difficulty doing even simple, routine tasks. Ordinary daily tasks at work or at home, or decision-making of any kind may become overwhelming or impossible. While victims experience confusion, they usually go through a period of denial or disbelief—that the incident took place, that it happened the way it did and that it happened to them. There is also a continual reliving of the event or of certain aspects of it, and a blocking of other facets. Sometimes when employees experience violence overload from persistent verbal abuse or harassment, they become resigned to the never-ending exposure to violence. Shock gives way to a gradual chipping away of their psyches. They become worn down.

Impact

The impact phase which follows shock is characterized by a period of anger and/or extreme anxiety. Often the anger is misplaced. Rather than being angry with the perpetrator of the violence, the person displaces the anger onto other people. The employer bears the brunt of the anger, for not having predicted the event, taken adequate precautions to protect employees, or for exposing them to danger. This stage is characterized by much soul-searching by victims, particularly about how they handled the situation. They experience uncertainty and self-blame. Soul-searching and doubts increase when the old "self" disappears and is replaced with a fearful and anxiety-prone persona. Survivors feel that they are on an emotional roller-coaster, over which they have no control. They feel depressed, hopeless, isolated and misunderstood. People who are unable to resolve their feelings about the experience stay in this second stage.

Recovery

The recovery phase takes place when feelings about what has happened begin to be resolved successfully. In spite of the fact that the recovery period may have taken a long time, it seems as though suddenly victims begin feeling better and they find they can resume some previous activities. The recovery is complete when they can put the incident behind them and get on with their lives. Their sense of perspective and control over their lives is restored. While they may never forget what happened to them and their attitude towards their job may change, they can resume their normal activities and even feel happy again.

HEALING PROCESS

Recovery from trauma or PTSD is a process. There is no magical formula. Traumatized people are unable to tolerate stress of any kind, since they have experienced an overload of stress. Batteries must be recharged, energy restored. This requires a stress-free environment. People in this temporary phase need to be constantly reassured because they feel vulnerable and out of control. They need encouragement, reassurance and the opportunity to talk repeatedly about their experience, until they get it out of their system. Trauma victims heal more quickly when surrounded by caring people who help them understand what has happened to them.

Traumatized people need counseling or therapy to help them recover. Recovery is most successful when counseling begins immediately after the incident and ends when the person resumes normal activities, and is symptom-free. Employees exposed to persistent violence such as harassment, or who have to appear in court often need additional support.

Victims of violence suddenly become more aware of the violence around them and alert to potential dangers. They become focused on what is important in life, reexamining their beliefs and values.

Healing is eased with management support and encouragement. Traumatized people need permission to grieve and time to heal. They also need practical help to enable them to continue working after the incident. Their special needs include: an escort to and from work, financial compensation for damages or losses, security measures, support to confront their aggressor or to press charges, and a gradual return to work.

Healing takes time and it hurts. It is often hard to see the light at the end of the tunnel. Recovery takes place when victims can come to terms with what has happened to them. They must stop blaming themselves either for what took place or for their reactions. Healing takes place when they can accept that "bad things do happen to good people" and even so, life can and does go on.

Dealing with the aftermath of a traumatic incident can be a long and difficult process. Violence alters our outlook about our life and our work. Sometimes this may result in deciding to leave a chosen career or job because it is too stressful or no longer enjoyable.

Strange though it may seem, trauma may actually have some positive aspects: It can be growth provoking, leading to a maturity and wisdom that inspires us to live our lives differently in the future. A harrowing incident may turn out to be a pivotal turning point in our lives. This realization and growth are also part of the healing process.

Employee-victims of violence have a lot to contend with. They have to deal with the psychological outcome of a traumatic incident, which changes their behavior and personality. When they are least able, they may have to deal with criticism or hostility from colleagues, family and friends. They may have to fight for their rights to health insurance, workers' compensation and sick leave: even their job may be at stake. They may also have to deal with a complicated, stressful judicial process. No wonder so many employees find the experience so traumatic.

During the difficult aftermath of the incident, victims need reassurance. They need to hear that their unusual, debilitating reactions do not make them weak, ineffectual or incompetent workers. They need assurance that this is a temporary (though possibly a lengthy) phase, and that eventually they will regain their self-control and self-confidence. Knowing that people are cheering them on is comforting and reassuring. Understanding, encouragement and support lessen the pain, shorten the recovery time and helps the recovery process.

OBSTACLES TO RECOVERY

An unsupportive workplace environment is probably the greatest obstacle to recovery. It causes employees to lose their enthusiasm for their jobs and to become disillusioned with their employer. A lack of support at work may lead employees to consider a total career change, because they believe they do not have what it takes to do the type of work they were doing at the time of the incident. They may re-evaluate their relationship with family and friends. They may also ponder whether they will ever again be independent, well-functioning human beings who can regain their personal power and control over their lives.

How we think people see us and think about us is important to our self-esteem. Employees frequently complain about people's negative attitudes and how this impedes their ability to recover. They complain that having to listen to and deal with insensitive, accusatory comments and negative attitudes. These are often worse than the actual incident. When an employer does not acknowledge the problem, downplays the incident or does not provide support, encouragement or reassurance, it is only natural for employees to feel isolated, hurt and resentful.

Since abused people feel so raw, they are hypersensitive to comments, gestures or attitudes. When an organization closes ranks, covers up, or sabotages attempts by victims or their supporters to confront the violence, the person suffers a secondary injury. The perception or realization that their employer and/or colleagues do not care may cause even more damage than the original event. Some employees never recover from the violence because of hurt suffered from callous people after the event.

Victimized employees quickly lose faith in the notion of a just world. When they are ridiculed, not believed or have to defend their actions, their disillusionment increases. Any perceived or actual lack of support and misunderstanding make them feel betrayed, ignored and bitter. All of this delays recovery and may even prevent it.

A management team that is slow to respond, is unsupportive or ignores the situation, causes employees to feel no one cares about their predicament or their welfare. They develop intense feelings of betrayal. This leads to disappointment, anger, frustration, abandonment, and finally an emotional withdrawal from the organization. Employee-victims often say, "If the organization does not care enough about me to do something about the situation and help me, why should I care about it? My attitude has changed. I'll do my job but that's all."

COMPLAINTS ABOUT MANAGERS

Stricken employees are acutely aware of nuances and are extremely sensitive to reactions of their employer and co-workers. They pick up on insincere gestures or statements. They know when someone is taking their concerns and interests seriously or when they are being paid lip service.

During my twenty-four years of work with employees who were either direct or indirect victims, I have heard many complaints about the way they are treated by their employer after an incident. The complaints can be summarized in eight statements.

- "I told my manager what happened and he did not believe me."
- "I was made to feel that what happened was my fault."
- "No one cares about what happened to me or what it did to me."
- "No one pays attention."
- "No one takes it seriously."
- "This could happen again. No one does anything about it."
- "Why doesn't someone stop what's going on?"
- "It's happened over and over, but nothing ever changes."

These complaints denote five basic themes about the attitude of employers:

- Employees are not believed.
- Employees are blamed.
- Employees are not given help.
- Nobody does anything to stop the violence.
- The offender is not punished.

These themes are aptly summed up in the words of one employee. She really expresses the views of employees everywhere, particularly when incidents are repeated and management is slow to react, or does not react at all.

Susan, a flight attendant, was a victim of sexual harassment by a passenger. Talking about the organization's response to her after the incident, she said: "Management just do not care. They do nothing to protect us. The customer is always right, and the harassment goes on and on. On top of it all, we are always blamed for the incident."

This theme of lack of caring is central to all employee complaints. Often employees do not feel supported by their supervisors and the organization and they do not feel protected. When employees see that things do not change, even when they draw management's attention to the problem, they become resigned, resentful and bitter. Not only do the employees suffer, but the organization suffers in low morale and reduced productivity.

ROLE OF MANAGEMENT IN RECOVERY

Management's behavior and reactions are central elements to employees' recovery and to morale, job performance and employee commitment. They have a key role to play in reducing the event's impact on all employees. A compassionate, supportive manager and a caring senior management team can make all the difference in diminishing employee reactions, reducing recovery time and influencing employees' productivity. When management provide adequate resources to help employees recover, employees can relax and focus all their energies on getting better. When management acts to protect their workforce, then employees can concentrate on their work.

An appropriate management response to the problem will ensure employees' commitment to the organization. Morale improves. The message quickly goes around the organization that "this is a management team that cares about us, does something about the violence, and helps us deal with it."

- 11 -
Family Affair: Workplace Violence and the Family

A complete analysis of workplace violence must include the connection between this issue and the family. The connection is twofold: workplace violence affects the family, and family violence affects the workplace. Helping families cope with the effects of work-related violence, and helping employees deal with family violence reduce losses and costs to an organization.

The family can be either a direct or indirect victim of workplace violence. Family members are direct victims when a workplace aggressor threatens them. They are indirect victims when their loved ones fear violence or experience it at work and bring the problem home with them.

The workplace can also be affected by family dynamics. Family stress, conflict, and especially conjugal and family violence spill over into the workplace.

WORKPLACE VIOLENCE AND THE FAMILY

When an incident takes place at work, the victim's family has to deal with the victim's overwhelming feelings, changes in personality and behavior, and routine. Sometimes victimized employees are so marked by violence they are unable to fulfill their family responsibilities. Although their family may try to be supportive they do not always know what to do to diminish the victim's initial distress, or how to handle longer-term trauma reactions. They are usually left to support the victim without guidance.

When employees experience a traumatic incident, everyone suffers—employees, their family and friends. The longer employees suffer from their physical and/or psychological injuries, the greater the strain on the family. As tension builds over time, the family unit becomes destabilized, and even traumatized.

A traumatized family goes through emotions and reactions paralleling those of the direct victim: shock, anger, fear, anxiety, tension, and a preoccupation with safety and security. The family's recovery is conditional on the victim's resilience.

When victims are unable to work the impact on the family is even greater. If medical insurance or workers' compensation benefits are delayed, or refused because the incident has not been accepted as a legitimate work accident, the family faces an additional crisis—a sudden reduction in financial resources.

The family suffers a double jolt from work-related violence. It must help its wounded member through the ordeal and cope with someone markedly changed by the incident. Moreover, while giving support to this person, family members must also deal with their own feelings and reactions about what has happened and adapt to the sudden changes in their routine and lifestyle.

FAMILY LIFE AFTER VIOLENCE

Frequently family members and friends are indirect victims of workplace violence. Since they were not present at the time of the incident, they are often the "forgotten victims" and not much is given to the impact on them.

Each morning families bid each other goodbye as they go to school, work or their other activities. When they gather together at night, they expect everyone to be the same. When a family member suffers a holdup, shooting or other crime or lives through months of bullying or sexual harassment at work, everything changes.

Family members ride a roller-coaster of emotions because of the incident. Relief, gratitude and joy over the person's escape from death or injury, is quickly replaced by anger and resentment.

Family and friends want to help the victim deal with the abuse or stress. However living with someone who is being victimized or has been traumatized is not easy. Watching a family member or friend struggle to recover can be exasperating. People who do not experience the violence themselves find it hard to understand why the person cannot simply forget what happened and move on. Patience often wears thin. Problems drag everyone down, causing family and friends to suffer with the victim.

When a child sees his mother or father crying, anxious and afraid, the child becomes similarly affected. When the child hears the reason for the parent's distress, he feels insecure and worries about his own safety and that of his parents. For example, young children of a holdup victim become easily frightened and often develop sleep and behavior problems because they believe that the "robber will come into my home and shoot mommy, daddy or me."

How workplace violence impacts on family life is highlighted in the following two examples.

Lucy, a 35-year old cashier was an easy-going person, content with her job and her family life. Her husband, Bob, had a good job as a factory supervisor. He worked a shift-rotation, and the family was well adjusted to the routine. Lucy worked full-time in a supermarket. Their three children, ten-year-old Donald, fourteen-year-old Fran and seventeen-year-old Denis were average students, involved with their friends and sports activities. Whenever there was a problem the children would go to mom first. Despite her busy schedule, she always seemed to have time for them. Bob and Lucy tried to decide things together especially when it came to the children. Although things were tight financially, they had a solid relationship and were a closely-knit family.

Things suddenly changed. One day, Bob received a telephone call from Lucy who said she had been in a holdup. She wanted him to take her home. When he arrived at the supermarket, she was giving the police a description of the robber. She was shaking and when she saw her husband, she started sobbing. He wrapped his arms around her and tried to calm her down.

When they got home, Lucy needed to talk about the holdup. She remembered having seen the robber in the store the day before and could clearly describe him. Throughout the evening and into the night, Lucy continued to shake and cry as she kept vividly reliving the scene of the gun pointed at her. Bob felt terrible and was furious because the supermarket had no security guard.

In the days that followed, everyone rallied around Lucy. She could not stay alone, so Bob and the children took turns staying with her. Lucy wanted to try to go to work three days later, but she became panicky and could not stay. She returned home after an hour, so shaken up that Bob had to call in sick so that he could stay with her.

A week later, Lucy began to meet with a trauma counselor provided by the company. She was determined to recover from the trauma. However, weeks later, she was still affected. The family worried about the changes in her, because even making a meal or doing the laundry seemed to overwhelm her. Donald told his father, "Mom cries all the time, it's scary. She was never like that before."

As the months went on, more changes occurred. Lucy could not go out of the house alone. Having identified the robber to the police, she became convinced he would find her and kill her. The children were getting tired of pitching in and Bob also began to feel the strain. He always had to arrange for someone to be with Lucy and he had to drive her everywhere. He knew the holdup had upset her and he wanted to be supportive. Yet as time went on, he was baffled by her reaction. He could not understand why she could not simply forget about it. When Bob would try to take Lucy shopping or distract her with suggestions of a movie, she would become angry. They fought more in the four months since the holdup than they had in the previous four years. Lucy was afraid someone would break into the house and harm her family. She became insistent about installing extra locks and an alarm system. She worried that something bad would happen to the children and did not want to let them go out alone.

Fran became angry with her mother because she was no longer interested in anything. Donald started having trouble sleeping and acted out at home. One day Lucy got a call from the principal telling her he had skipped school. This made his parents furious and even more upset. Denis spent less and less time at home. When he was around, he was the one person who rushed to his mother's defense because he wanted to protect her.

Lucy constantly argued with everyone and was difficult to be around. Bob and the children were tired and fed up with her and her problems.

It took a year of intensive therapy before Lucy recovered and could return to work. Only then could her family put the holdup behind them and get on with their lives. While Lucy was suffering from the debilitating effects from the holdup, her family had also become traumatized. Only when she had recovered could the family move forward.

In the following situation the family had to deal with grief, as well as a major upheaval in their lives.

Dominique, a 45-year old taxi driver, was shot to death during a night-time robbery. His wife Marguerita and their three children, aged nineteen, sixteen and thirteen suddenly found their life in chaos. Not only did the family have to deal with Dominique's horrible death, they also had to endure a dramatic change in their lifestyle. Without the money Dominique earned, they could not afford their house. Three months later they moved to a small apartment. Their savings had been spent and no other source of income being available, Marguerita had to quickly find a job. Before long her youngest child started displaying aggressive behavior toward her and her eldest began using drugs. Beside her own grief and her children's problems, Margueita had to deal with the family's financial crisis.

Their grief and trauma were heightened because of the financial crisis that caused irrevocable damage to the family.

Another source of stress for families is when violence continues over time. Bullying, stalking or abuse of power take their toll on the family, since they may have to deal with someone whose behavior changes over time. Fear, powerlessness and a preoccupation with the incident consume both the victim and family. Faced with the realization that complaining or reporting the abuse could result in reprisals, people choose to remain silent. The prospect of a worsening situation, possible dismissal and loss of income are immobilizing factors.

Even if the employee experiences no direct violence, the risk of an incident may have a profound impact on the family. They worry about the type of work their parent, spouse or child does. Many families know that cashiers, nurses, social workers, police, prison guards, taxi drivers and teachers are high-risk occupations for violence. Media reports with graphic pictures drive the point home and force the families to consider the risks. They worry whether their own loved one will suffer a similar fate.

FAMILIES AS TARGETS

Families sometimes become unwilling targets for violence, for the most part used as a means to coerce the victim into compliance. Holding family members hostage to extort large sums of money from the business, or threatening an employee's children to pressure the person to act against their will are two examples of this. A third example is when a disgruntled person targets an employee's family as an act of revenge.

Janice, a 36-year old social worker was acting on a case of child abuse. After she had taken the child into protective custody, the child's father threatened to kill her and her family. Because of the man's history of violence and his criminal record, Janice was terrified that he would harm her and her children. After he made the threat, the man disappeared. For their own protection, Janice and her three children aged ten, twelve and fourteen had to move out of their home and go into hiding. For four weeks they lived in unfamiliar surroundings with severe restrictions to their activities. The children could not even go to school. Janice had good reason to worry: the police strongly linked the man to a multiple murder case. Four weeks after his threats, he was found dead. Janice and her family returned home and the children returned to school and resumed their regular routines.

This family suffered directly from workplace violence, totally disrupting their lives. Until the man's death, they lived with the constant fear of being hurt or killed.

Another way families can become victimized is when they bear the brunt of their loved ones' emotions. Consider the impact on families from persistent violence, such as harassment or stalking.

Employees may stay in jobs where they are abused because of a restricted job market. More often than not though, it is their bruised psyches that prevent them from moving on. When the stress builds up at work and they are unable to confront their aggressors, those people closest to them, that is, family members, may inadvertently become targets of victims' frustration, anger and stress. Even if they can control their feelings and do not take their anger out on their families, the enormous stress and preoccupation with the harassment will affect everyone, especially the children. Workplace violence takes its toll on the family, just as it takes its toll on the victim.

HELP FOR TRAUMATIZED FAMILIES

When workplace violence occurs, regardless of the type of victimization, the home atmosphere becomes charged. Family members end up reacting to each other's emotions and behavior. The longer the situation persists, the greater the tension.

Families react to crises differently. Some people become overly protective, others pull away. Some are able to rally around and give support, others may be unable to tolerate the stress.

Family distress adds to the victim's stress and vice versa. It is therefore important to view and treat the incident as a family crisis rather than just an individual crisis. Employers must remember this when they plan a violence response program to help workers experiencing on-the-job violence. The program should extend to family members.

Support for families is often overlooked because everyone focuses on the victim. However, unless family members are involved in the counseling, they cannot fully appreciate what is happening. Without really knowing how to help, they often become discouraged by changes to the victim's personality and behavior, or slow recovery. In the case of Lucy, her husband was involved in her therapy, which relieved some of the tension between them.

Engaging the entire family in therapy would have helped the family better understand and deal with their emotions. They would have also learned how they could better help her. This support would have hastened Lucy's recovery and decreased the trauma on the family overall.

FAMILY VIOLENCE AND THE WORKPLACE

Just as work violence affects the family, family life affects the workplace, sometimes to the point where the workplace becomes an unwitting target for family violence.

Employees who have family problems tend to take the problems to work with them, or at the very least, the tension they feel. Frustration over unresolved problems, or an inability to cope with life or family pressures, may turn an even-tempered employee into a bully.

Chapter 3 focused on the factors that contribute to workplace violence. Family dysfunction, exposure to violence as a child, and poor parental role modeling in anger management and conflict resolution affect people's behavior, even at work. When employees grow up in violent homes or live in violent relationships, they tend to be more tolerant of abuse at work. If they are not strong enough to stop abuse in their personal relationships, they will more than likely be unable to assert themselves and stop abuse at work.

Furthermore, people who are angry and aggressive at home tend to carry their anger, hostility and lack of respect into the workplace. Their colleagues, and even their manager, become the targets of their abusive behavior. This is one way family dynamics play out in the workplace.

Sometimes conjugal violence spills over into the workplace. An employee is harassed, stalked or threatened at work by an abusive spouse or partner. At times, other employees become his ill-fated targets. Domestic violence has been identified as a significant security problem at the workplace, according to the Pinkerton survey previously referred to.[1] How conjugal violence affects the workplace is highlighted in the following examples.

An estranged boyfriend sent nude pictures of his former girlfriend to her employer in an attempt to embarrass and discredit her, and get her fired.

A disgruntled husband, furious over his wife's decision to divorce him, continually harassed her at her workplace and threatened to kill her. When management tried to protect her by having her colleagues and supervisor answer her phone, her husband threatened their lives.

Sometimes the threats and fury turn to homicide. Male partners in particular, who are determined to kill their female partners, do not necessarily wait for them to get home.

The cost of conjugal violence in the workplace should be a concern to all senior management groups. It is estimated that employers lose between $3 and $5 billion every year in absenteeism, lower productivity, higher turnover and health and safety costs because of domestic violence.[2] Moreover, of working women who are victims of domestic violence: 96% experience problems at work due to abuse, 74% are harassed while at work by their abuser, 56% are late to work, 28% leave work early, and 54% miss entire days of work.[3]

FAMILIES AND WORK—A VITAL LINK

The connection between what goes on in the family and what goes on at work should not be underestimated. Family violence contributes to the problem of workplace violence. Violence at work contributes to family discord and instability.

We need to better understand how anger and frustration is transferred from one place to another. When employees suffer abuse at the workplace, they cannot leave their problems at work. Moreover family dynamics have a significant impact on work attitude, behavior and relationships. To fully address the issue of workplace violence strategies that include the family context must be considered. These strategies include:

- Extend employee assistance coverage to family members.

- In the event of a violent incident, extend trauma counseling to family members and provide them with documentation outlining the company's policy to help employees deal with the aftermath and how families can help.
- Train managers in early detection of domestic violence and how to refer employees for help.
- Create a security plan to deal with incidents of domestic abuse at work.
- Encourage victims of conjugal violence to access the employee assistance program.
- At the first incident of abusive workplace conduct, insist on a change in behavior, and encourage the employee to access the employee assistance program to help achieve this change.

By taking account the reality of the family situation and developing better security and support strategies for employees, the connection between family violence the workplace can be better controlled.

- 12 -
Management Guide: Dealing with Incidents and Preventing Violence

A management team that has not yet had to handle an episode of workplace violence is fortunate. One day, however, this might change. Senior management may be faced with the task of investigating complaints of sexual harassment, bullying, abuse of power or assault. They may have to support and comfort an employee who was harassed, or discipline another employee who exhibits abusive behavior. They may also have to intervene when clients become verbally abusive or threaten or physically attack their staff. Or they may be called upon to manage a major crisis as a result of a bomb threat, industrial accident, shooting or murder, or possibly even a terrorist attack. Then, a well-designed response and action plan is essential.

Too often workplace violence is managed after the fact, rather than with a proactive approach. As with all problems, the best way to manage it is to be prepared. This means picking up the cues that warn of potential hot spots, responding quickly to problem situations and setting up violence prevention mechanisms. In these ways a vigilant organization can reduce the risks of violence.

This chapter focuses on proactive measures to address workplace violence. The responses and strategies will help organizations avoid the negative comments and criticism toward management, expressed in the following examples.

"I was blamed for the incident. Instead of supporting me, my supervisor and department manager insinuated that I provoked the violence. They made me feel it was my fault. I was the victim and it was my fault. I love my work but I'm so angry. I don't have any respect for management. How could they treat me like this?"

"No one understood what I went through. People laughed at my fears. I got the message, 'Don't complain.' The first time I reported the

death threat to my supervisor, I was told it did not mean anything, nothing was going to happen to me and I should forget about it. My supervisor's life wasn't threatened, mine was. How can everyone be so sure nothing will happen? There's no support around here. I can't even talk about it. The message is: 'If you can't handle it, it's your problem.' The attitude shocked me. If they don't care about me, why should I care about them?"

"I went through the most frightening incident of my life and no one cared. When I couldn't go in to work the next day, no one called me. Two days later my supervisor telephoned, but it was to tell me it would be better if I came back to work. Nobody talked to me about the incident. Oh yes, they asked me how I was, but I could see they really didn't want to hear about it. I gave so much to this place. It really hurts to be treated this way."

"My supervisor is constantly on my back, yelling at me and belittling me. It got to a point when I couldn't take it anymore. I knew before I even went to labor relations to report her behavior that I wouldn't get any help. I was told that perhaps it would be better if I asked for a transfer or even considered if I was the right type of person to work here."

"We have to put up with so much abuse and violence from patients and no one stops it. We are not even allowed to talk about it. The last time I raised the issue at a meeting, I was told that it was part of my job and I had better grow up. My manager then changed the subject. Everything is always our responsibility and our fault. No one wants to listen. No one stops the violence, and it goes on and on. What's the matter with our administration? They refuse to accept incident reports and we're not allowed to file workers' compensation claims. They want to pretend life is peachy around here when it's the pits."

TOWARD POSITIVE ACTION

The first step in managing the problem is to accept that in many industries and workplaces, violence is a fact of life. If you refer to the *Workplace Violence Continuum* presented in Chapter 2, it becomes clear that managing violence means managing all types of violence: verbal and psychological as well as physical. In broad terms, managing violence in the workplace is about organizational change and development. This means ensuring organizational structures, policies and practices promote respectful attitudes and behavior among employees, between employees and clients, and in fact with every person who comes into contact with the organization. To this end, the following practices must become an integral part of the operations and culture of all workplaces.

- Establish a customer-based service model.
- Respect customers and consumers and insist on the same behavior towards employees.
- Denounce all types of violence by clients, toward clients, or between employees.
- Build a respectful organizational culture that appreciates employee diversity and contribution.
- Train supervisors and managers to become positive leaders, coaches and role models for change.
- Promote employee participation in problem-solving and decision-making.
- Empower employees to take ownership of problems and to find and implement solutions.
- Encourage consensus-building and teamwork.
- Focus on how results are achieved as much as the results themselves.
- Include principles of respect, tolerance and collaboration in the mission statement and daily operations.
- Recognize and reward team players and consensus-builders.

Many organizations would have to make drastic changes in their daily operations to do these things. This would involve the way employees work together, how they deliver their service or products, how they interact with their clients and how they perform their jobs. Across North America and in many other parts of the world, some visionary CEO's and senior management teams have already grappled with the complex problems caused by violence, and created more effective organizations.

SUCCESS STORIES

What do success stories look like? Two of them are models for what can be done about violence in the workplace, how organizational change can come about and the benefits of the change.

A community health center had a long history of internal strife that was seriously affecting employee morale and its service delivery. A small but powerful group of employees were disrespectful, hostile and abusive toward management. They challenged every new decision and action, and sabotaged anything they did not like. These same workers also terrorized many of their colleagues: no one wanted to tangle with them. In essence they controlled the organization. Victimized employees were too frightened about reprisals to lodge formal complaints but they privately pleaded with management to stop the abuse.

Fear, anxiety and a preoccupation with these problems took precedence over work. The disruptive employees created a crisis in leadership and in service delivery. Previous administrations had tried unsuccessfully to discipline these employees and had wanted to fire them, but as the organization was unionized, firing the troublemakers was almost impossible. The managers had difficulty handling the continual stress, hostility and abuse from their employees. The troublemakers literally forced seven executive directors to resign over a twelve-year period and caused numerous resignations within the management team.

Six months into his position, a new executive director realized that he had to resolve the problem otherwise he too would be forced to resign. He invited his management team to work with him in tackling the problem. With the help of a consultant, they learned about workplace violence and developed a strategic plan to gain control of the situation. They first built a profile of the patterns of abuse. These included incidents of harassment, intimidation, subtle threats, non-compliance with management requests, refusal to accept work assignments, disruptive and abusive behavior and passive resistance to change. They then discussed how the abusive behavior affected their ability to manage the organization and the effect on service delivery. They examined their management styles and the way they had been approaching the problem. As they became clearer about their roles, they learned to communicate more assertively with employees. They also learned how to cool down on-the-spot situations of abusive behaviors and to resolve conflicts in non-adversarial ways. The management team developed a coordinated and consistent approach to handling employee insubordination and disputes.

As the management group became more empowered, they could see changes in their relationships with each other and with their subordinates. The new anti-violence policy developed by an Occupational Safety Committee, including union and management representatives, itemized clear sanctions for offenders. The agency made it clear that violence of any kind would not be tolerated. The management team firmly confronted abusive employees and began using the disciplinary process. They also began to pass on their new communication and conflict resolution skills to other employees who in turn began to confront their bullying colleagues. Rather than allowing employees to complain and dump the problem on management, they encouraged and supported employees' own attempts to deal with their colleagues. Soon staff and supervisors were working together to resolve conflicts with disruptive and abusive co-workers.

Two months after they had begun the process, the management team began to feel empowered and successful. Then on two separate occasions within a three-week period, clients threatened the lives of two employees who had been helping them. Management took swift decisive action. The executive director himself confronted the clients about the threats and told them clearly that their actions were unacceptable and would not be tolerated. In one case, he resolved the problem by organizing an immediate appointment with a psychiatrist for a psychotic patient. In the other situation, he first warned the client he was going to report him to the police. He then lodged a joint agency-employee criminal charge against the client. In both situations, the actions stopped the violent behavior. The executive director also provided counseling for the employee-victims, took precautionary security meas-ures for them and for their families, and was present and supportive throughout the police investigation and legal procedures.

The message quickly spread throughout the organization that this executive director and his management team were different. They had been successful in transmitting the message that violence would not be tolerated, offenders would be punished and employees supported. Management saw positive changes-in their relationships with staff, in general morale and in job performance. Their confidence grew in their ability to be an effective management team since they had been able to control and effectively manage internal violence. Staff had move energy and thus more time to take care of their clients.

In a public utility company, the union and management were both concerned about the high number of harassment complaints by employees against their co-workers. When they began to collaborate on resolving the problem, they realized that the organization was plagued with problems of widespread discrimination and harassment, which was demeaning and hurtful to the individual and disruptive. The harassment of employees was a work hazard, similar to an occupation-al disease or injury. They decided to affirm the right of employees to work in a harassment-free environment.

By working together, management and union set about to improve the work environment. They developed an anti-harassment policy, which gave employees the right to refuse to work when they perceived a situation as unsafe. Harassment was defined to include remarks or actions that were demeaning, or undermined the dignity and work of a colleague. They put in place a simple procedure that immediately removed the targeted employee from the harassing situation with no loss of pay; provided for an immediate investigation, and stipulated appropriate disciplinary measures. The issue of false accusation made with malicious intent was counterbalanced by a provision in the policy for action against the complainant.

Management mandated specific people to administer the complaint process. They conducted an awareness campaign throughout the entire organization. They set up mandatory workshops at all levels to *introduce and explain their new anti-harassment policy and provided ongoing orientation sessions for all new employees. They also distributed a policy manual and posters to publicize and inform employees about the program.*

Management and union collaborated by adopting a unified position against harassing behavior, through a Respect at Work policy. Over time they were able to transform a hostile and dangerous environment into one which welcomed diversity. They successfully made the organization an example for respectful workplace conduct.

These two examples show the extent to which organizations can become stagnated by internal problems of violence and how things can improve. Willingness to confront the situation, build partnerships, produce a clear anti-violence policy, provide training and support victims was a major step towards solving the problem of violence in the organization. A strategic plan with clear goals enabled management to change the culture in their organizations. Empowered management groups were thus able to say no to violence and curtail it.

VIABLE SOLUTIONS

Where does a senior manager begin? How can one avoid the type of negative staff comments cited earlier in the chapter and become a success story? It means focusing on three specific areas:

- Managing Violent Incidents
- Preventing Violence
- Developing Effective Programs and Services

The following guide will help managers bring about organizational change and create a respectful workplace, thereby reducing incidents. We will examine each of these areas.

Managing Violent Incidents

The issues involved in managing violent incidents are:
- Defusing Explosive Situations
- Managing the Employee-Offender
- Dealing with Dangerous Clients or Patients
- Handling the Aftermath of Violence
  - Initial Response toward Employees
  - Follow-up Actions
  - Help for Families
- Violence Resulting in Death
- Caring for Management
- Management Action Review

Defusing Explosive Situations

It is not easy to manage a problem of violence. While most managers do not expect to have to deal with someone who brandishes a knife or threatens to shoot, anyone may come face-to-face with an employee or client who loses control.

The key to defusing a threatening or volatile situation is to manage it. Angry outbursts and threatening comments or behavior should always be taken seriously. They should receive immediate attention and a planned response. It is far better to defuse angry outbursts and hostile conflicts quickly than wait to see what will happen. Ignoring them and simply hoping the anger will dissipate will not resolve anything. The objective of any intervention is to defuse a highly charged or explosive situation quickly and restore calm.

Below are suggestions on how to deal with angry, hostile people who may potentially lose control and resort to more extreme forms of violence. An early, planned action by management will decrease the risk of an escalating and perhaps life-threatening situation.

- **Take complaints seriously**. Enable the person to present his grievances at the earliest opportunity. Try to find a viable solution to correct or resolve the problem.

- **Do not argue**. Do not get into a shouting match or confront someone who is losing control. Do not become emotional. Assure the person that you understand his point of view and that you are there to help. Stay calm, use a subdued voice and maintain quiet control. Make no sudden or hostile movements. Be firm but try to solve the person's problem quickly. Tell him how you plan to do this step-by-step.
- **Back down**. This is important especially if someone is armed and looking for a fight. Try to be helpful. Let the person talk about his complaints. Apologize (profusely if necessary) for any real or perceived wrongs. Convince the person you understand and will resolve the problem. Then resolve it!
- **Take death threats or veiled remarks seriously**. These are the cues that first warn of trouble. Listen attentively to the other person's concerns. Be firm, but find a solution. Take security precautions.
- **Convince the person the problem can be resolved**. Give assurance that you are there to resolve the problem and how you will do this. Then resolve it!

Managing the Employee-Offender

Many people believe that the best way to manage internal violence is to screen out potential troublemakers and not hire them in the first place. For example, many workplaces, in the United States, favor conducting a "Risk Assessment" as part of their hiring interviews to screen out chemically dependent, violent or disturbed people. While this may help to some degree, it does not guarantee that all potential abusers will be identified. Nor will this resolve the organizational and personal problems that lead employees to lose self-control. Life and work stresses can easily cause a stable employee to become volatile. For this reason, managers should expect to have to deal with abusive employees or clients. Employees who become severely troubled by personal or family difficulties or substance abuse problems during the course of their employment may also be a cause for concern.

When disruptive behavior, verbal abuse or harassment occur, the manager must be able to handle the offensive behavior quickly to reduce the risk of escalation. The manager must assess and minimize the threat to himself, to other employees and to property.

Abusive behavior is best handled by consistent, firm action. A planned intervention with an offending employee has several objectives:

- Stop the offensive behavior immediately.
- Investigate the complaint, provide the offender with an opportunity to present his/her case.
- State that the behavior is unacceptable and will not be tolerated. Apply suitable and safe discipline.
- Help the offender learn more appropriate behavior. Provide help to resolve problems that led up to the behavior.

Abusive employees should be managed the same way employers manage problem drinkers or drug abusers in the workplace. The objective should not be to fire the person unless the behavior presents a risk to other people's safety or to the organization's property, or unless the actions are criminal in nature. The objective should be to develop a plan that will pick up on the early cues that warn of violence, immediately stop the behavior, and improve the person's performance.

An employee who physically attacks or threatens another staff member should be dealt with severely but fairly. No workplace should tolerate any form of menacing behavior. Corrective or disciplinary action should include an assessment of the employee's risk for further violence and the employee's access to weapons. Firing a disgruntled employee may lead to further problems. If terminating employment is necessary, it should be handled cautiously and with the goal of cooling down volatile emotions. For example, suspending the person with pay pending an investigation takes care of the employee's immediate concern about finances and gives him a chance to respond. It also buys time. In this type of situation, the manager should always work with the human resources department, employee assistance program, and if necessary an out-place-ment service. If anyone feels there is a risk of extreme violence, then working with the company's security officer and police is essential.

The following are important points to consider when dealing with the offender.

- **Assess the risk for violence**. Avoid the trap of refraining from taking action by denying there is a problem.
- **Listen to cues that warn of trouble**. The cues are there in speech and actions (e.g. "I have a gun permit," "I have ways of punishing you"). Picking up the cues is the first step to manage violence.
- **Deal immediately with death threats and life-threatening behaviors**. Report threats to the police and work collaborative-ly with them to handle the offender. This reduces the potential for the offender to carry out the threats or for the incident to escalate out-of-control.
- **Obtain coaching to deal with disruptive, emotionally dis-turbed or malicious employees**. The objective should be to pre-vent any escalation of violence, to stop the behavior and calm the situation. A manager who is unsure of how to do this should get help. It is also important to know how to confront the employee in a positive way, how to handle the process calmly, and how to develop an action plan. Do not be afraid or reluctant to consult specialists for advice or to be coached in handling the situation.
- **Treat abusive behavior as a job performance issue**. Getting along with colleagues, superiors and clients and having a posi-tive attitude are as much a part of job performance as carrying out concrete job tasks. Making conduct part of a performance appraisal review transmits a powerful message about behav-ioral expectations. It also raises the level of work behavior. When the onus is placed on the offender to change unacceptable conduct and there is clarity about what must change, the person is disciplined for bad behavior and re-educated.
- **Use disciplinary means to deal with abusive, disruptive or violent behavior**. Deal openly with the behavior and act quick-

ly to stop it. Document offensive behaviors with the date, time, description and outcome of the incidents. Hold regular disciplinary interviews using documented information. Stick to the facts. Do not accept excuses for the behavior. Make it clear that the conduct must stop and demand a change. Credit the employee for past or current good performance and achievements. Clearly explain the consequences if the behavior does not change. Be consistent in words and actions. Apply the same standards throughout the organization.

- **Treat the employee-offender with respect**. Be polite and respectful throughout the initial exchange and subsequent contacts and demand the same respect in return. Managers and staff all want to be treated with respect.
- **Offer counseling**. Direct the employee to the employee assistance program or, if the company has no program, arrange for the employee to receive counseling. Make it clear that the employee has to learn to deal with anger and conflict more effectively, and needs to address personal difficulties or problems. If the employee is mentally ill or has a substance abuse problem, a medical examination and treatment should be required before the employee is allowed to return to work. Reassure the employee about his job, but at the same time, monitor the situation carefully to ensure the employee follows through with the treatment.
- **Credit the person when positive behavior changes occur**. Encourage, compliment and reinforce the positives. This will give the person an incentive to continue to improve. If there is no change in attitude or behavior, take further disciplinary action as indicated.
- **Address stressors that cause tension and conflict**. Abusive behavior and violent episodes can sometimes be signs of frustration. Listen to what is being said. Often complaints are justified. Inattention to problems increases frustration, stress and anger. Many fatal outbursts could have been prevented if only the employer had taken the offender's complaints seriously. Addressing and resolving problems relieve employee stress and

improve organizational effectiveness. If a problem cannot be resolved, explain why. Ensure the employee understands, then ask for his help to resolve the problem. If he refuses to cooperate, then dismissal may have to be considered.

- **Pay attention to the termination process**. Although there is no fail-proof way to fire a problem employee, some ways are better than others. The goal is to be as humane as possible. Termination of employment should be a process and not a sudden action for which neither the employer nor employee is prepared. Employers who are worried about potential risks when terminating a violent employee should get help to prepare for the termination interview from an out-placement service or mental health professional. The organization should also provide the dismissed employee with counseling immediately after the termination interview to help deal with the shock of dismissal and the anger and depression that follows.

Dealing with Dangerous Clients or Patients

When a client becomes violent and targets an employee, it is most often due to dissatisfaction with a service or product, a perceived or actual injustice or an unresolved conflict. He may also have a grudge against an employee or with the organization. These problems can be managed. This is different from a situation where a deranged individual, often a stranger, targets employees and the organization.

The majority of client-generated attacks against organizations can be avoided. Discontented customers should not be avoided. Rather, management must find ways to pay better attention to the way it delivers goods and services, how it handles complaints, and the way it settles disputes. Many clients become furious, and go on the attack, not only because they are volatile people, but because no one pays attention to them and their complaints. They want to be heard!

Management should encourage employees to report angry, hostile clients or threats, especially when they are afraid. Fear is a powerful feeling that warns of danger. Managers need to give direction and provide backup and support. Employees need training to handle disputes, especially those involving highly abusive or volatile customers. They should never be left on their own to deal with emotionally charged situations. A manager should be ready to intervene diplomatically and promptly. The involvement of a person of higher authority is often what is needed to calm an enraged person. The best way to deal with dangerous people is to intervene immediately. This does not mean only at the first outburst but at the earliest cues that warn of trouble brewing. Being alert to the cues and acting on them is a critical step in reducing violence. How the incident is handled is important especially when an employee must continue to deal with the abusive person in the future.

Handling the Aftermath of Violence

This section provides practical guidelines for the manager who has to intervene after a violent incident. It looks at the initial response and follow-up actions toward the victimized employee or employees. It also describes specific actions organizations can take to help traumatized employees and their family members. It provides suggestions for actions if the violence results in death. It offers practical self-help strategies for management to help them through a stressful incident. Lastly, important elements about workplace violence presented in different sections of this book are summarized. These actions and strategies will help the person charged with the responsibility of developing a response plan after a violent episode, do it effectively.

Initial Response toward Employees

Experiencing any kind of violence is usually traumatic, particularly an incident that is perceived to be, or is, life-threatening. A manager who hopes to assist employees who have been attacked or threatened must know what, when and how to do so.

The immediate goal should be to decrease the immediate shock. The action must be swift. The most crucial time for taking action is immediately after an incident and during the first 24 hours. The following actions provide immediate support for employees and reduce some of the risks of long-term trauma.

- Ensure the immediate safety and security of affected employees and others in the area.
- Provide immediate medical attention if someone is injured. Check the state of other employees as well.
- Move distressed employees to a quiet, comfortable, protected area and separate them into small groups. Stay with them and attend to their basic needs (blanket, warm drink. Never give alcohol.)
- Allow people to cry. Reassure them repeatedly that they are now safe and make sure that they are.
- Encourage employees to talk about the incident. However never force them if they refuse. Be a good listener.
- Accept employees' interpretation about what happened. Do not cross-examine or blame them.
- Make sure employees can handle a police interrogation, if the police have been called in.
- If police reports need to be filled out, help people to do so. If charges are pressed, ensure that the organization presses charges along with the victims, or, if this is not possible, accompany them and provide support and legal counsel.
- Make sure employees call their families as soon as they are able to, especially if the incident is reported in the media.
- Allow employees to go home if this is what they want, but only after they have calmed down. Provide transportation if needed. Make sure someone is at home and urge distraught employees who live alone to have someone spend the night with them.
- Call several times to find out how employees are doing. These calls will demonstrate that you care, and are reassuring and comforting.
- Immediately after the incident, arrange for employees to access the employee assistance program or provide professional counseling by an experienced trauma counselor.
- If several people were involved, arrange (within 24-48 hours after the incident) for group crisis counseling (i.e. critical incident stress debriefing) by an experienced mental health professional.
- Fill out incident reports and workers' compensation claims.

- Ensure that other employees working in the organization are all right. Provide an opportunity for them to talk about what happened and reassure them that the situation is under control. Be sure to address their needs.

Follow-up Actions

- If people do not come in to work the next day, call and find out why. Do not force employees to work if they do not feel they are able to. Arrange for them to receive professional help, and encourage them to return to work when they are ready.
- Assist and support employees with police and security investigations.
- Reduce workloads for distressed employees. Relieve as much stress as possible by addressing their needs.
- Ensure that stressed employees take frequent breaks.
- Listen to employees when they want to talk about the incident, even if their comments are repetitious. Provide opportunities for this exchange.
- Pay special attention to employees' needs for security. Do what is necessary to reassure them.
- If victims make requests to which the organization is unable to respond, explain why. Encourage staff to collaborate with management to find alternate solutions to their requests.
- Include employees in decisions about their welfare.
- Take employees' concerns and fears seriously. Demonstrate understanding and a desire to help by positive, timely action.
- Keep employees informed about court appearances, status of police investigations, etc., and offer legal assistance.
- Provide time for all employees to discuss the incident, how they can help each other and how further incidents can be prevented.

Help for Families

Keep in mind that workplace violence impacts on employees' families. Managers need to think about the role that families have in helping victimized employees recover, and also how to help the family. Understanding, support and involvement by the family will reduce employees' recovery time.

Consider the following actions to help decrease stress on family members.

- **Provide information**. Ensure that families are aware of the facts and know what is being done to help the employees. Inform them about security arrangements. Address their specific needs and concerns.
- **Provide direction and guidance**. Engage family members in the employees' recovery. This will enable them to become coaches and will help to reduce the intensity of employees' stress reactions.
- **Pay attention to the risk of family trauma**. Families can become immobilized. When this happens, victims' distress increases, impeding their recovery. Providing financial, material and psychological support to employee-victims and to their families will decrease everyone's stress and reduce recovery time.
- **Pay attention to family stress**. Extend the use of the employee assistance program to immediate family members. This will help reduce personal stress and resolve family issues related to the crisis.

Violence Resulting in Death

Organizations should plan for crises and be prepared if catastrophe strikes. Violent death hurls employees (including senior management) into immediate, severe shock and chaos. A predetermined crisis plan can help the organization navigate the crisis in an orderly manner. This will also reduce the intensity and duration of people's distress.

In order to diminish the impact of the incident, employees throughout the organization should receive reassurance, support, information and professional assistance to deal with the event. Help should be immediate and concentrated.

There are important principles for effective crisis management. A control center should be established, under the complete and absolute authority of one person, who will delegate tasks to other team members. The greater the control over external events, the quicker the organization will be able to regain its equilibrium. In the absence of a public relations officer, someone other than the designated leader, should be spokesperson. Others should be assigned responsibility for answering the telephones and dealing with anxious calls from family and friends.

Keeping employees informed helps them regain their sense of control. After the injured are dealt with, and police and rescue personnel have gone, priority should be given to providing psychological help for employees. Group sessions are helpful in these situations. They allow employees to discuss their feelings and raise concerns, and for counselors to identify individuals needing personal attention. Group intervention also allows for the natural support group to develop. Individual counseling is necessary for severely affected people.

In the days and weeks following the incident, when the organization begins to regain control and get back to normal, people who coped well initially may begin to show signs of strain, and become ill. Long after its normal operations resume and the public forgets about the incident, the organization can still be reeling from its effects. For this reason, continued counseling and other support should be made available for employees who may still be distressed. The human resource department is particularly important during and after a crisis because it can help with such things as benefits and job reassignments.

Caring for Management

When senior management are intensely involved in a violent situation, they often forget that they need similar support and counseling to that arranged for their employees. Employees throughout the organization may experience psychological shock or stress from a disturbing incident. Management at all levels, from the immediate supervisor to the CEO, may be overwhelmed or similarly affected by what has happened.

Management must take care of their employees, provide leadership to contain the violence, protect their staff and make the workplace safe. Hiring a consultant to help manage the crisis or talking with their counterparts in another organization, which has been through a similar experience, will greatly assist them in planning a strategy. This will save time and money and will also reduce pressure and stress.

Management Action Review

During and after a minor or major crisis, the immediate supervisor is the primary person to respond to employees. He must know how to handle the situation. Responding to distraught employees is a difficult task, even more so for supervisors uncomfortable dealing with employees' emotions, or who similarly distressed. Following predetermined guidelines will help supervisors understand normal reactions to trauma and how to help their employees.

The negative impact of violence and the possibility of secondary injury can be decreased by following the DO and DO NOT lists. While some of these tips have already been suggested earlier in this book and in this chapter, they will serve as a convenient checklist for handling the aftermath of a dangerous, violent or serious traumatic situation.

The "Do" list:

- Remember that there are many types of violence that affect people.
- Recognize that people have different perceptions about and reactions to violence and danger.
- Remember to take each threat seriously: accept every threat at face value and take action.
- Implement security measures when appropriate.
- Understand that affected employees are more sensitive to people's reactions and may "overreact": be supportive.
- Offer employees the same support you would expect in a similar situation.

- Encourage employees to talk about what happened.
- Let employees know you are concerned about their well-being.
- Allow employees to participate in safety and security decisions.
- Avoid discussions about employee responsibility until they have recovered.
- Keep affected employees informed about the status of the situation.
- Keep employees informed when police investigations involve them.
- Understand that employees may be angry with you and other managers.
- Provide counseling resources for all employees, and encourage employees to use them.
- Provide group debriefing sessions within 24-48 hours.
- Reduce workloads of distressed employees.
- Follow-up with concrete actions to let employees know you care.
- Keep families informed and extend support services to include them.
- Talk openly with staff about the risks of on-the-job violence.
- Encourage staff to collaborate in plans/actions to deal with violence.
- Conduct an operational debriefing at a senior level to improve the organization's response.
- Remember to take care of yourself.

The "Do Not" list:

- Trivialize the incident or pretend nothing happened.
- Blame the victim.
- Insinuate that employees provoked the incident.
- Scoff at employees' expressions of fear.
- Expect employees to be able to function fully right away.
- Push people to resume work if they say they are unable to do so.
- Adopt the attitude that victims are taking too long to recover.
- Give the impression victims are sick or mentally ill.

- Forget people on sick leave because of the incident.
- Ignore what happened or minimize how employees were affected.
- Refuse to listen to employees who need to talk about the incident.
- Disregard employee complaints of abuse or internal conflicts.
- Disempower employees in a moment of crisis by making decisions for them.

Preventing Violence

> The issues involved in controlling and preventing violence are:
> - Organizational Change
> - Cultural Change

Although the workplace may never be totally free from all forms of violence, most can be eliminated. There are no miracles or quick fix. However some actions can effectively reduce the frequency of incidents, cool off potentially dangerous situations, help victimized employees and help reduce an organization's exposure to violence. These strategies require changes to the organization's functioning and culture. Eliminating violence from the workplace begins with a change in employee behavior. It means setting up mechanisms to ensure change. Finally it means educating the workforce about what is expected from them.

Organizational Change

To reduce violence and promote a violence-free environment, an organization should:

- **Conduct an audit of violence**. Assess employee, management and client attitudes and behavior to determine the level of violence that is tolerated. Conduct a survey or run focus groups to take a pulse of the workplace culture, using the results to guide the change strategies.

- **Adopt an organizational philosophy of zero tolerance for violence**. Take a tough stand against violence of any kind. Make zero tolerance everyone's responsibility. Involve as many of the workforce as possible to create a snowball effect in promoting a violence-free work environment. Encourage employees to suggest ways to eliminate abusive, disruptive conduct and to promote mutual respect at work. Involving employees in the process will increase their commitment and reduce resistance for change.
- **Develop a strategic plan**. Involve a cross-section of employees in the process. Ensure that the CEO oversees, or at the minimum, supports the process. Include all employees and customers in the plan.
- **Create structures to manage the action plan**. A coordinated effort will help create a violence-free work environment. Bringing all existing policies, programs, or offices together will ensure a coordinated, inclusive initiative. (e.g. health and safety, offices to deal with sexual harassment, diversity, diversity initiatives).
- **Implement a customer service model**. Work with employees to improve customer service and strive for excellence. Improve operations and resolve organizational irritants to support this goal.
- **Collaborate with employees**. Work with employees to develop strategies to deal with abusive clients or patients or potentially dangerous situations. Use employees' concerns, worries and fears to develop innovative prevention strategies. Collaborate on changing working conditions that will decrease risks to safety and security.
- **Change organizational structures, policies and practices**. Align systems and practices with the violence-free work environment policy. Make the organization a model of civility. Promote principles of respect, tolerance, teamwork, collaboration and consensus-building with employees and clients. Change organizational values, culture, practices and operations

that allow intolerance and resentment. Link the human resource function with daily operations.

- **Develop a participatory management style**. Encourage employee input in operational decision-making (e.g. high-performance work teams, shared decision-making, consensus-building). This allows employees to control their work environment and assume responsibility for attaining objectives related to performance and service delivery. Allow employees to learn from their mistakes.

- **Protect employees and the organization**. Improve security and modify operations and labor practices. Alter operational irritants and human resource management practices which alienate employees and clients and cause frustration, resentment and anger. Reduce the potential for reprisals by being clear, yet empathic when dealing with disgruntled employees and in handling layoffs and dismissals. Adopt a fitness-for-work policy that ensures employees are physically and psychologically fit to do their jobs.

- **Use mediation and alternate dispute resolution**. Work towards a non-adversarial approach to resolve disputes between employees, between employees and management, and with customers. Ensure that all parties can live with the solutions. Mediation and alternate dispute resolution enable people to settle conflicts in a non-aggressive way. It creates order, respect and harmony. Traditional conflict resolution practice uses power and coercion, leaving people to feel angry and resentful. Alternate dispute resolution uses consensus-building and other win-win strategies to settle disputes. This contains the conflict and decreases the potential for uncontrolled outbursts or violence.

Cultural Change

- **Change attitudes**. Ensure the CEO and management team act as role models in civility and refuse to tolerate abusive conduct of any kind, from anyone. Establish strong, effective leadership by ensuring that a management team values positive attitudes, respectful conduct, open communication and win-win conflict resolution. The principles of collaboration, respect, fairness and tolerance should form the basis of management's leadership style, practices and actions.

- **Celebrate diversity and employee appreciation**. Harness and celebrate the diversity of the workforce. Create a work environment where employees can fully exploit their diverse talents and skills. Recognize and pay tribute to excellence in employee contributions.

- **Launch and promote an anti-violence campaign**. Promote a zero tolerance for violence campaign among employees and clients by setting aside a special day. Distribute brochures and display posters in waiting rooms and washrooms, in the cafeteria and in publicity materials. Refuse to support or become affiliated with organizations, people or public actions that demonstrate, support or promote any kind of violence. Support causes that promote peaceful coexistence and tolerance, respect and dignity of people.

- **Develop a code of conduct**. Clear guidelines will promote mutual respect and set standards for employee and client conduct. The code should define violence and state the consequences of abusive, harassing and violent behavior. Stress individual and group responsibility. Outline procedures to deal with abusive clients or employees. This should include pressing charges against people who threaten or assault an employee, or whose behavior or activities are against the law. Outline steps for investigating complaints, protection for complainants and due process for accused offenders. Emphasize fairness, equity and consistency for all types of offenses and all offenders. Give a signal to all stakeholders that violence of any kind is unacceptable and will not be tolerated. Include in the code of conduct corrective disciplinary measures to stop abusive behavior. Apply sanctions fairly and equitably. Educate the workforce about expectations for conduct.

- **Reaffirm that violence is not part of the job**. Support staff who deal with angry, volatile clients or dangerous situations. Make the reporting of incidents easy for staff. Provide training and coaching to help them deal with abusive or dangerous situations.

- **Deal with change as a process**. Changing an organizational culture, changing the way people talk to each other and treat each other is a *process*. This process involves educating senior management first and then the entire workforce to the benefits of civility. When senior management participate in training in civility, it sends a powerful message to the workforce that this is something everyone has to be involved in and that the leadership has made a commitment to change. In building a respectful work environment, the organization will benefit from a renewed allegiance from its workforce.

Effective Programs and Services

Programs and services that reduce employee distress after incidents are:
- Assistance for Employees
  - Employee Assistance Program
  - Critical Incident Stress Debriefing
  - Trauma/Grief Counseling
  - Training
- Assistance for Managers
  - Crisis Response Team and Plan
  - Consultation in Crisis Management and Organizational Change
  - Mediation
  - Training and Coaching

Making services and resources available for employees who experience stress and frustration from professional and personal difficulties, is as important as knowing what to do during or after an incident. Prevention is always the best strategy. The following services and practices successfully reduce stress on employees after incidents, and reduce stress overall.

Assistance for Employees

Employee Assistance Program (EAP)

An Employee Assistance Program is a confidential, professional counseling service employers provide to employees and members of their immediate families. Except in extreme circumstances as a condition to continued employment, (e.g. treatment for substance abuse, problems with anger), accessing EAP is voluntary. Counselors help employees deal with stress related to addiction problems, personal and family crises, and work-related difficulties. The EAP provides a safety net to cool off potentially volatile behavior of stressed or desperate employees who are overwhelmed by personal or work-related problems.

Critical Incident Stress Debriefing (CISD)

A Critical Incident Stress Debriefing helps employees who are distraught because of a life-threatening event. A CISD is a unique one-time intervention used to reduce the initial overwhelming emotions that come from being exposed to traumatic events such as violence, accidents, or death. A CISD is best performed within 24-48 hours of the incident. Individual employees and groups of employees can benefit from this intervention. Depending on the nature of the incident and the extent of the shock waves, employees other than those directly affected may also benefit from a debriefing. Everyone connected to the incident should be included in a mandatory session to eliminate any stigma. People do not have to talk, just be present.

The goals of the CISD are to:

- Help people talk about the incident and deal with their intense emotional reactions.
- Reassure people that their reactions are normal.
- Help people understand the effects of trauma.
- Review stress management techniques and coping skills.
- Encourage group support.
- Identify high-risk individuals needing further help.

A CISD should be conducted by a qualified, experienced mental health professional. Reliable resources would be an employee assistance program counselor, a professional experienced in trauma or grief counseling or a counselor who works with victims of crime.

Trauma/Grief Counseling

Trauma counseling should be available to employees and family members for as long as they suffer reactions from the incident. Trauma counseling differs from a CISD (a one-time intervention) in that it is often needed either to prevent post-traumatic stress reaction or to treat it. Ideally, counseling should begin as soon as any symptoms occur and continue until the employee has fully recovered, is back on the job and functioning normally. When a traumatic incident occurs, counseling should also extend to employees' family members. EAP counselors routinely help employees deal with trauma associated with industrial accidents, suicides, violence and sudden death. Individual or high-risk employees can obtain help by contacting the EAP directly. Supervisors can facilitate or encourage a referral to the EAP. Employees can also contact mental health centers specializing in helping people recover from the aftermath of trauma.

Training

Training employees who interact with the public (e.g. call centers) or work with a violent population (residential child care workers) is essential to help them learn ways to diminish risks to their safety. Employees should learn:

- About the risks of on-the-job violence.
- How to identify danger signals or cues.
- How to modify their own attitudes, behavior and actions in order to defuse highly-charged emotions and reduce risks to their safety.
- Self-protection strategies.
- How to manage anger, their own and the other person's.
- Conflict resolution techniques and mediation skills.

- Self-care strategies to cope with the aftermath of incidents.

Equally important are training programs to alter behavior, change negative attitudes and conduct and learn about civility, tolerance and diversity. Seminars, workshops, lunchtime presentations, keynote addresses, discussion groups and special days are useful methods to accomplish this. Using a group facilitator in meetings and for role modeling will enhance teamwork and positive behavior, and create a healthier workplace culture. Training in anger management and conflict resolution focuses attention on how people handle anger and how to deal more effectively with conflict. This reduces internal conflicts that can lead to crises, and improves the way people treat and relate to one another. To effectively develop strong teamwork and improve productivity, the organization needs to train employees to improve their communication skills and to learn how to build consensus and resolve problems. Training should include basic values such as respect for gender and cultural diversity, and expected workplace conduct.

Assistance for Managers

Crisis Response Team and Plan

Being prepared and knowing who does what and how to do it are critical elements for containing and managing a crisis. This means having a carefully selected team in place with clear roles and responsibilities. This Crisis Response Team will enable the organization to respond quickly and regain its equilibrium, even in the aftermath of a devastating crisis. Having a list of useful resources and telephone numbers available will save time and reduce panic. Every organization needs a Crisis Response Team and a Crisis Response Plan. The time to put this together is before it is needed, when people are calm and able to think logically about how best to manage a potential crisis.

Consultation in Crisis Management and Organizational Change

If managers are uncertain about how to handle an incident or deal with the aftermath of violence, they should work with a specialist in this field. Even a telephone consultation can provide direction and invaluable assistance to the manager who wants to resolve a problem but does not know how. Being coached or guided through the process can save the leadership considerable time, effort and dollars, by making sure all the necessary steps are in place. If management want to develop a plan to promote a violence-free environment, it would be wise to get some help. The plan must be adapted to an organization's mission, culture and context. Colleagues in other organizations who have faced similar crises can provide valuable information about how to handle the situation and suggest professional resources.

Mediation

Making a mediation service available for employees and consumers to resolve disputes, as well as training employees in conflict resolution techniques are two low-cost measures to solve problems. Peer-mediation programs, where employees are trained and serve as mediators, are also effective, cost-efficient ways to resolve problems and restore harmony to the workplace.

Training and Coaching

It is essential to set up a training program or provide coaching so that supervisors and managers can become role models of desired behavior. They need to also learn how to manage disruptive behavior, harassment and other forms of workplace violence. Training and coaching managers to be effective communicators and consensus-builders, and to be positive role models, will create a respectful workplace environment. When managers model desired behavior abuse decreases overall.

Areas for skill development:

• Understanding the manager's role in improving safety and managing violence.

- Improving communication and supervisory skills.
- Mediating solutions in employee conflicts.
- Building consensus and teamwork.
- Handling abusive, disruptive and disturbed employees and clients.
- Using constructive and safe discipline to stop abusive conduct.
- Managing crisis situations.
- Being a role model in civility and creating a respectful work environment.

COST OF INACTION

Whenever the subject of managing workplace violence comes up, it is amazing how quickly organizations derail the idea of taking constructive action because of money. Money and budget constraints are obvious factors in addressing any organizational issue. The key factor here is not money, but a willingness to face the problem and make a commitment to change. These points are highlighted in the following example.

An electronics company solicited help on how to handle a major restructuring that would result in large numbers of layoffs. Over the years the company had been through a lot of internal tension and management-staff strife. The executives were worried about how employees would handle this latest blow. But although they sought advice, they never seriously considered the plan recommended by the consultant that detailed strategies to deal with anticipated employee disgruntlement and a method to humanely handle the layoffs. They disregarded the plan because they thought the consultant's recommendations were excessive. Moreover they did not want to incur the extra expenses involved.

Four months after the layoffs, an ex-employee entered the premises and shot and killed one of the executives. It was later learned that all the warning signs had been evident, in the killer's reaction to the layoff, his desperate life situation and in his letters to management. These had all been ignored.

In addition to the executive's tragic death and loss to his family, many other lives were damaged by the incident. Some employees went on extended sick leave; others quit. Performance deteriorated and for months the company suffered from low morale and poor performance. It took years to replace the executive, his knowledge and experience. The organization paid out huge sums of money in health benefits, replacement costs, legal fees and public relations. Moreover, the company's image became tarnished when employees and the public discovered that the cues had been there and senior management had not followed the advice they had sought and had been given.

This company paid dearly for its hard-line approach to the lay-offs and its mistakes in dealing with employee disgruntlement. In this situation, the cost of inaction turned out to be significantly greater than the cost of activating the plan.

When organizations are faced with problems of potential violence, the CEO and the senior management team have a choice. They can decide whether to be proactive or reactive. They can either pay to implement a plan that will possibly prevent the problem from worsening or they can pay afterwards.

Managing the aftermath of a crisis is costly. Moreover the organization may feel the effect of tarnishing an image that has taken years to build. The organization will hobble along with reduced productivity, poor morale and loss of expertise and knowledge. Having a plan is like insurance-you pay for it in case you need it, while hoping you don't. It is a precautionary measure.

It is true that prevention, in terms of changing an organizational culture, resolving problems, supporting employees and promoting civility costs thousands of dollars. However, the cost of dealing with a crisis resulting from a shooting spree or murder may well run into hundreds of thousands or even millions of dollars. Violence is expensive: preventing violence is costly, but the cost of inaction is prohibitive. In addition to all of this, there is the possibility of litigation for negligence, due to failure to inform or to adequately protect employees.

Companies that take a proactive approach when dealing with violence find that it pays off dividends. By acknowledging a problem and taking the type of action described in this chapter, management will reap the rewards. Employees will feel more secure in the knowledge that their employer cares and is concerned about their welfare. They will appreciate working for an organization that values tolerance, respect and collaboration and promotes these principles in their daily operations and labor relation practices. They will form a closer bond with their employer and become even more devoted to their work. This will result in a motivated, energetic workforce and will translate into improved organizational performance and efficiency.

CONCLUSION

Changing an organizational culture from one of tolerance for violence to one that promotes civility and values respect, pays huge dividends. It shows in the way people work together: collaboration, civility, teamwork and tolerance for diversity. Moreover, the time that managers spend handling employee problems and complaints will decrease, allowing everyone to focus more on the work they were hired to do.

Many organizations take action against violence, not only because they know it makes good business sense, but because they have a strong social conscience. A violence-free environment enables employees and consumers to feel secure, bolsters morale and allows everyone to get on with their work. Positive corporate action develops stronger allegiances and personal commitment, thereby improving productivity.

It is up to the organization's leadership to manage violence in the workplace. To get this problem under control, everyone must be proactive. It starts with the leadership. The CEO and his executives, mid-level managers and supervisors must take a stand against violent behavior and provide the direction to deal decisively with violence when it occurs and promote a respectful workplace culture.

Given the pervasiveness of violence in our society, it is evident that most workplaces will be confronted with similar problems. We need a concerted effort and well-planned strategy to control it, which includes abusive and harmful employees and taking a hard-line position toward threatening, abusive clients. The CEO and senior management team must set an example for proper conduct. They must demand that everyone accept responsibility for this problem and work together to overcome it.

Employees should never have to accept violence as part of their jobs. Employers should not have to stand for the reckless destruction of their property or harm to their workforce. Violence can undermine and completely destroy a business that took a great effort to build.

If you are a CEO, executive, manager or supervisor, it is up to you to decide what to do about this problem. If you value civility, you will want to lead your organization in this direction. The resolution to workplace violence is possible. All it requires is a determined leader.

- 13 -
Forward Thinking:
The Civility Revolution

Throughout this book a case has been made that violence is ingrained in organizational culture and shapes the way we do business and our relationships at work.

This is a macro-level problem affecting not only our work but the way we live our lives. Although violence is a social problem that rational people denounce, efforts to deal with it have resulted in band-aid solutions rather than long-term resolution of the problem. Since we do not get to the root causes, we are not successful in containing violence.

To advance as a society, we must tackle the darker side of human nature—the violence within us and around us. Moreover we must acknowledge the extent to which violence is a part of our everyday existence and culture.

The evidence is clear. Communities all over the world experience riots, street crime, drug wars, gang fighting and youth violence. Behind closed doors, conjugal violence, child abuse and elder abuse shatter the façade of blissful family life. The deterioration of the traditional two-parent family, with its extended support network, has created hardships. Morality has eroded. This is exacerbated as a result of the weakening influence of institutions, such as the church and schools, which in the past bound people, families and communities together. Job instability, unemployment and poverty create high levels of frustration, powerlessness and hopelessness. All this sets the stage for conflict, alienation and violence.

Ours is a strange society. We abhor violence on the one hand, but support it on the other. We support a *violence culture* that creates an even greater violence-oriented society. In so many ways we not only permit abusers to get away with their actions, but we make it possible for them to gain positions where they wield even more power.

An example which highlights this issue occurred in 1993 widely televised and unprecedented U.S. Supreme Court nomination hearing of Clarence Thomas, who had been accused of sexual harassment by a former assistant. His appointment amid so much controversy makes for interesting reflection. If Professor Anita Hill's charges of sexual harassment were true, as has been proposed in "Strange Justice," (a book by Jane Mayer and Jill Abramson resulting from their investigative analysis of the version of both parties[1]), then what strange justice indeed. Aside from not believing the victim, we would have elevated an abuser to an even more powerful position. Furthermore we would have a Senate Committee nominating such a person to a position dedicated to uphold the nation's morality. What would this mean?

What does it mean to the average person and to society in general when an American President or other heads of state are caught lying? What is the impact of politicians remaining in power after they have been found guilty and convicted of robbery, drunk driving or spousal abuse? What does it mean when sports heroes sexually or physically assault women or boys or are prosecuted for murdering an estranged female partner? What message do young people receive when a sports figure threatens the life of a commissioner during a labor contract dispute or when entertainers, who are heroes to our young people, are charged with cocaine trafficking, drunk driving or sexual abuse of a minor?

If we believe that the future of humankind lies in the hands of our children, what messages are being received by these actions? How can we expect children to value human life and to believe in civility when the example of entertainers, sports heroes, politicians and media, would have them believe that violence brings power and control, money and fame? Why should they behave differently when they witness and experience adult brutality and cruelty in all its permutations, when they encounter it at school and when pro-gun lobbyists tell them that carrying weapons is a constitutional right?

VIOLENCE INDUSTRY

If we do not realize how much violence is central to our lives, just consider our thriving violence industry. War toys, violence in movies, music and video games are just a few products created to satisfy the unquenchable thirst of consumers.

Our love-hate relationship with violence results in contradictory messages. We say we abhor it, but make excuses for aggressors' behavior. We dream of a society without it, but are addicted to violent television programs and films. We love the fighting in sports, which we regard as integral to the game. We say we want to keep violence out of our backyards, but we refuse to take measures to curb the availability or production of firearms. We want the violence to stop, but do not sufficiently include subjects that would teach our children, at an early age, how to coexist in a peaceful society.

In so many ways we tolerate violence. We have fostered a violence industry that is an economic success. Among the heroes and role models we revere are people who have little regard for the sanctity and dignity of human life. How will violence stop? When we decide that we no longer want to live this way, say "no more violence" and work together to make it stop.

This is a social problem for which we must share a collective responsibility. Indirectly we are all victims, because violence creates fear, and negatively affects how we think, act, work and live. Violence has curtailed our freedom to such an extent that many of us fear going to work or sending our children to school. Others are too afraid to walk outside or even to stay alone at home.

BREAKING THE SILENCE

No matter where the violence occurs, the average person feels powerless when faced with it. When we are confronted with too much violence, we become indifferent, apathetic and immune to it. When we do not see abusive situations for what they are, we inadvertently allow violence to escalate. This happens in our families and in our workplaces.

This passive acceptance that violence as a way of life creates a code of silence. The silence enables workers' compensation programs to exclude "soft" forms of violence as a category of workplace injury. It gives abusers permission to continue to target their victims. It allows victims to be hurt, to feel guilty and live in fear, or to be scapegoated and punished. The silence also lets violence do its work—damage our spirit by destroying the best in what people have to give and undermining the well-being of our families, workplaces, communities and society in general.

Although violence in the workplace is now recognized as a pervasive global problem, our tolerance for, and desensitization to violence prevent employees and management from coming to grips with the depth of the problem. The truth of what life is actually like for employees and how much violence is part of the organizational culture is obscured by a conspiracy of silence in which most of us are active players.

While the collusion may be partially unconscious, we all conspire in one way or another to keep this issue hidden. We suppress the truth to allay our fears and quell our anxieties about a problem too distressing to think about or to confront. With violence so normalized and glorified in our daily lives, abuse has become accepted as normal behavior in the workplace. Many people consider violence to be part of their jobs or accept that it is normal to work in an abusive environment.

The strong taboo against speaking out prevents us from taking firm action. CEO's, executives, senior management and even frontline employees do not "see" the violence because they have been socialized to accept abusive behaviors and practices. Therefore bullying, harassment and abuse of power thrive. When leaders do acknowledge violent incidents within their organizations, they are usually externally-perpetrated, such as armed robbery or attempted murder. Or, it is easier for them to "see" the violence when it is perpetrated on staff by a client or customer. However, internal violence is the hardest to acknowledge, understand and root out.

In the coming years we will be confronted by even more threats to the stability of work organizations. The worst threats will not be the result of terrorist actions impacting on the workplace, nor will they be from robberies, crimes by strangers, or abuse by clients. The real problem is now and will continue to be violence internal to the organization.

INTERNAL VIOLENCE THE BIGGEST CHALLENGE

When internal violence occurs, the entire workforce—front-line workers, management, executives, boards of directors, CEO's and government officials—collude individually and collectively, albeit at times inadvertently, to allow it to thrive. As an individualistic society, we place self-interests, personal needs and desires above the interests of the collective. We have difficulty in satisfactorily resolving interpersonal conflicts so that both parties feel like winners. We show little concern for other people's problems and suffering, making excuses such as not having the time or energy, when in fact we really do not care enough about what happens to our co-workers. This may work until we become victims ourselves.

Our tendency is not to want to get involved when a colleague is the target of abuse. We isolate employee-victims. By shrugging off our collective responsibilities and adapting an attitude of indifference, we add to their injuries. Since we are insensitive to their suffering or plight, we fail to give them the moral and emotional support and understanding they need to successfully recover. As a result, victims feel frustrated, angry and fearful. Abusers continue their behavior, picking targets at will. Victims become even more victimized or they seek revenge and go on the offensive. The cycle continues.

If ever there was a health and safety issue around which employees and management should unite, it is workplace violence. Although in recent years many unions and professional associations have adopted this problem as a cause celèbre, we still do not yet have enough positive initiatives and collaborative efforts by organized labor, trade associations, management and individual workers to bring about widespread change. By failing to unite and speak out against workplace violence in all of its permutations, everyone gives permission for it to continue.

As a collectivity, we accept the premise that abusive behavior and violence are part of the job: it is what one has to put up with to hold down a job. We are wrong. Dealing with violence is not part of a job description, with the exception of those agencies whose specific task it is to control and combat violence.

By becoming desensitized to the violence in our culture, we cease making demands on people to change their behavior. This stops us from advancing as a society. Feeling helpless and apathetic, we abandon our ideals—for peace and respect—and continue to be at risk.

We frequently chastise others for their behavior while ignoring our own roles in creating or perpetrating violence. Too often employees are abusive toward management and co-workers, just as the latter are abusive toward them. Employees are disrespectful and impolite toward their own consumers, who are then insulting and rude toward them. No matter who is abusive first, once the other party joins in, the cycle of violence continues and escalates.

Unless there is a change in the thinking, attitude and behavior of the entire workforce, violence will escalate, eventually destroying even more lives and playing greater havoc with our lives.

Our failure to accept our individual and collective responsibilities has created an impasse. Unless we understand our own contribution to the problem, nothing will change. When we admit our own wrong-doing and realize that some seemingly innocuous behaviors are unacceptable, positive change will come about. When a critical mass decides that they do not want to work with people who are abusive, then a culture change will take place.

Strong collaboration between employees, organized labor and management can bring about this change. This collaboration could resolve many abusive situations. It could bring about unprecedented peaceful coexistence and cooperation on the work front.

Acknowledgment means confronting some harsh realities about the work we do and how we live our lives. It also means admitting we are part of the problem, since by our attitudes, behavior and intolerance we often contribute to the escalation of violence. This means we have to question our personal values and goals. We have to think about the part we play in creating the kind of society we live in and our contribution to our work environment.

Since we are trapped in the cycle of violence, our workforce is made up of many fearful, battered employees, who are often more preoccupied with how to protect themselves than with their job performance.

To end the cycle of violence, everyone has to break the code of silence and initiate change. Understanding, awareness and discussion will alleviate the fear. Acknowledging the problem will enable us to work toward change. It will lead us to a reexamination of the way we relate to each other, the values we admire, how we achieve power and the way we behave in pursuit of our goals and aspirations.

WHAT CAN WE DO?

At times we are all guilty of some sort of abuse. Being part of an individualistic society, we often believe we have an inherent right to think of ourselves first, or to pursue anything we want, even at the expense of others. We are territorial animals who value our individual rights and often shrug off our collective responsibilities. If there is something we do not like, we get angry and tell someone off. If we do not get our own way, we attack.

Many of us have difficulty understanding and dealing with our own anger. We adopt the attitude that if "I do not like what you are doing to me, you are going to get it" rather than "I do not like what you are doing to me and I am going to tell you and ask you to stop." It is not the expression of our anger that is the problem. It is the way we express it, how we let power and control get the best of us, and how we are motivated by revenge.

Before we can tackle the larger issues in workplace violence we must look inward and undergo a self-examination. Ask yourself the following questions: How do I communicate with my colleagues, superiors and subordinates? What happens when I get angry or cannot get my own way? How do I handle my need for success, power and control? Do I know how to solve conflicts in non-aggressive ways so that the other person and I both come out as winners? Do I treat people with the same courtesy and respect that I expect from them?

Everyone needs to ponder these questions. Self-reflection and a better understanding of our needs, goals and dreams can lead to important changes in our feelings, thinking and behavior. When a sufficient number of us change our thinking and attitudes, we will create a force strong enough to demand similar changes in others.

As with any social problem, a momentum eventually develops, producing a powerful pressure to change. This has already happened in some abusive workplaces. Attitudes and workplace policies on racism, gender inequality and sexual harassment are changing because of social pressure. The winds of change will be hard to stop once people realize and actively accept the fact that abuse of any kind is inappropriate and disruptive, and that offensive behavior does not have to be and will not be tolerated.

It is important to understand that no one changes from one day to another. It is a process. However, the more respectful you are, the more respectful you will be treated. The more you openly express concern about violence, the more you will become a leader against violence. The more you are willing to speak out, and collaborate with others, the more we will be able to create a safe and secure work environment and even a more tolerant society. Understanding the problem and working toward solutions will empower you and your colleagues. As an individual and part of a collectivity you will recognize your right to live and work in an environment free from violence and fear. You and your colleagues help us become part of a "Civility Revolution."

ROLE OF MANAGEMENT

Little can happen without leadership. Employers who do not acknowledge the existence of internal violence are robbing their organizations of energy and the best in their people. Management have the responsibility to take the lead and say no to violence, to support their employee-victims and to set higher standards on conduct. Management have the responsibility to create a work culture that denounces abuses of any kind towards anyone.

Business leaders must demonstrate their leadership in words and in deeds because they, above all, have the power to effect change. From a business viewpoint, the issue is not whether management should put energy, time and money into addressing this problem, but how much and when. Energy, time and money are already wasted by a lack of attention to this problem. It comes down to a question of priorities and choices. Management can take a little time and spend a small amount of money to understand and address the problem before it escalates into a crisis. Or they can ignore the problem and continue to suffer from lost productivity and a demoralized workforce. They can pay huge sums for stopgap measures, crisis management and litigation and negligence costs.

No workplace is immune from intolerance and abuse. However most only change when forced to do so. For example, most workplaces now have a sexual harassment policy. How did this happen? What was the impetus to implement this policy? It could have been in response to an incident affecting female members of their workforce, one which probably cost the company a considerable amount of money. It is possible that some companies understand that this was the right thing to do and did it. Others may have wanted to prevent an incident from happening. However, most organizations did not change until they were forced to, adopting sexual harassment polices in response to legislation. Gains have been made with regard to regulations and procedures regarding sexual harassment, discrimination and equity practices. They will also be made with regard to problems of violence. If companies do not make it clear to their employees that abusive behavior is unacceptable, legislation will eventually provide the push to make it happen.

As companies continue to streamline their operations to make them more viable in a global economy, they will make decisions that are in the best interests of the business but not necessarily of

their workforce. The practice of streamlining operations and eliminating positions or closing plants in North America and reopening
them in third world countries may ensure a business' survival or
increase its profitability. However, large-scale layoffs or the elimi-
nation of positions produce desperate, unemployed people.

Decision-makers must think about this. They must also pay
greater attention to the *way* they handle dismissals and ensure these
are done in as fair and humane a way as possible. Job firings on a
Friday afternoon with a couple of hours notice or no notice at all, or
massive layoffs announced just before Christmas are not the way to
treat employees and their families. These insensitive practices incite
people to anger and even to violence. It also incites anger in the survivors who, while feeling fortunate that they still have a job, must
do more but with the same salary.

Visionary leadership means moving towards a more collaborative management style, to create a different kind of workplace culture. It values the individual. By involving people at all levels of the
organizational hierarchy and inviting them to make a contribution,
employees feel important, proud and respected. Business leaders
can profit from this: they can achieve their goal of excellence, and at
the same time, they may even save lives.

ROLE OF ORGANIZED LABOR

Society as a whole has gained due to organized labor's struggle
to implement workers' rights and health and safety measures. They
are to be given credit for having broken the silence around workplace violence and for having demanded that employers fulfill their
responsibility regarding the protection of their workers. It is largely through the initiatives of organized labor to educate their members and pressure management for change, that this problem has
even gained recognition.

Labor's continued involvement is needed to effect further
change. Their collaboration with management on joint projects
increases employee and management commitment to each other
and creates opportunities for a respectful working environment.

Cooperation is a key to many issues, including better performance and finding solutions to tough problems.

Labor's continued role in creating a different kind of workplace culture is vital. They must continue to be vigorous in monitoring externally-generated violence and active in raising the consciousness of their members on this issue. Labor needs to expand its collaboration with management to create a safer work environment and to serve as a catalyst for change with regard to abusive behavior. However, for its own credibility around this issue, labor must also reconsider some of their own practices and behavior around disputes and strikes. Strong-arm tactics and overt or covert forms of violence that are tacitly sanctioned by some unions in order to settle disputes must stop. Unions must address present day workplace issues with a modern outlook and approach. Confrontation and violence are no longer pressure tactics that will win disputes, especially over the long-run. Nor are they in the best interests of their own members. It also sends a negative message to the public.

Unions must address some difficult dilemmas and positions. For example, in their desire to stand by their members in grievance procedures, unions often support and defend members who are violent toward other workers, clients or management. When they become aligned with the aggressor, unions not only support and give tacit approval to abusive and violent behavior, they inadvertently maintain that such behavior is correct and acceptable. When they back abusive people in a grievance procedure, they block attempts by management to deliver the message that this conduct is unacceptable. However, when the union has to grieve on behalf of a member who is a victim of violence, they expect the offender to be thoroughly punished. These contradictory positions give mixed messages, block constructive action and sabotage a zero tolerance for violence policy.

The involvement of organized labor is essential for the eradication of workplace violence. They must continue to break the silence and play a key role as agents for change. At the same time they have to resolve their inconsistencies in their attitudes towards all forms of workplace abuse and violence.

ROLE OF OTHER TRENDSETTERS

Although one would assume the responsibility for resolving workplace violence begins and ends with management and labor, this discussion would not be complete without some further reference to the link between workplace violence and violence in society in general. We must briefly look at the roles of several other important sources in creating and perpetuating the problem of violence.

Our education systems are at the heart of the violence issue. Any change in the way people treat each other and deal with each other must begin at an early age. It is in the school system that new trends in social tolerance, collaboration, anger management and positive conflict resolution must develop. While many schools are already carrying out programs in dispute resolution, this is not enough. Young people need to be thoroughly sensitized to the extent to which violence permeates our lives and theirs. They need to understand, to see and to be exposed to the benefits of peaceful coexistence. We must help them learn how to remain competitive as individuals but still accept a greater social responsibility for other people. They must be taught lessons in civility, and respect for others and for the dignity of human life.

The role of organized religion should not be forgotten. Although religious institutions have lost influence and respect over the years, society needs staunch moral and spiritual leadership. While our religious leaders should rightfully fulfill this role, they need to seriously reflect upon their own preachings, conduct and actions. They, of all our leaders, should be above reproach. The many revelations in recent years of financial irregularities lead one to view religion as a commercial enterprise. Add to this the public disclosure of sexual abuse toward minors by members of the clergy, and the disquieting silence of the religious hierarchy: we have an erosion of the morality and credibility of organized religion. War and murder in the name of religion, racism and hate crimes supported and often times even promoted by leaders of various religions throughout the world, present a contradiction in the role of religion and what it stands for—namely the teaching of peace and love for all people. Our religious leaders must set the example, so that we can have role models whom we respect, believe in and whose spiritual and moral guidance we are willing to follow.

The role of arts and entertainment is a critical force in creating change. Gratuitous violence on television, music, films and sports leads us to become immune to all things violent. While it could be argued that artists, entertainers, creators, writers and producers give us violent entertainment to satisfy consumers' appetite, they too must recognize that they have a social responsibility and demonstrate leadership in decreasing violent content in entertainment. As part of their responsibility they can take the initiative in this area and self-regulate the content of their programs. While enormous amounts of money are made supporting the themes of violence, money can also be made by offering programs without violence

The media has the power to influence attitudes, to educate and to change behavior. Watching the way journalists report stories of workplace violence and how they treat violent incidents in general, we can only conclude that they accept violence as a fact of life. A violent incident is sensationalized rather than its impact described. Journalists are important catalysts for change and have exposed workplace violence as the major occupational hazard it has become. Yet they often overlook the pattern in the stories they report and seldom present the broader perspective through an analysis that binds all the stories together. We need their help in the effort to grasp the global pattern of workplace violence and find the solutions.

It must be said, however, that like the rest of us, journalists and camera crews build an invisible shield which allows them to report on the most gruesome situations without having to think too deeply about risks to their own lives. Distancing themselves is the only way they can continue to expose themselves day after day to dangerous situations and heart-wrenching incidents. At the same time, the stories they write about and the pictures they give us include more than the facts. More often than not they include the gory details, because sensationalism is what sells. This makes good business sense.

The media play an important role in desensitizing us and furthering violent causes. When they present us the news, they choose the focus and the angle of the stories. War enters our living rooms and pictures of bombings flash on our screens, which many people watch with their children. The competitiveness of television ratings drive the media to sensationalist news reporting because the prize is increased advertising revenue. Violence sells. Terrorists attain instant notoriety and free publicity the world over because of intense media exposure. Sometimes media attention even creates or provokes more hostility in conflicts, because widespread exposure to the cause adds fuel to the fire. If terrorists were to not receive worldwide attention, who would know about their cause? Is it possible that they would be less inclined to embark on a violence crusade, if they knew they would not make the evening news?

Politicians have a dismal record when it comes to legislation and programs to stop violence. Political leaders must stand up to gun lobbyists, because supporting gun control will decrease crime, injury and murder. They need to break down the euphemism "guns don't kill, people kill" by understanding that people will not kill as easily if guns are not available to them. They need to show positive leadership in violence management by committing more financial resources to stop the flow of drugs, and to coordinate programs and develop a comprehensive strategy to diminish violence in our society. They need to demonstrate civility and be exemplary role models for proper conduct, and demonstrate dignity and respect for human life. They need to work to build a culturally diverse society as a global community and to say no to violence and show us that they mean it.

All these groups have a crucial role to play in halting violence because they are society's leaders. What they do influences how we think and inspires our behavior. Their values and actions shape the moral attitudes of society, public opinion and our conduct.

EMPLOYEES' BILL OF RIGHTS

If we really want to tame the beast why not have a bill of rights for employees as we have a bill of rights for citizens? Employees have the right to:

- Be treated with respect and dignity by colleagues, superiors, subordinates and clients.
- Work in an environment free from intimidation, fear and all forms of violence.
- Work in an environment where the prevailing attitude is one of respect and zero tolerance for violence.
- Expect action to be taken to protect them when violence occurs.
- Expect their employer to adopt a position against all forms of violence and to sanction offenders swiftly and decisively.
- Refuse to work, without loss of pay, if at risk either physically or psychologically.
- Say no to violence and expect others to do the same.
- Deal with anger, dissension and differences in a constructive way.
- Expect understanding and support from co-workers and management when they are exposed to violence.
- Be able to explain events and facts about the violent incident without being interrogated.
- Be provided with security, medical and legal help and psychological counseling to assist them in dealing with a violent episode in the workplace.

CREATE A CIVILIZED WORKPLACE

The resolution of workplace violence involves choices. Continued tolerance and apathy toward violence will expose us to even more incidents and increase the risk to our lives. We must recognize that workplace violence occurs because of fundamental imbalances and problems in our organizational structures and practices; in the way we do business and in the way we behave. Violence will decrease when we pay attention to not only doing our jobs, but also to how we get things done and how we work together.

In tough economic times, business leaders focus time, energy and money on re-engineering their organizations, in order to streamline their operations and make their businesses more competitive and cost-efficient. In the same spirit, we need to work toward a re-engineering of workplace relationships and conduct. We need a new workplace culture that combines the best of values and thinking of both men and women. We need to take people's strengths in problem-solving and achieving results and combine this with other people's strengths in setting up the processes to achieve them. Men and women should not be in competition with each other or see each other as threats but rather as having valued, complementary skills.

Changes in attitude and behavior will occur only when existing male-dominant values and thinking mesh with female values, when participatory management styles and alternative dispute resolution approaches are fully integrated into the workplace. Violence will be controlled when it is understood in the full context of a business issue and when management take a strong leadership position to stop it and expect their co-workers to do the same.

Workplaces of the future that will excel are those that are successful at achieving their goals, while at the same time paying close attention to the way they carry them out. Selling a product, nursing a patient, and teaching a student should involve excellence in the product as well as excellence in the way the product is delivered. This means achieving excellence in communication, teamwork and problem solving.

Successful companies will be those which can harness the positive energies of their workforce and make their employees feel that they have a direct stake in what happens to the organization. It means challenging people, making them reach their maximum potential and always treating them with dignity and respect.

If we were able to create truly positive work environments, we would not need to regulate behavior at work through codes of conduct and sexual harassment policies. The workforce would become self-regulatory, because fundamentally people want to belong to and fit in with the culture of the dominant group. The more people are empowered and treated as adults, the more their self-confidence and performance will strengthen. The more employees achieve their maximum potential and collaborate with colleagues, the more we will be able to create challenging, vibrant, superior work organizations. Such workplaces thrive on employee contributions, productivity and commitment.

Combating workplace violence involves change. It involves a commitment to change. All employees must develop an ability to function well in teams, know how to build consensus and become adept at alternate conflict resolution. While we may never be able to eradicate all types of violence employees are exposed to, a changed workplace culture will have a positive impact on how we deal with problems of violence. Every positive action we take is another step forward in controlling violence in our workplaces and in our society.

Every manager must be involved in creating a new type of workplace culture, because management have the power to influence and shape the conduct of the total workforce. When management will act as role models in civility, respect, consensus-building and peaceful dispute resolution, their employees will then follow their lead. Everyone wants to emulate the behavior of a charismatic leader.

There needs to be a single message about workplace violence, one that is consistent and clear. Abusive behavior of any kind is not to be tolerated in the workplace, any more than it should be tolerated in our homes, and in our communities. We do not have to stand passively by and watch how violence destroys the heart and soul of our organizations and the lives of our employees. We all have the power to say no to it and to change.

A simple effective action gets us started. It means believing, supporting and practicing zero tolerance for violence of any kind in our workplaces. This means each of us must do our part. Every small change leads to another. If you decide today to work on being more respectful of your colleagues, you will be contributing to the change. If you decide to commit yourself to be a little nicer to one person a day, to say something positive to someone who is having a bad day, or apologize when you know you did wrong, you will advance the cause. If you are joined by others in doing these simple things, then the chances for success will be great. Eventually all the little changes will produce a snowball effect, leading us closer to a more respectful workplace.

Each of us should be able to go off to work every day truly believing and confidently saying to ourselves:

> I have the right to be safe and secure at my place of work and in the work I do. I have the right to be treated with dignity and respect. I have the right to demand this of others and to make the same demand on myself. By doing this, I will help create a civilized workplace.

Notes

CHAPTER 1

1 U.S. Department of Justice. (March 1998). "Violence by Intimates: Analysis of Data on Crimes by Current or Former Spouses, Boyfriends, and Girlfriends." Washington, D.C.: Bureau of Justice Statistics.

2 National Clearinghouse on Child Abuse and Neglect Information. "Child Maltreatment 2001: Summary of Key Findings." U.S. Dept. of Health and Human Services. www.nccanch.acf.hhs.gov/pub/factsheets/canstats.cfm

3 National Center on Elder Abuse. (1995-1997). "Statistics: Elder Abuse in Domestic Settings." National Study of Domestic Elder Abuse. Washington, DC.

4 Top grossing movies for 2002, 2003 in the U.S.and Globally. www.IMDb.com

5 The Associated Press, Canadian Press.

6 National Institute for Occupational Safety and Health (NIOSH). (August 1994) "Occupational Injury Deaths of Postal Workers-United States, 1980-1989." MMWR Vol. 43, No. 32. Division of Safety Research, Center of Disease Control.

7 Bureau of Labor Statistics. (2002). "Fatal occupational injuries by occupation and event or exposure." www.bls.gov/iif/peoplebox.htm#faqd
Also Sygnatur, Eric and Toscano, Guy. (Spring 2000). "Work-related Homicides: The Facts. Compensation and Working Conditions. www.bls.gov/opub/cwc/archive/spring2000art1.pdf

8 Occupational Safety and Health Administration. (September 2003). Safety and Health Topics, "Workplace Violence." U.S. Department of Labor. www.osha.gov

9 Latest statistics as of January 24, 2004. "WTC death toll drops by three." Associated Press: As reported in The Gazette, Montreal.

10 Pinkerton, Top Security Threats. (2003). "2002 Survey of Fortune 1000 Companies." Pinkerton Consulting and Investigations Inc., USA.

11 Duhart, Detis. (December 2001). "Special Report. Violence in the Workplace, 1993-99." *A National Crime Victimization Survey Report*. U.S. Department of Justice, Washington, DC: Bureau of Justice Statistics. NCJ-190076.

12 European industrial relations observatory on-line. (2002). "Unions demand 'zero tolerance' of workplace violence." European Foundation for the Improvement of Living and Working Conditions. www.eiro.eurofound.ie/2002/12/feature/uk0212104f.html

13   U.S. Department of Justice. "Indicators of School Crime and Safety, 2001 & 2003." and Press Release, October 31, 2001. BJS202/307-0784. Bureau of Justice Statistics. www.ojp.usdoj.gov/bjs

14   Ibid., Press Release.

15   U.S. Department of Justice. (2002). Federal Bureau of Investigation. "Uniform crime reports. Bank robberies in the United States, 2001." www.fbi/gov/ucr/cius_02/htm/web/specialreport/05-SRbankrobbery.html

16   Canadian Bankers Association, Toronto, Ontario.

17   Duhart, Detis. (December 2001). "Violence in the Workplace, 1993-99." Op. cit.

18   Paoli, Pascal. (December 2000). "Violence at Work in the European Union, Recent finds." *SafeWork. Third European Survey on Working Conditions.* European Foundation for the Improvement of Living and Working Conditions, Dublin, Ireland. International Labor Organization. www.Ilo.org/public/english/protection/safework/volence/eusurvy/eusurvey/htm

19   International Labour Organization (ILO). (1998). "Violence on the Job – a Global Problem." Press Release. Geneva. www.ilo.org/public/english/bureau/inf/pr/1998/30.htm

20   World Health Organization. (May 10, 2002). "New research shows workplace violence threatens health services." Press Release WHO/37. www.who.int/inf/en/pr-2002-37.html

21   Duhart, Detis. (December 2001). "Special Report. Violence in the Workplace, 1993-99." Op. cit.

22   Ibid.

23   International Labour Organization (ILO). (1998). "Violence on the Job – a Global Problem." Op.cit.

24   Duhart, Detis. (December 2001). "Special Report. Violence in the Workplace, 1993-99." Op. cit., and International Labour Organization (ILO). (1998). "Violence on the Job - a Global Problem." Op.cit.

25   European industrial relations observatory on-line. (2002). "Unions demand 'zero tolerance' of workplace violence." Op.cit.

26   Bachman, Ronet. (1994). "Violence and Theft in the Workplace." *National Crime Victimization Survey.* U.S. Department of Justice, Office of Justice Programs. Washington, DC: Bureau of Justice Statistics.

27   Northwestern National Insurance Company (NWNL). (1993). "Fear and Violence in the Workplace." Minneapolis, Minn: NWNL.

28   Paoli, Pascal. (December 2000). "Violence at Work in the European Union, Recent finds." Op.cit.

29   International Labour Organization. Safework. "Introduction to violence at work." ILO, Geneva. www.ilo.org/pulbic/english/protection/safework/violence/intro.htm

30   Heyes, Derrick. (August 2001). "Preventing Workplace Violence. Towards an Aggression-Free Workplace." Conference Board of Canada, August 2001. www.conferenceboard.ca

31   Keashly, Loraleigh. (2001). "Interpersonal and systematic aspects of emotional abuse at work: the target's perspective," *Violence and Victims*, vol. 16 (3): 233-268.

32   Paoli, Pascal. (December 2000). "Violence at Work in the European Union, Recent finds." Op.cit.

33   Sheehan, M., McCathy, P., Baker, M. and Henderson, M. (2001). "A model for assessing the impacts and costs of workplace bullying," paper presented at the Standing Conference on Organisational Symbolism (SCOS), Trinity College, Dublin, 30 June to 4 July 2001. As reported in Mayhew, Claire and Chappell, Duncan. (August 2001). "Occupational Violence: Types, Reporting Patterns and Variations between Health Sectors." The University of New South Wales.
     www.who.int/violence_injury_prevention /injury/en/Wvstateart.pdf

34   Many articles on the Internet have used these figures. The author attempted to substantiate them without success. However, Salomon Smith Barney is just one example of a settlement of over $1 million.

35   Geller, Adam. (December 18, 2002). "Salamon must pay $3.2 M is Sex Harassment Case." The Associated Press. Reprinted.
     www.law.com/jsp/article

36   Capozzi, Michael. (October 15, 2001). "Insuring the threat of workplace violence." (Risk in Focus), Risk & Insurance.
     www.findarticles.com/cf_dls/mOBJK/14_12/83804364/p1/article.html

37   World Health Organization. (May 10 2002). "New research shows workplace violence threatens health services". Press Release WHO/37.
     www.who.int/inf/en/pr-2002-37.html

CHAPTER 2

1   Post-traumatic Stress Disorder (PTSD) first appeared in the DSM-IV edition of the Diagnostic Manual of the American Psychiatric Association.

2   Random House Webster's College Dictionary. (2001). New York, NY: Random House Inc.

3   This definition has been modified from the definition that appeared in the first edition of *Taming the Beast*. The author acknowledges the work of the Task Force on Violence of Batshaw Youth and Family Services, Montreal, Quebec. Their deliberations and clarification of the definition of violence for their own organization helped the author clarify this definition.

CHAPTER 3

1   Bachman, Ronet. (1994). "Violence and Theft in the Workplace." *National Crime Victimization Survey*. U.S. Department of Justice, Office of Justice Programs. Washington, DC: Bureau of Justice Statistics.

CHAPTER 4

1   Pinkerton, Top Security Threats. (2003). "2002 Survey of Fortune 1000 Companies." Pinkerton Consulting and Investigations Inc., USA.

2   Farnham, Alan. (December 1990). "Read This or We'll Cut Off Your Ear."
    Fortune Magazine.
3   PricewaterhouseCoopers. (June 22, 2003). "2003 Global Economic Crime
    Survey," in association with Wilmer, Cutler and Pickering.
    www.pwcglobal.com
4   Gary Schaefer. (July 2, 2003). "Japan's bosses are becoming bullies."
    Associated Press, published in The Montreal Gazette.

CHAPTER 5

1   Duhart, Detis. (December 2001). "Special Report. Violence in the
    Workplace, 1993-99." *A National Crime Victimization Survey Report*. U.S.
    Department of Justice, Washington, DC: Bureau of Justice Statistics.
    NCJ-190076.
2   International Labour Organization (ILO). (1998). "Violence on the Job – a
    Global Problem." Press Release. Geneva.
    www.ilo.org/public/english/bureau/inf/pr/1998/30.htm
3   Sygnatur, Eric and Toscano, Guy. (Spring 2000). "Work-related Homicides:
    The Facts." *Compensation and Working Conditions*.
    www.bls.gov/opub/cwc/archive/spring2000art1.pdf
4   Occupational Safety and Health Administration (OSHA). (May 2000).
    "Risk factors and Protective Measures for Taxi and Livery Drivers." U.S.
    Department of Labor.

CHAPTER 6

1   USA Weekend. August 13-15, 1993 Issue.
2   International Labor Organization. (May 29, 2003). "Violence and Stress in
    the Workplace: The Education Environment."
    www.ilo.org/public/english/dialogue/sector/themes/violence/educat.htm
3   U.S Bureau of Justice Statistics. (Nov. 18, 2003). "Indicators of School Crime
    and Safety: 2003." Department of Labor, Office of Justice Program.
    www.ojp.usdoj.gov/bjs/
4   Josephson Institute of Ethics. (2001). "Report Card on the Ethics of
    American Youth 2000. Report # 1: Violence, Guns and Alcohol" as report-
    ed in the National School Safety Center Review of School Safety Research.
    www.nssc1.org
5   Ibid.
6   Nansel, T., Overpeck, P., Pilla, R., Ruan, W., Simons-Morton, B., Scheidt, P.
    (April 25, 2001). "Bullying Behaviors Among US Youth: Prevalence and
    Association With Psychosocial Adjustment," *Journal of the American Medical
    Association*, as reported in the National School Safety Center Review of
    School Safety Research. 2001. www.nssc1.org
7   Huston, A.C., Donnerstein, E., Fairchild, H., Fashbach, N.D., Katz, P.A.,
    Murray, J.P., Rubinstein, E.A., Wilcox, B.L., & Zukerman, D. (1992). "Big
    World, Small Screen: The Role of Television in American Society." Lincoln,
    NE: University of Nebraska Press.

8   United Federation of Teachers (UFT). (1996). "Report of the School Safety Department for the 1995-96 School Year." New York, NY: UFT.

9   Ibid.

10   United Federation of Teachers. (2004). "Incidents Against City School Educators Skyrocket Nearly 40 Percent." United Federation of Teachers – News and Issues, January 29, 2004.
     www.uft.org/?fid=304&tf-1774&nart=1099

11   BBC News. (January 27, 2004). "Review of school violence figures." BBC News.
     http://new.bbc.co.uk/go/pr/fr/-/2/hi/uk_news/scotland/3433501.stm

12   United Federation of Teachers (UFT). (1994). "Report of the School Safety Department for the 1992-93 School Year." New York, NY: UFT.

13   Roark ML. (1993). "Conceptualizing Campus Violence: Definitions, Underlying Factors, and Effects." *Journal of College Student Psychotherapy*; 8(1/2): 1-27 as reported in InfactsResources. (July 2002). The Higher Education Center for Alcohol and Other Drug Prevention.
     www.edu.org/hec/pubs/factsheets/fact_sheet4.html

14   Task Force of the National Advisory Council on Alcohol Abuse and Alcoholism. (2002). "A Call to Action: Changing the Culture of Drinking at U.S. Colleges." National Institute on Alcohol Abuse and Alcoholism. (NIH Publication No. 02-5010).

15   InfactsResources. (July 2002). The Higher Education Center for Alcohol and Other Drug Prevention.
     www.edu.org/hec/pubs/factsheets/fact_sheet4.html

16   Amanda, Gerald. (1994). "Coping with the Disruptive College Student: A Practical Model." The Higher Education Administration Series. Asheville, NC: College Administration Publications, Inc.

CHAPTER 7

1   World Health Organization. (May 10, 2002)."New Research Shows Workplace Violence Threatens Health Services." Press release, WHO/37.
     www.who.int/

2   Bureau of Labor Statistics. (2001). "Survey of Occupational Injuries and Illnesses, 2000." U. S. Department of Labor, as reported in Occupational Safety and Health Administration, "Guidelines for Preventing Workplace Violence for Health Care and Social-Service Workers." (2003 Revised). OSHA 3148. U.S. Department of Labor.
     www.osha.org/publications/osha3148.pdf

3   Occupational Safety and Health Administration, "Guidelines for Preventing Workplace Violence for Health Care and Social-Service Workers." (2003 Revised). Op. cit.

4   Duhart, Detis. (December 2001). "Special Report. Violence in the Workplace, 1993-99." *A National Crime Victimization Survey Report*. U.S. Department of Justice, Washington, DC: Bureau of Justice Statistics. NCJ-190.

5   Health and Safety Executive. (October 1999). "Violence at Work: Findings from the British Crime Survey." Home Office Information and Publications Group: Research, Development and Statistics Directorate, London. As reported in Cooper, C. and Swanson, N. "Workplace violence in the health sector, State of the Art."
     www.who.int/violence_injury_prevention/injury/en/Wvstateart.pdf
6   World Health Organization. (May 10, 2002). "New Research Shows Workplace Violence Threatens Health Services." Press release, WHO/37. www.who.int/
7   Information from International Labour Organization (ILO), World Health Organization (WHO), International Council of Nurses (ICN) and Public Services International (PSI). www.who.int
8   See for example: Lion, J.R., Snyder, W., Merrill, G.L. (1981). "Underreporting of assaults on staff in a state hospital." *Hospital and Community Psychiatry*. 32: 497-498, and Fottrell, E. (1980). "A study of violent behaviour among patients in psychiatric hospitals." *British Journal of Psychiatry*. 136:216-221.
9   Service Employees International Union (SEIU). (1993). *Assault On The Job*. Washington, DC. and the Canadian Union of Public Employees (CUPE). (1994). *Action Kit: Help Check Violence at Work*. Ottawa, ON.
10   Engel, Frema & Marsh, Shirley. (February 1986). "Helping the Employee Victim of Violence in Hospitals." *Hospital and Community Psychiatry*. Vol. 37, No. 2.
11   As reported in Mayhew, C., and Chappell, D. (December 2001). "Internal Violence (or Bullying) and the Health Workforce" *Taskforce on the Prevention and Management of violence in the Health Workplace. Discussion Paper No. 3*. The University of New South Wales. www.who.int
12   Engel, Frema & Marsh, Shirley. Op. cit.

CHAPTER 8

1   International Labour Organization. Safework. "Introduction to violence at work." ILO, Geneva.
     www.ilo.org/pulbic/english/protection/safework/violence/intro.htm
2   Canadian Union of Public Employees (CUPE). (1999). "1999 CUPE Work Environment Survey – Ontario Social Services: Overloaded and Under Fire." Ottawa, ON: CUPE.
3   Canadian Union of Public Employees (CUPE). (1993). Survey Results: Violence Against Social Service Workers. Ottawa, ON: CUPE.
4   Duhart, Detis. (December, 2001). "Special Report. Violence in the Workplace, 1993-99." *A National Crime Victimization Survey Report*. U.S. Department of Justice, Washington, DC: Bureau of Justice Statistics. NCJ-190076.
5   London Borough of Haringey. (1986). *Guidelines to Staff to Assist in the Management of Aggressive Behaviour by Clients or Members of the Public*. London, England: Social Services Dept.

6   International Labour Organization (ILO). (1998). "Violence on the Job – a Global Problem." Press Release. Geneva.
     www.ilo.org/public/english/bureau/inf/pr/1998/30.htm
7   Occupational Safety and Health Administration, "Guidelines for Preventing Workplace Violence for Health Care and Social-Service Workers." (2003 Revised). OSHA 3148. U.S. Department of Labor.
     www.osha.org/publications/osha3148.pdf

CHAPTER 9
1   U.S. House of Representatives. Abuse of Elderly Is Staff Special Investigations Division Committee on Government Reform.
     www.house.gov/reform/min/pdfs/pdf_inves/ pdf_nursing_abuse_rep.pdf

CHAPTER 11
1   Pinkerton, Top Security Threats. (2003). "2002 Survey of Fortune 1000 Companies." Pinkerton Consulting and Investigations Inc., USA.
2.   Business and Professional Women (BPW/USA). (2003). "101 Facts: Domestic Violence and the Workplace". Sources: Workforce Development Group: *Domestic Violence Affects Corporations 2001*. Statistics. American Institute on Domestics Violence.
     www.bpwusa.org/content/PressRoom/101 Facts/101_violence.htm
3   Ibid

CHAPTER 13
1   Mayer, Jane & Abramson, Jill. (1994). Strange Justice: The Selling of Clarence Thomas. New York, NY: Houghton Mifflin.

Additional References

Amada, Gerald. (1992). "Coping With the Disruptive College Student: A Practical Model." *Journal of American College Health*. Vol. 40. March.

Arthurs, H.W. (1994). *Integrity in Scholarship*. A Report to Concordia University by the Independent Committee of Inquiry into Academic and Scientific Integrity. Montreal,QC: Concordia University.

Atkinson, Joan. (1991). "Worker Reaction to Client Assault." *Smith College Studies in Social Work*. Vol. 62, No. 1. November.

Bernstein, Albert J. & Rozen, Sydney Craft. (1992). *Neanderthals at Work*. New York, NY: Ballantine Books.

_____. (1989). *Dinosaur Brains: Dealing with All Those Impossible People at Work*. New York, NY: John Wiley & Sons.

Brown, Robert, Bute, Stanley & Ford, Peter. (1986). *Social Workers at Risk*. London, Eng: Macmillan.

Byham, William. (1998). *Zapp! The Lightning of Empowerment*. New York, NY: Ballantine Books.

California State. Department of Industrial Relations. (1993). *Cal/OSHA Guidelines for Security and Safety of Health Care and Community Service Workers*. Medical Unit, Division of Occupational Safety and Health. San Francisco, CA.

Canadian Union of Public Employees (CUPE). (1987). *Stopping Violence at Work*. Ottawa, ON: CUPE.

Clemmer, Jim. (2003). Leader's Digest. Toronto, ON: TCG Press.

_____. (1999). Growing the distance Toronto, ON: TCG Press.

Cornelius, Helena & Faire, Shoshana. (1990). *Everyone Can Win. How to Resolve Conflict*. Australia: Simon & Schuster.

Covey, Stephen. (1992). *Principle-Centered Leaderhsip*. NewYork, NY: Simon & Shuster.

Cowan, John Scott. (1994). *Lessons from the Fabrikant File: A Report to the Board of Governors of Concordia University*. Montreal, QC: Concordia.

Deal, Terrence & Kennedy, Allen A. (1982). *Corporate Cultures: The Rites and Rituals of Corporate Life*. Reading, Mass: Addison-Wesley.

Depree, Max. (1989). Leadership is an Art. New York: N.Y. Dell.

Department of Health and Social Security. (1988). *Violence to Staff, Report of the DHSS Advisory Committee on Violence to Staff*. London, Eng: HMSO.

Dziech, Billie Wright & Weiner, Linda. (1990). *The Lecherous Professor. Sexual Harassment on Campus*. Chicago, IL: University of Illinois Press.

Elgin, Suzette Haden. (1987). *The Last Word on the Gentle Art of Verbal Self-Defense*. New York, NY: Prentice Hall.

Figley, Charles. (1989). *Treating Stress in Families*. New York, NY: Brunner/Mazel.

_____, Ed. (1985). *Trauma and Its Wake. The Study and Treatment of Post-Traumatic Stress Disorder, Vol.1*. New York, NY: Brunner/Mazel.

Fisher, Roger & Ury, William. (1981). *Getting to Yes. Negotiating Agreement Without Giving In*. New York, NY: Penguin Books.

Fox, James. (1996). *Trends in Juvenile Violence*. A Report to the United States Attorney General on Current and Future Rates of Juvenile Offending. College of Criminal Justice. Boston, Mass: Northeastern University.

Herman, Judith Lewis. (1992). *Trauma and Recovery*. New York, NY: BasicBooks.

Insurance Journal. (2002). *AIG's American International Companies Unveils Workplace Violence Insurance*. Wells Publishing.
www.insurancejournal.com/news/newswire/nationa/2002/11/15/24373.htm

Kadel, Stephanie & Follman, Joseph. (1992). *Reducing School Violence*. Southeastern Regional Vision for Education, Florida Department of Education, and the School of Education, University of North Carolina at Greensboro.

Lanza, M.L. (1976). "The Reactions of Nursing Staff to Physical Assault by a Patient." *Hospital and Community Psychiatry*. Vol. 133:422-425.

Madden, D.J., Lion, J.R., & Penna, M.W. "Assaults on Psychiatrists by Patients." *American Journal of Psychiatry*. Vol. 133, No. 4:422-425.

Metropolitan Life Insurance Company (1993). *The Metropolitan Life Survey of The American Teacher 1993: Violence in America's Public Schools*. New York, NY: Louis Harris and Associates Inc.

National Coalition Against Domestic Violence (NCADV). (1996). *Facts about Domestic Violence*. Denver, CO.

Newsweek. *Violence In Our Culture*, April 1, 1991, pp. 46-52.

Nicarthy, Ginny; Gottlieb, Naomi, & Coffman, Sandra. (1993). *You Don't Have to Take It*! Seattle, CA: Seal Press.

NIOSH. (2002). Violence. *Occupational Hazard in Hospital*. Cincinnati, OH: National Institute for Occupational Safety and Health.
www.cdc.gov/niosh/2002-101.html

Norris, Dan. (1990). *Violence Against Social Workers: The Implications for Practice*. London, Eng: Jessica Kingsley Publishers.

Ochberg, Frank. (1988). *Post-Traumatic Therapy and Victims of Violence*. New York, NY: Brunner/Mazel.

Pavela, Gary, Ed. (1993). "Academic Integrity: Part 1." *Synthesis Law and Policy in Higher Education*. Vol. 5, No. 1. Spring.

Poyner, Barry & Warne, Caroline. (1988). *Preventing Violence to Staff*. Health & Safety Executive. London, Eng: Tavistock Institute of Human Relations.

_____. (1986). *Violence to Staff. A basis for assessment and prevention*. London, Eng: Tavistock Institute of Human Relations.

Ryan, Kathleen D. & Oestreich, Daniel K. (1991). *Driving Fear Out of the Workplace*. San Francisco,CA: Jossey-Bass.

Sagen, Maile-Gene & Schwartz, Barbara A. (1992). *Campus Violence: The University of Iowa Response.* The University of Iowa: Office of the University Ombudsperson.

Shields, Glenn & Kiser, Judy. (2003). "Violence and Aggression Directed Toward Human Service Workers: An Exploratory Study," Families in Society: The Journal of Contemporary Human Services: Vol.84, No.1.

Sorenson, Susan & Brown, Vivian. (1990). "Interpersonal Violence and Crisis Intervention on the College Campus." *New Directions for Student Services.* No. 49, Spring.

Spilhaus, Sally, Chair. (1994). *Task Force to Review Policies Pertaining to Rights, Responsibilities and Behaviour.* Internal document. Montreal, QC: Concordia University

State of Washington, Department of Labor and Industries. (1993). *Study of Assaults on Staff in Washington State Psychiatric Hospitals.*

The Chilly Collective, Eds. (1995). *Breaking Anonymity, The Chilly Climate for Women Faculty.* Wilfred Laurier University Press.

Toscano, Guy & Weber, William. (1995). *Violence in the Workplace.* U.S. Department of Labor. Washington, DC: Bureau of Labor Statistics.

Travis, Carol. (1982). *Anger. The Misunderstood Emotion.* New York, NY: Touchstone.

U.S. Department of Justice. (1998). Recommendations for Workplace Violence Prevention Programs in Late-Night Retail Establishments. Washington, DC: Occupational Safety and Health Administration. OSHA 3153.

United States Senate. (1992). *Violence Against Women: Victims of the System.* Hearing before the Committee on the Judiciary. One Hundred Second Congress, First Session on S.15. Serial No. J-102-10, April 9, 1991. Washington, DC.

Walker, Lenore. (1979). The Battered Woman. New York, NY: Harper & Row.

Wigmore, Dorothy. (1995). "Taking Back the Workplace" in *Invisible.* Eds: Messing, Karen, Neis, Barbara & Dumais, Lucie. Charlottetown, P.E.I.: Gynergy.

About the Author

Frema Engel shows people how they can use charm and grace to disarm and win over difficult antagonists. She promotes a more harmonious workplace by gently building attitudes and behaviors that resolve conflict and foster a community spirit. Years before workplace violence became a public issue, Frema was giving keynote addresses, developing training programs and coaching corporate and public sector leaders on how to reduce violent incidents and eliminate chronic conflicts.

Frema is a proponent of building collaboration and civility to create excellence in organizations. She uses her twenty-five years experience as organizational consultant, trainer, leadership coach and professional speaker to help employees in every industry resolve crises and use them as an opportunity for change. She has counseled and trained thousands of employees, managers and executives how to effectively stop abusive behavior and develop positive work relationships. *Taming the Beast* is a synthesis of this rich experience.

Frema has authored numerous publications on workplace conflict and peace building: more than a dozen professional and newspaper articles, two industry-specific books as well as contributing author in two books. For two years she also wrote a weekly newspaper column about workplace issues. Journalists often call upon her professional expertise, frequently interviewing and quoting her on radio, television and in print.

Frema's Montreal-based firm Engel & Associates specializes in action-based training, organizational development and crisis management. She earned a Master of Social Work degree at McGill University and later lectured there and at University of Montreal. She is a member of the Canadian Association of Professional Speakers and the International Federation of Professional Speakers.

KEYNOTE ADDRESSES, TRAINING & CONSULTING

- Do you want to disarm difficult antagonists with charm and grace—and win them over?
- Do you want to know how to identify hot spots and never have them happen again?
- Do you want to learn how the *Four R's for Violence Prevention* can dramatically change behavior in your organization?

Increase the level of respect and collaboration at your workplace.

Engel & Associates offers keynote addresses, interactive workshops and targeted consulting.

For your next:
- Professional meeting or conference
- Training program
- Executive or management retreat

Find out about our customized solutions tailored to your needs.

Programs and services:
- Risk assessment
- Crisis management
- Leadership enrichment
- Management coaching
- Customized training programs
- Conflict resolution and mediation
- Organizational change management

Call Engel & Associates at (514) 989-9298
or toll-free at 1-800-363-6435

E-mail: frema@fremaengel.com
Website: www.fremaengel.com